Creative PAINTING for Scrapbookers

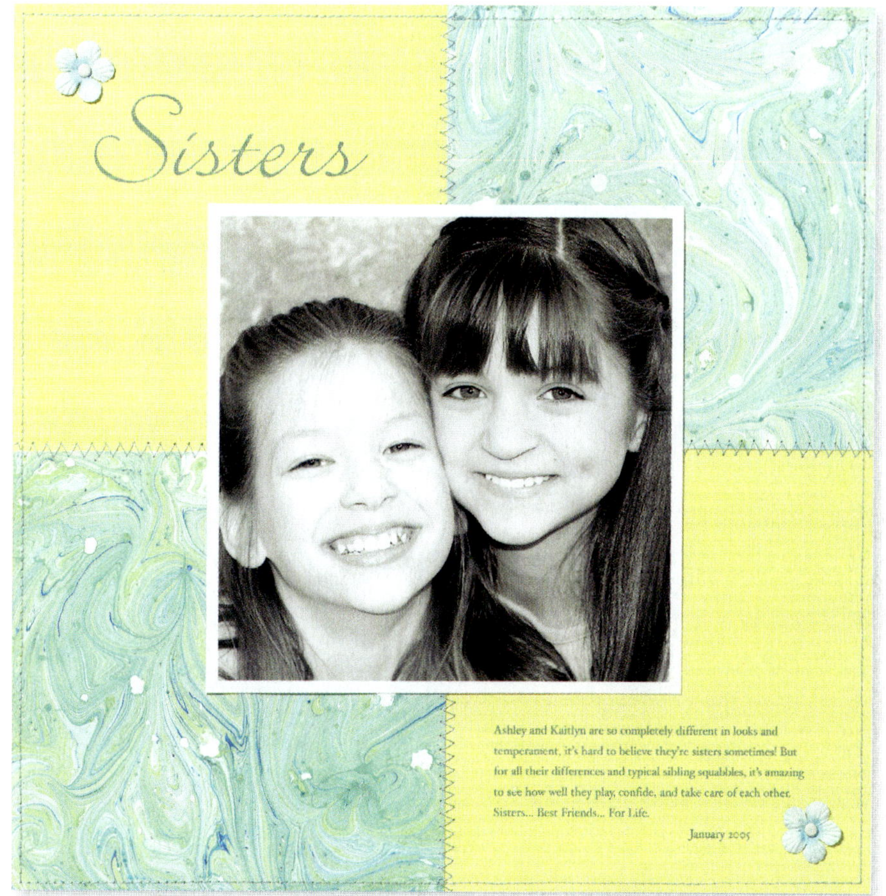

Step-by-Step Projects for Dazzling Page Effects

Lori Bergmann

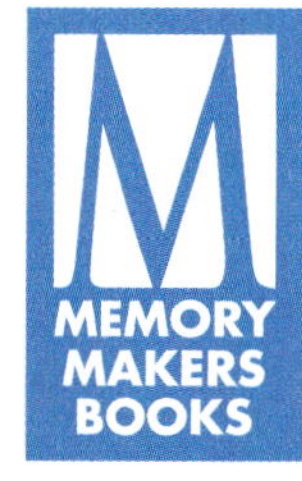

Denver, Colorado

Author & Artist Lori Bergmann

Managing Editor MaryJo Regier

Editor Amy Glander

Art Director Nick Nyffeler

Graphic Designers Jordan Kinney, Robin Rozum

Art Acquisitions Editor Janetta Abucejo Wieneke

Craft Editor Jodi Amidei

Photographer Ken Trujillo

Contributing Photographers Lizzy Creazzo, Jennifer Reeves

Editorial Support Karen Cain, Emily Curry Hitchingham, Dena Twinem

Hand Model Jeanne Karalus

Memory Makers® *Creative Painting for Scrapbookers*

Published by Memory Makers Books, an imprint of F+W Publications, Inc.
12365 Huron Street, Suite 500, Denver, CO 80234
Phone 1-800-254-9124
First edition. Printed in the United States of America.
10 09 08 07 06 5 4 3 2 1

Library of Congress Cataloging-in-Publication Data

Bergmann, Lori, 1964-
Creative painting for scrapbookers : step-by-step projects dazzling page effects / by Lori Bergmann.
p. cm.
ISBN 1-892127-66-0
1. Photograph albums. 2. Scrapbooks. 3. Painting--Technique. I. Title.

TR501.B47 2005
745.593--dc22

2005054482

Distributed to trade and art markets by
F+W Publications, Inc.
4700 East Galbraith Road, Cincinnati, OH 45236
Phone (800) 289-0963
ISBN 1-892127-66-0

Distributed in Canada by Fraser Direct
100 Armstrong Avenue
Georgetown, ON, Canada L7G 5S4
Tel: (905) 877-4411

Distributed in the U.K. and Europe by David & Charles
Brunel House, Newton Abbot, Devon, TQ12 4PU, England
Tel: (+44) 1626 323200, Fax: (+44) 1626 323319
E-mail: mail@davidandcharles.co.uk

Distributed in Australia by Capricorn Link
P.O. Box 704, S. Windsor NSW, 2756 Australia
Tel: (02) 4577-3555

Memory Makers Books is the home of *Memory Makers*, the scrapbook magazine dedicated to educating and inspiring scrapbookers. To subscribe, or for more information, call 1-800-366-6465.
Visit us on the Internet at www.memorymakersmagazine.com.

This book is dedicated to my wonderfully supportive family: my best friend and always encouraging husband, Kraig, and my lovely daughters, Kaitlyn and Ashley, who are my favorite subjects to photograph and scrapbook. I could never have realized my long-standing dream of writing a book without your love, patience and understanding—I am one blessed wife and mom! And to my own mom, for giving me a portion of your creative genes and to my dad, who I know would have been so proud to share this accomplishment with me.

And I would like to thank the wonderful designers who contributed their talents to this book, my friends who are a constant source of inspiration and fun, and to the community of women around the world who have always made me feel privileged to be a part of this amazing sisterhood of scrapbookers!

Table of Contents

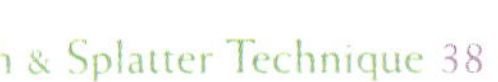

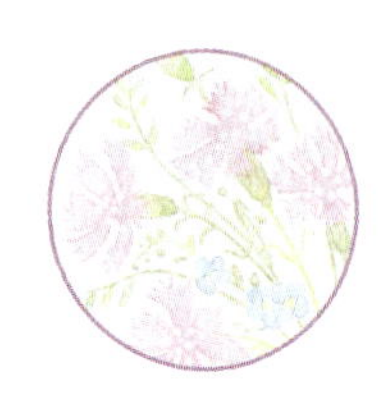

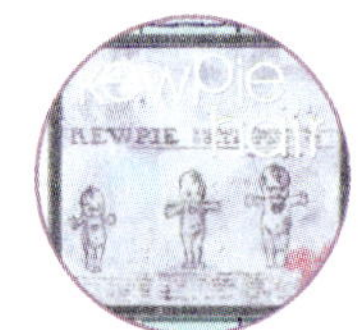

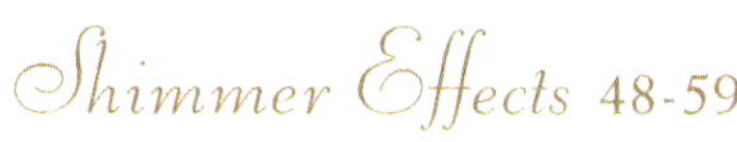

Shimmer Effects 48-59

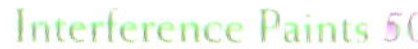

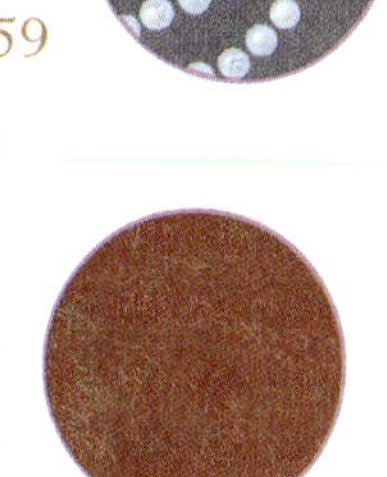

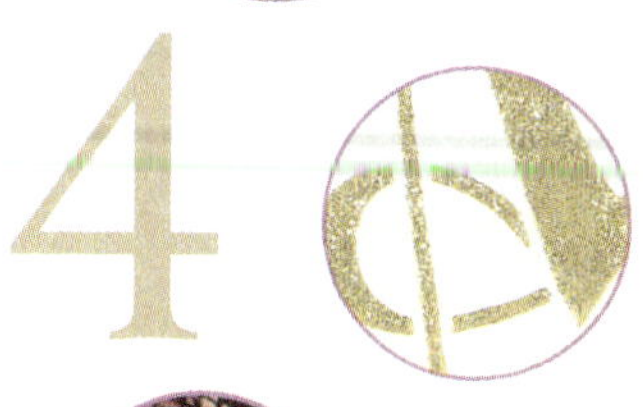

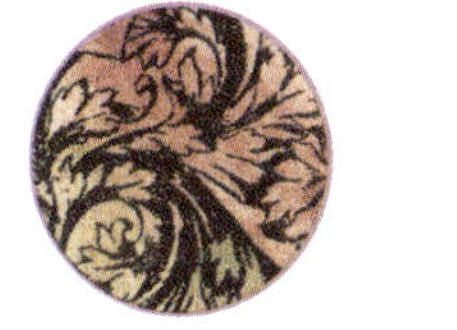

4

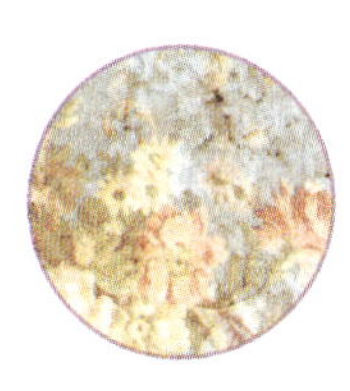

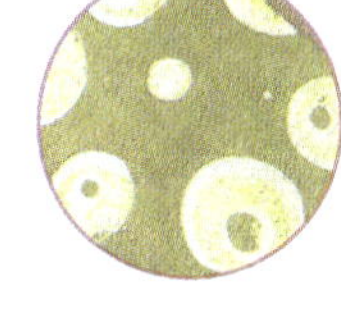

Dyes 60-71

5

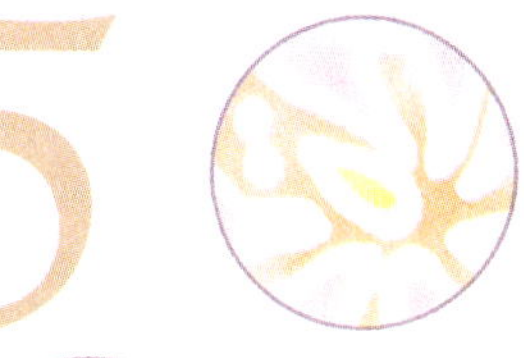

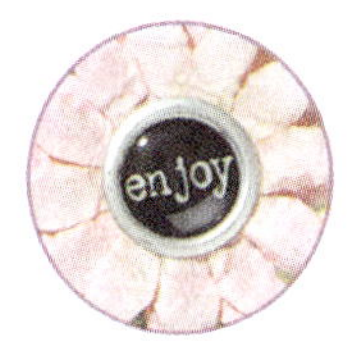

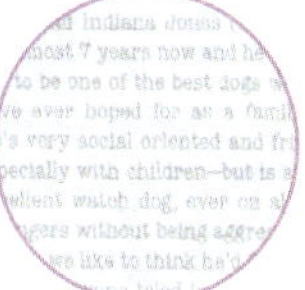

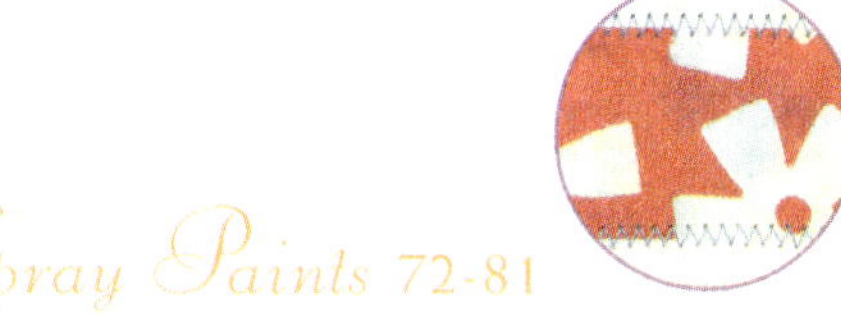

Spray Paints 72-81

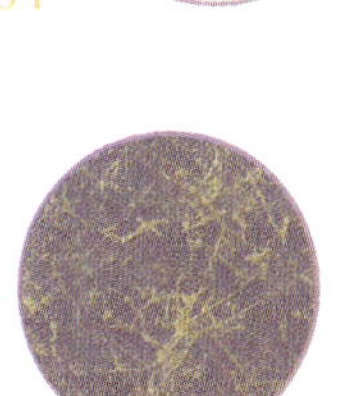

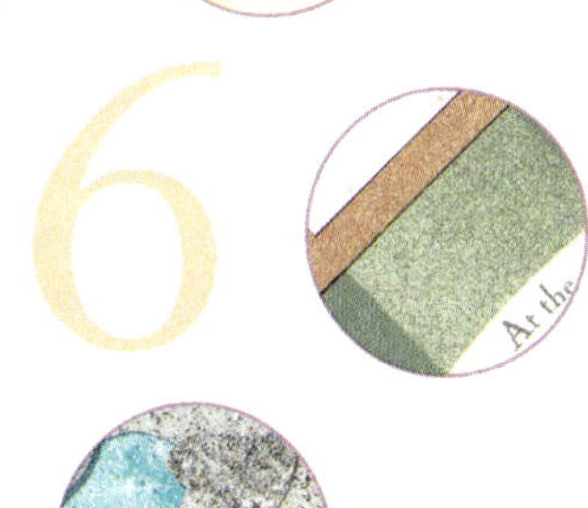

6

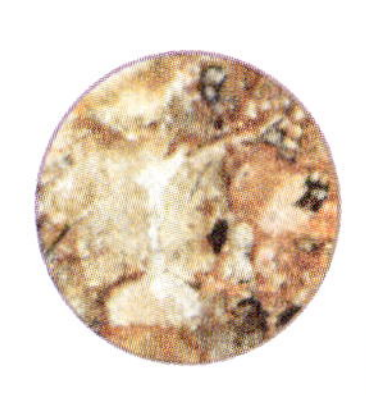

Specialty Paints 82-91

7

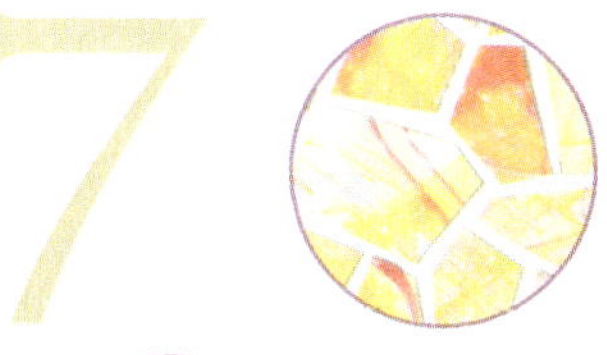

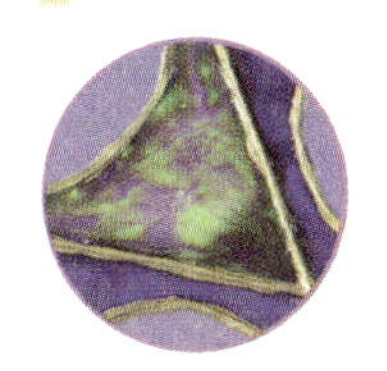

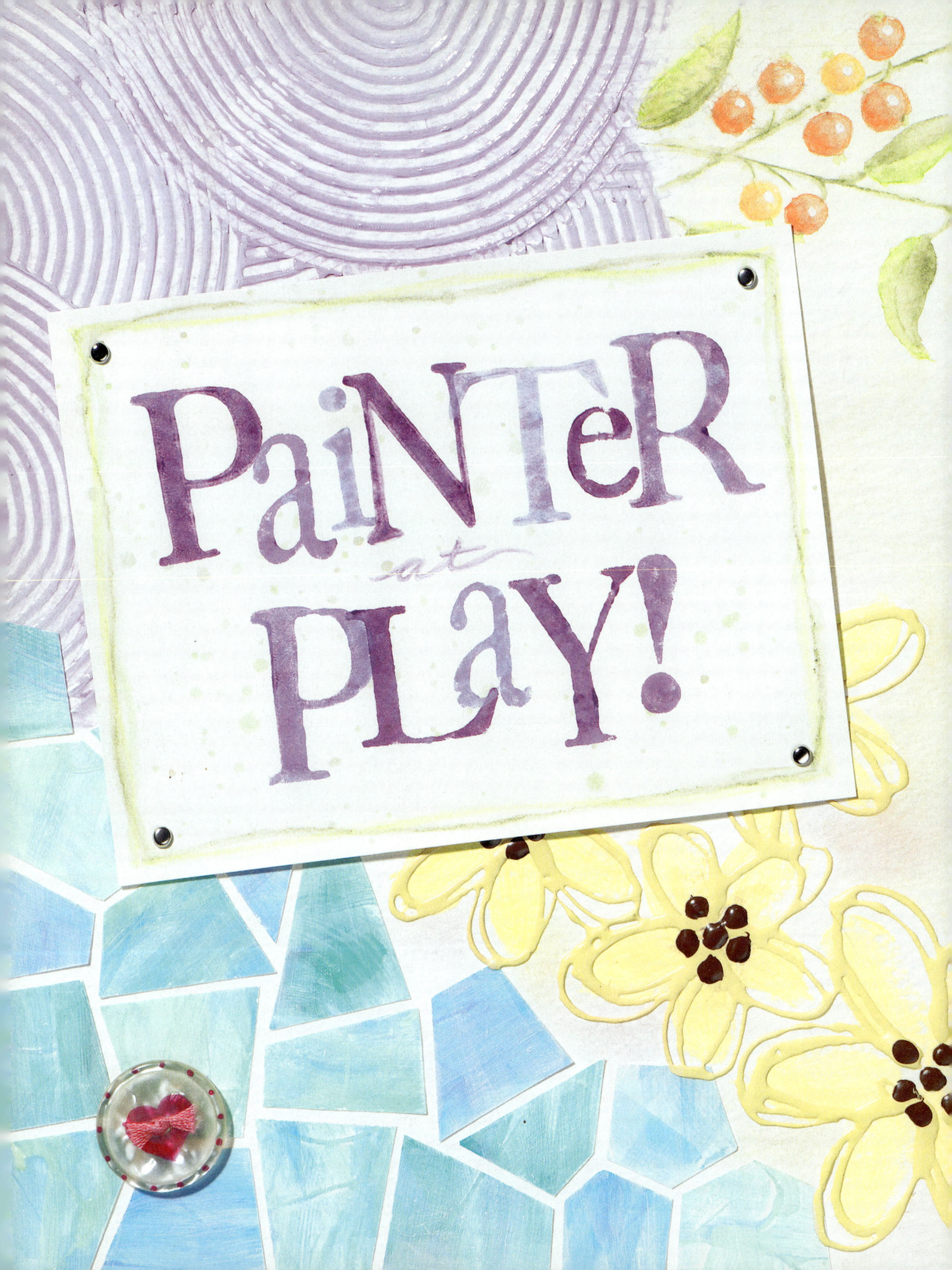
PaiNTeR
at
PLaY!

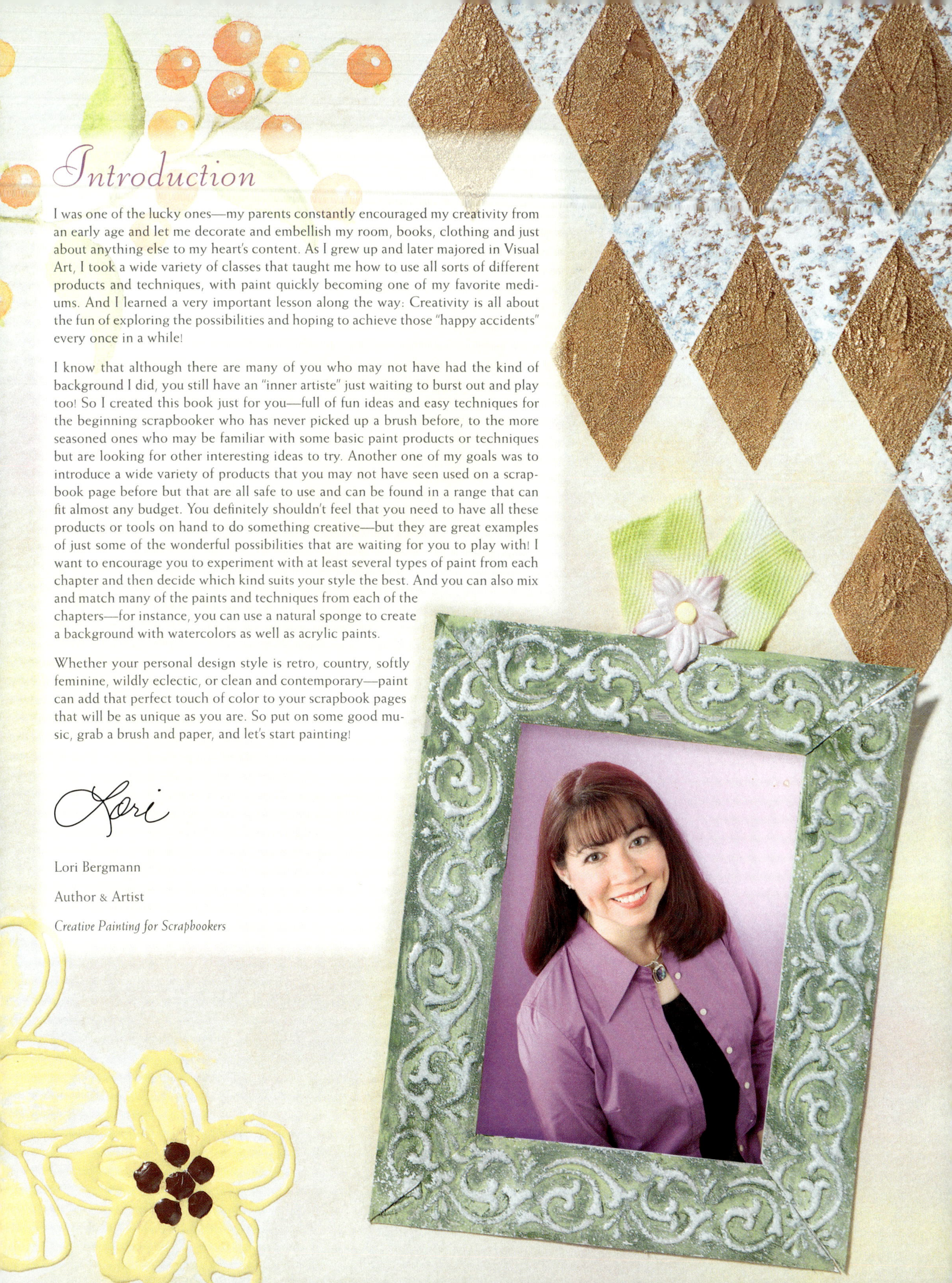

Introduction

I was one of the lucky ones—my parents constantly encouraged my creativity from an early age and let me decorate and embellish my room, books, clothing and just about anything else to my heart's content. As I grew up and later majored in Visual Art, I took a wide variety of classes that taught me how to use all sorts of different products and techniques, with paint quickly becoming one of my favorite mediums. And I learned a very important lesson along the way: Creativity is all about the fun of exploring the possibilities and hoping to achieve those "happy accidents" every once in a while!

I know that although there are many of you who may not have had the kind of background I did, you still have an "inner artiste" just waiting to burst out and play too! So I created this book just for you—full of fun ideas and easy techniques for the beginning scrapbooker who has never picked up a brush before, to the more seasoned ones who may be familiar with some basic paint products or techniques but are looking for other interesting ideas to try. Another one of my goals was to introduce a wide variety of products that you may not have seen used on a scrapbook page before but that are all safe to use and can be found in a range that can fit almost any budget. You definitely shouldn't feel that you need to have all these products or tools on hand to do something creative—but they are great examples of just some of the wonderful possibilities that are waiting for you to play with! I want to encourage you to experiment with at least several types of paint from each chapter and then decide which kind suits your style the best. And you can also mix and match many of the paints and techniques from each of the chapters—for instance, you can use a natural sponge to create a background with watercolors as well as acrylic paints.

Whether your personal design style is retro, country, softly feminine, wildly eclectic, or clean and contemporary—paint can add that perfect touch of color to your scrapbook pages that will be as unique as you are. So put on some good music, grab a brush and paper, and let's start painting!

Lori

Lori Bergmann

Author & Artist

Creative Painting for Scrapbookers

Basic Scrapbook Supplies

Basic Tools

Cutting Mat 1

Paper Trimmer 2

Grid Ruler 3

Scissors 4

Journaling Pen 5

Pencil 6

Craft Knife 7

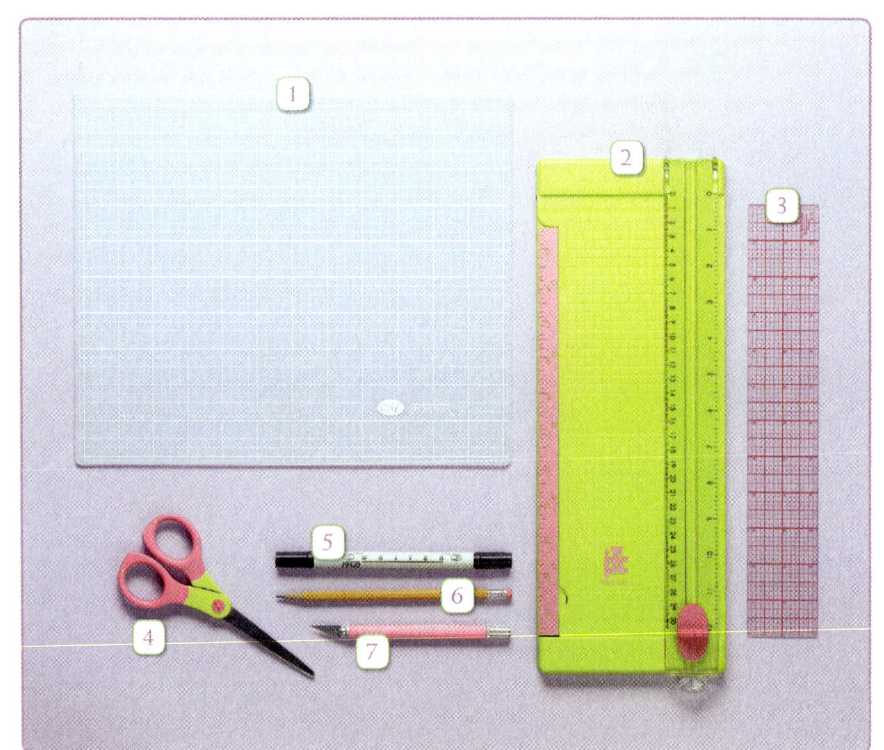

General Adhesives

Liquid Adhesive 1

Stencil (Repositionable) Spray Adhesive 2

All-Purpose Spray Adhesive 3

Silicone Dots 4

Permanent Adhesive Tape Runner 5

Photo Tab Adhesive 6

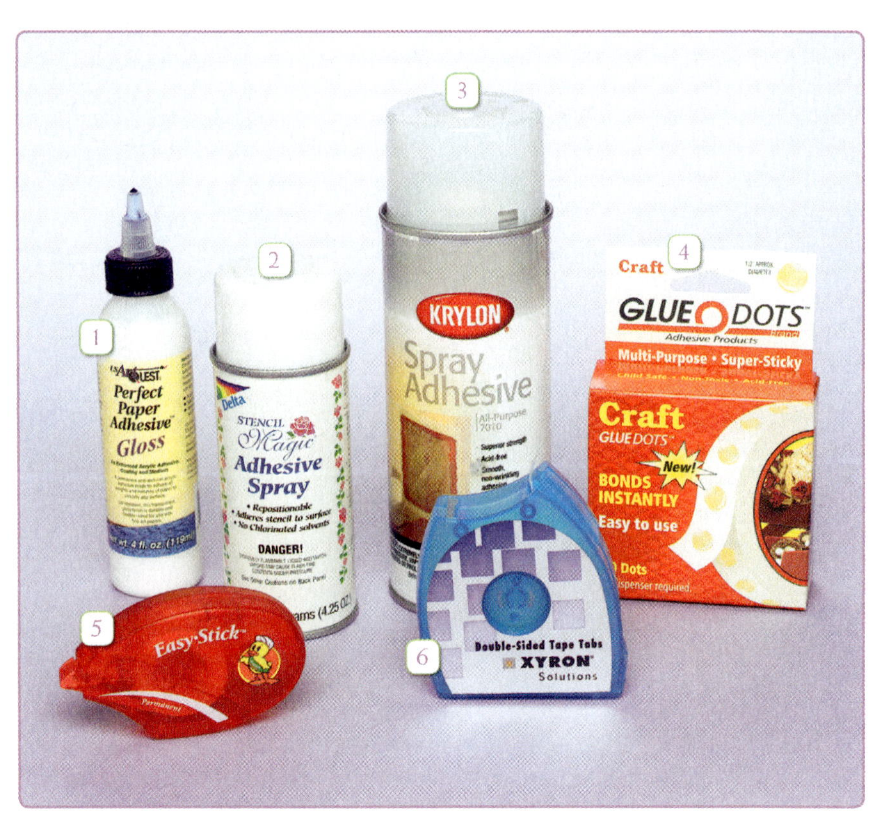

Basic Painting Tools

These are some of the tools I recommend using to create many of the projects in this book, but it's not necessary to have all of them in order to have fun painting. Feel free to experiment and use similar tools you may already have on hand to play around with the various mediums and techniques, and then invest in more specific tools as you need them.

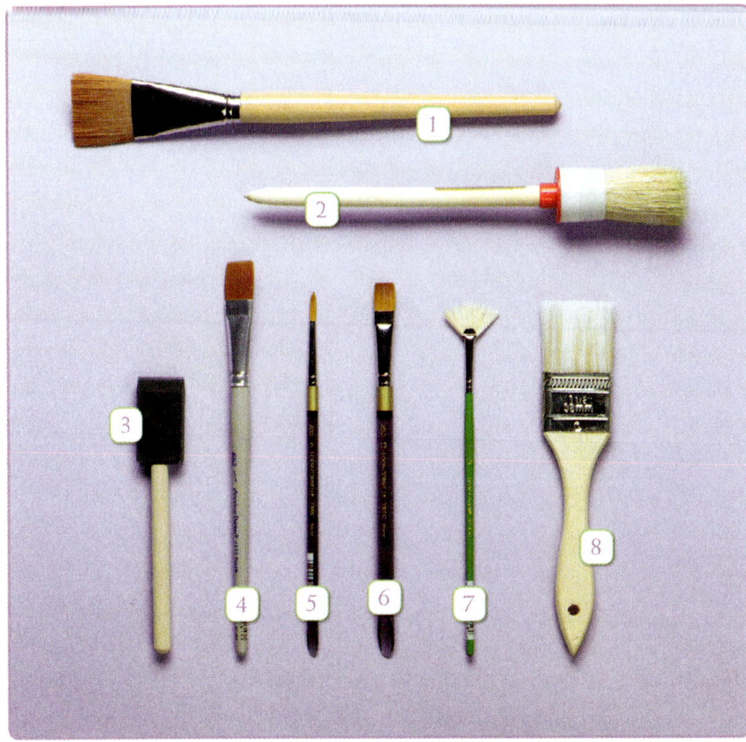

Brushes

1 Wash Brush

2 Stipple Brush

3 Foam Disposable

4 Flat/Shader Brush

5 Round Brush

6 Flat/Shader Brush

7 Fan Brush

8 Rough Disposable

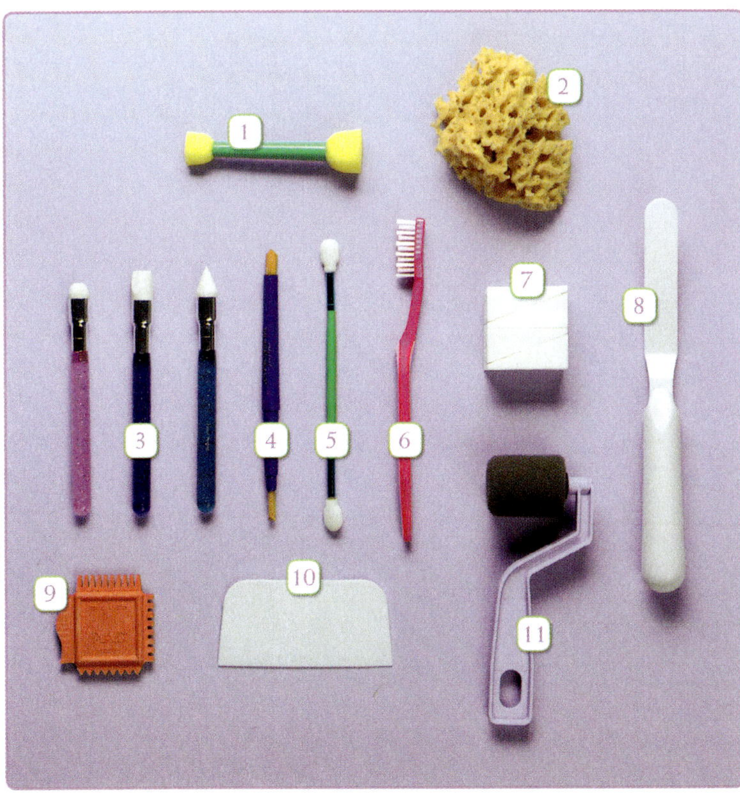

Other Applicators

1 Sponge Tool

2 Natural Sea Sponge

3 Foam Brushes

4 Incredible Nib

5 Foam Applicator

6 Toothbrush

7 Foam Wedges

8 Palette Knife

9 Faux Finish Comb

10 Palette Knife

11 Paint Roller

Basic Painting Tools

Miscellaneous Painting Supplies

1 Disposable Pans

2 Paint Palette

3 Painters Tape

4 Paint Remover Wipes

5 Mist Bottle of Water

6 Newsprint

7 Painters Rags

8 Mixing/Storage Containers

9 Paper Towels

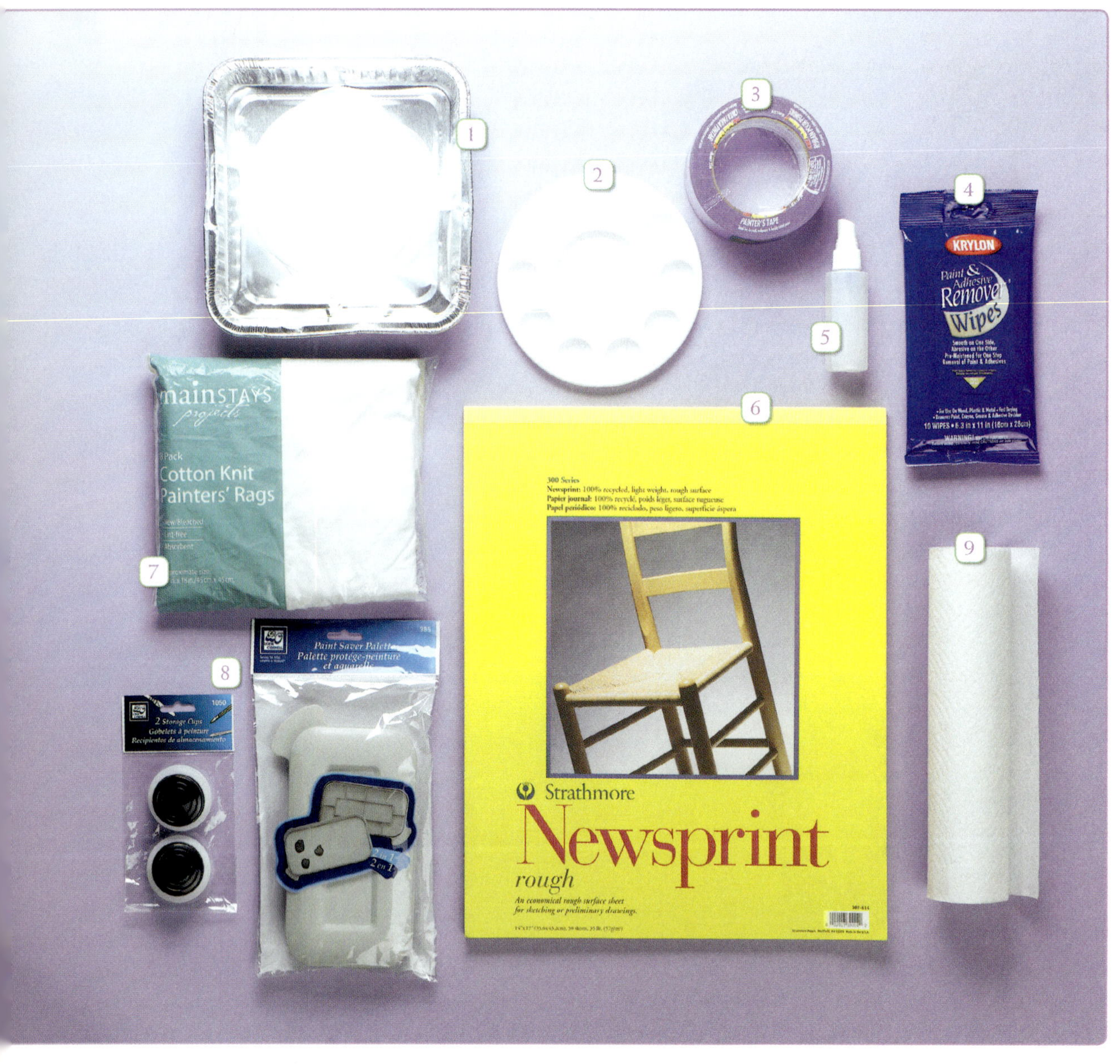

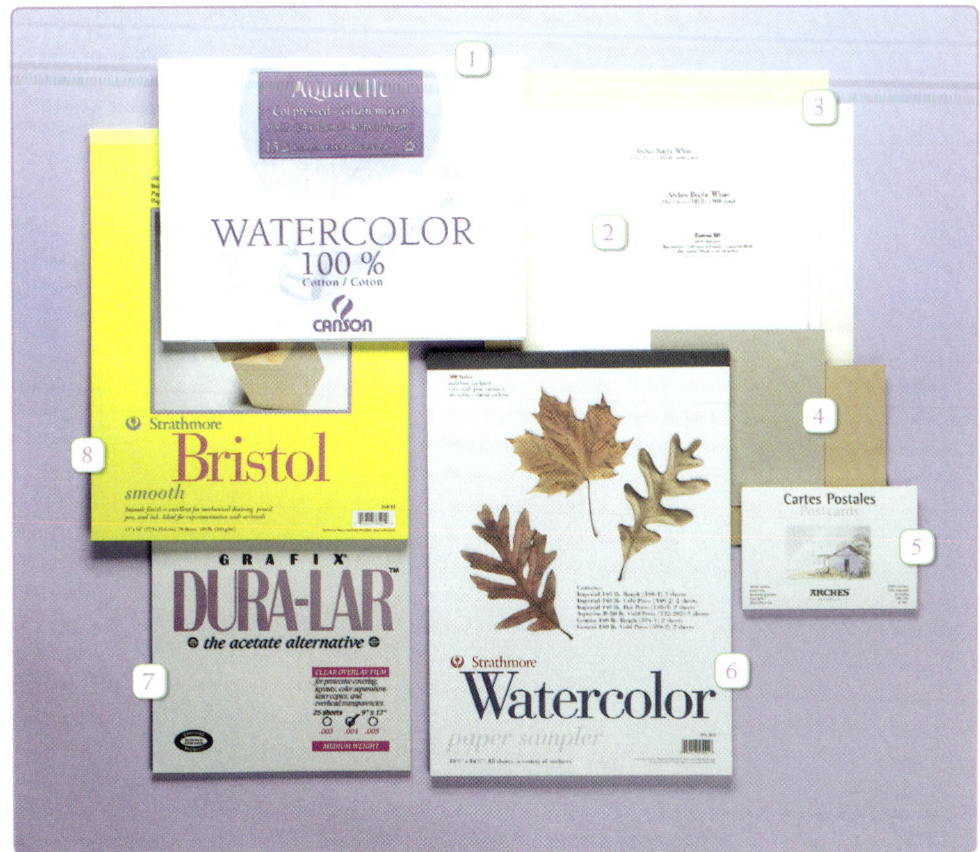

Painting Surfaces

1 Watercolor Paper Block

2 Watercolor Paper (individual sheets)

3 Heavyweight Cardstock

4 Chipboard

5 Watercolor Postcard Pad

6 Watercolor Paper Pad

7 Wet-Media Film

8 Bristol Paper

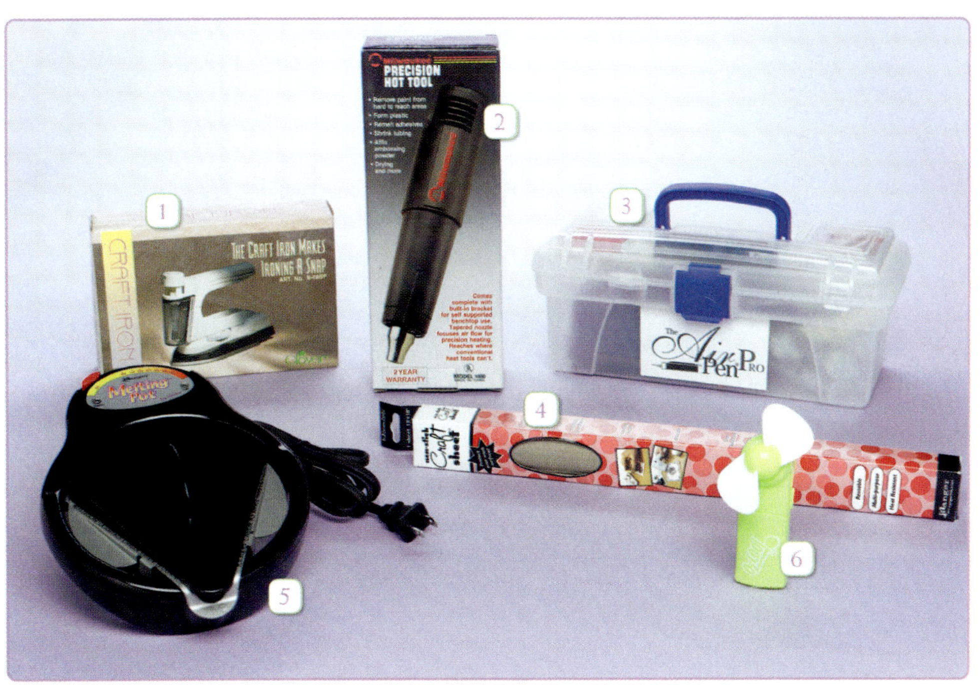

Other Useful Tools

1 Craft Iron

2 Heat Tool

3 AirPen Pro

4 Nonstick Craft Sheet

5 Melt Art Pan

6 Mini Fan

1

Acrylic Paints

If you've never tried your hand at painting before—let alone on your scrapbook pages—then acrylic paints are one of the easiest types to start working with. They're affordable, easy to find, come in a wide array of colors and dry quickly. Some of the best features of these versatile paints are that they can be applied to virtually any type of surface, can be mixed with many other mediums and dry to a flexible, permanent finish so that you don't have to worry about cracking or flaking paint in your albums. Also, no matter what type or brand of acrylic paint you choose to buy, they are all water-based for easy cleanup and are inherently acid-free. Some manufacturers have even formulated paints with less water specifically for scrapbookers and paper crafters to minimize warping on thin surfaces such as vellum and patterned paper.

Within the acrylic paint family, there are also different types with special characteristics. The fluid type that can be easily poured from a bottle is the most common and is used mainly in these first two chapters. There are also acrylics with a stiffer, creamier density and dimensional paints that can be thinned to use with the same techniques as well as used full-strength to create some other really interesting effects.

Acrylic paints can be found in several levels of quality and price, ranging from a professional artist grade, to a lower craft/value grade. As with most other paints, the price of the product is a usually a reflection of the ingredient quality and the manufacturing process used to create it. For example, an artist grade paint will be more expensive because it has a concentrated amount of high quality pigments, while a children's craft paint will be formulated with lower quality pigments and more "filler" products, which may affect the longevity and fade-resistance of your design. I would recommend using medium- to high-quality paints that have been made for decorative painters and professional artists to ensure your scrapbook designs will last for many future generations to enjoy.

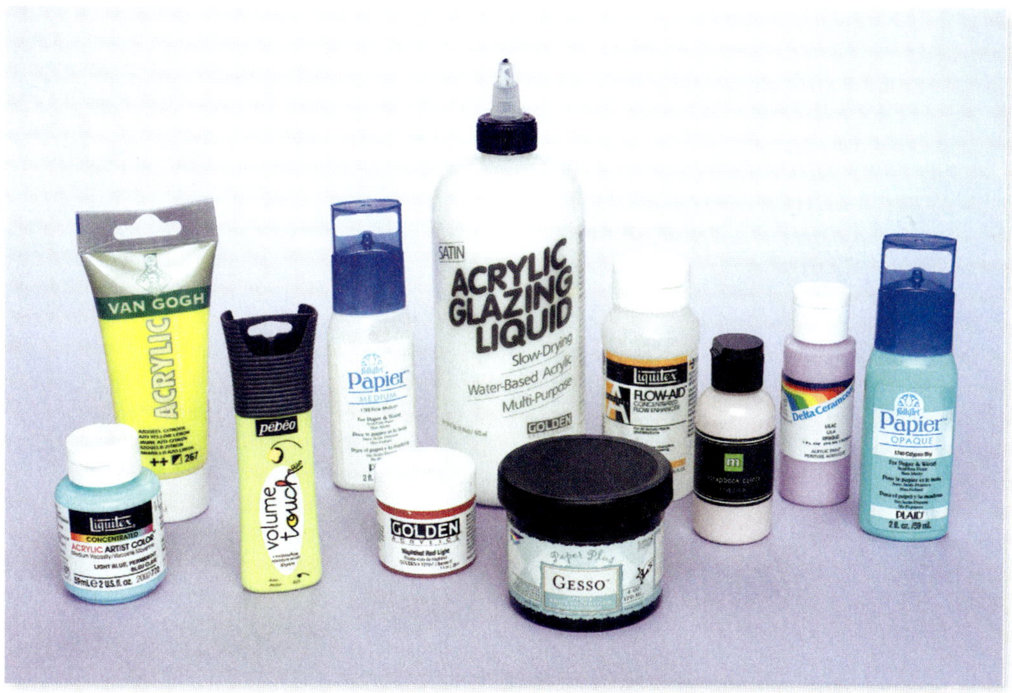

Featured Supplies

Gesso

Artist Quality Paints

Craft Paints

Dimensional Paints

Flow Medium

Glazing Liquid

Dry Brushing

I had several photographs of my girls having fun during a "garage shoot" and was stumped as to how to design a spread that would work with the different colors and expressions. The solution was a clean, graphic design with a variety of layered, dry brushed elements that were inspired by the colors in their clothing. I love how the textured cardstock and papers come to life with just a smidge of paint!

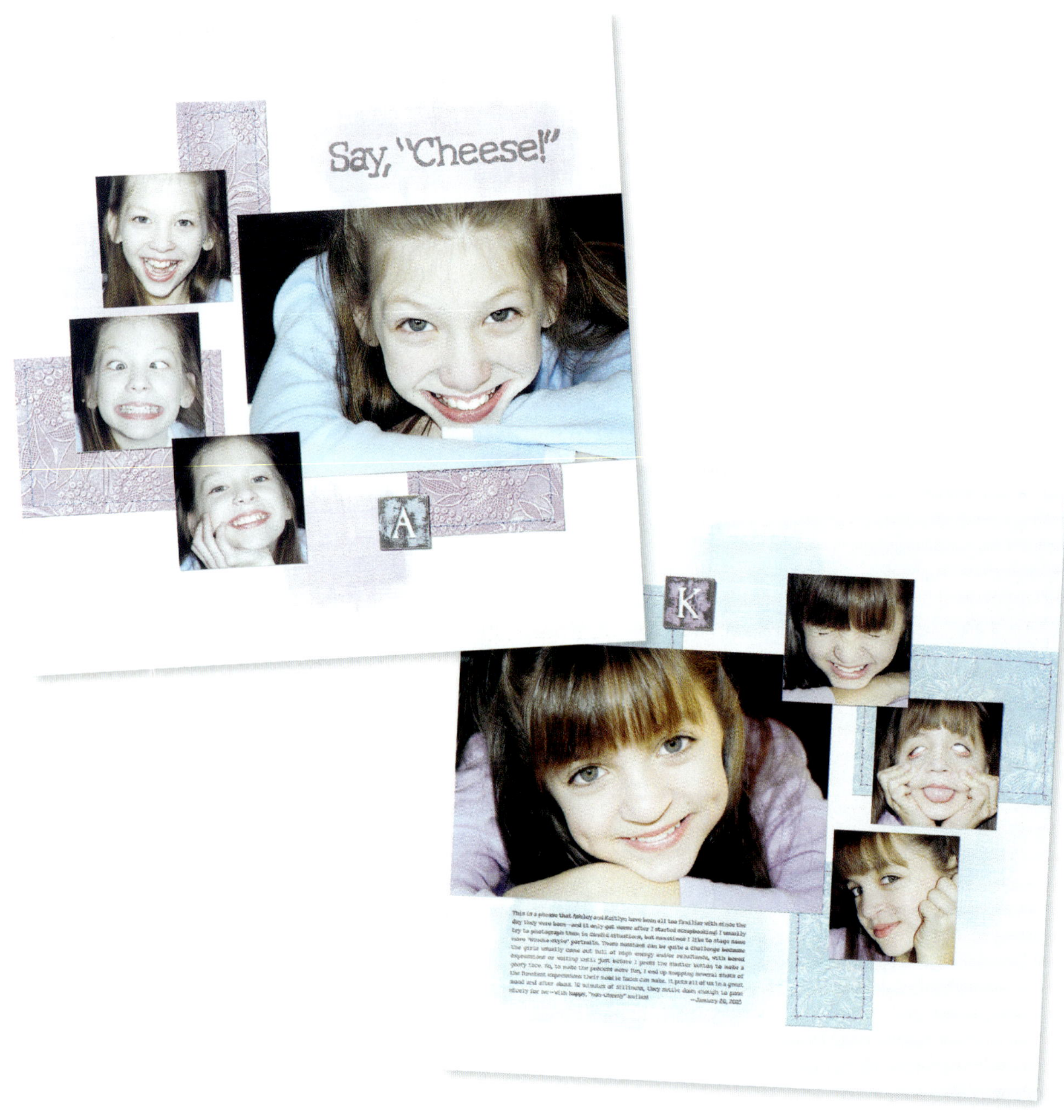

Say, "Cheese!"

Supplies: Pale lilac, demin blue, blue mist and white Ceramcoat acrylic paints (Delta); American Painter 1" wash brush, Spongit tool (Loew-Cornell); embossed papers (Provo Craft); textured cardstock (Bazzill); metal letters (Making Memories); sewing thread (Coats & Clark); glue dots (Glue Dots International)

Dry brushing is one of the easiest ways to give a layout some "artistic flair" by quickly altering papers or embellishments with just a brush, a little paint and a delicate touch. It's important to make sure your brush is as dry as possible so you don't end up with those dreaded paint globs or cause thinner paper to warp. Simply dip the tip of the brush into the paint and lightly brush off any excess onto a paper towel before applying the paint to your surface. This technique is especially dramatic when used over anything that has a slight texture or raised pattern, but also works well on smooth surfaces like plain cardstock because the brush strokes create a visual texture that will add interest to just about any kind of design. Another advantage of dry brushing is that because the paint is applied so thinly, it will dry in a matter of minutes, and you can complete a layout very quickly.

Tips & Tricks

- *I used a page layout program to create the basic design and journaling to make it easier to mirror image all my shapes and print my text perfectly onto the painted blocks. I also used it as a pattern with a light box underneath my cardstock as I painted.*
- *If you don't have the exact color you need, don't be afraid to mix a small batch of custom color. I mixed two blue paints to get a shade that matched the embossed paper and then saved it in an airtight container. I also wrote the "recipe" for my custom mix (2 drops Blue Mist + 1 drop Denim Blue) on the container in case I ever need to make that color again.*

Other Ideas to Try . . .

1. Create a plaid design using a combination of different brush types and/or widths.
2. Layer two or three shades of the same color over each other in a swish-style pattern.
3. Create a spotted background with a round foam applicator tool or the tip of a brush handle.
4. Tone down and soften bright papers or printed designs with light or dark paint colors.

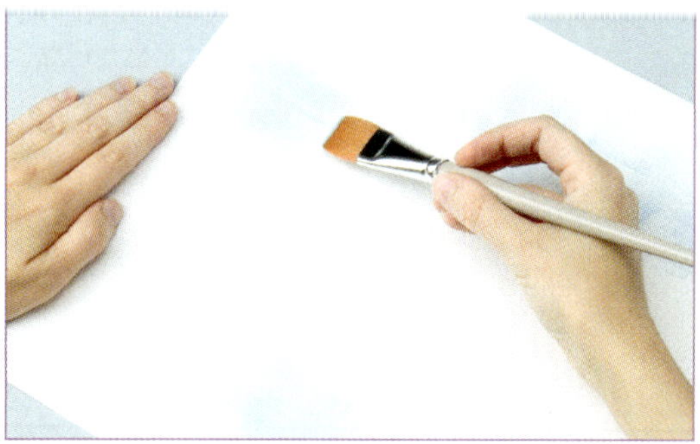

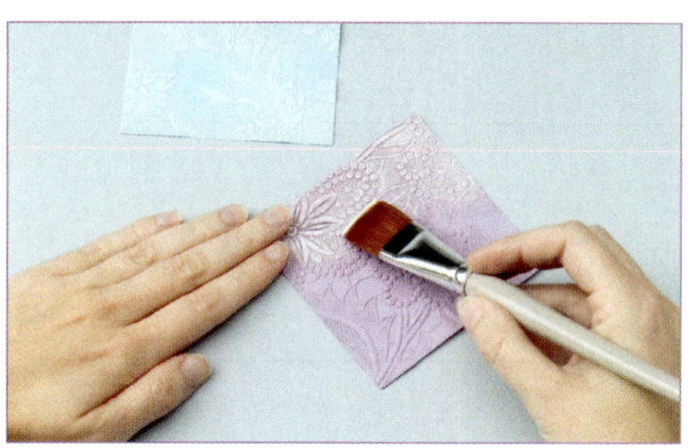

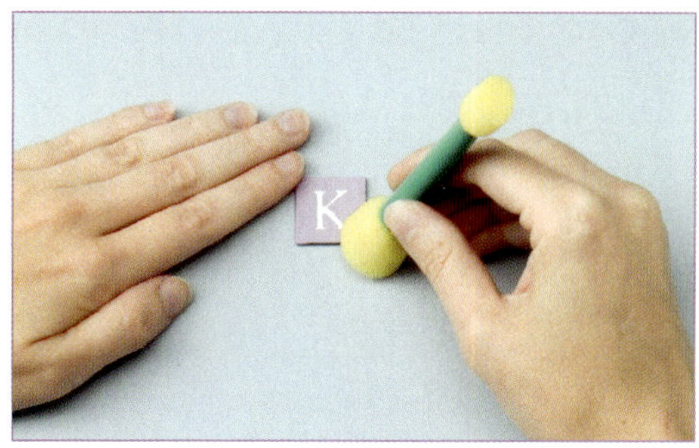

1

Lightly brush paint onto textured cardstock and allow to dry. Print text over the painted areas by running paper directly through your printer.

2

Brush white paint over embossed paper so that only the raised areas are highlighted. Once dry, trim into rectangles and sew to the background with a contrasting thread color.

3

Create a distressed metal letter accent by painting in the recessed shape, then sand off excess paint so that just the letter remains white. Using a sponge tool, lightly tap second color onto the accent, being careful not to get any into the white letter. Sand again until you get a worn, distressed effect.

Scumbling

This photo of my youngest daughter taken the day we brought her home from the hospital is one of my all-time favorites. I wanted to create a layout that conveyed a soft, gentle feeling, and the pastel painted background and pretty painted metal accents do just the trick! I also used a Photoshop watercolor filter on the focal photo and sanded the edges.

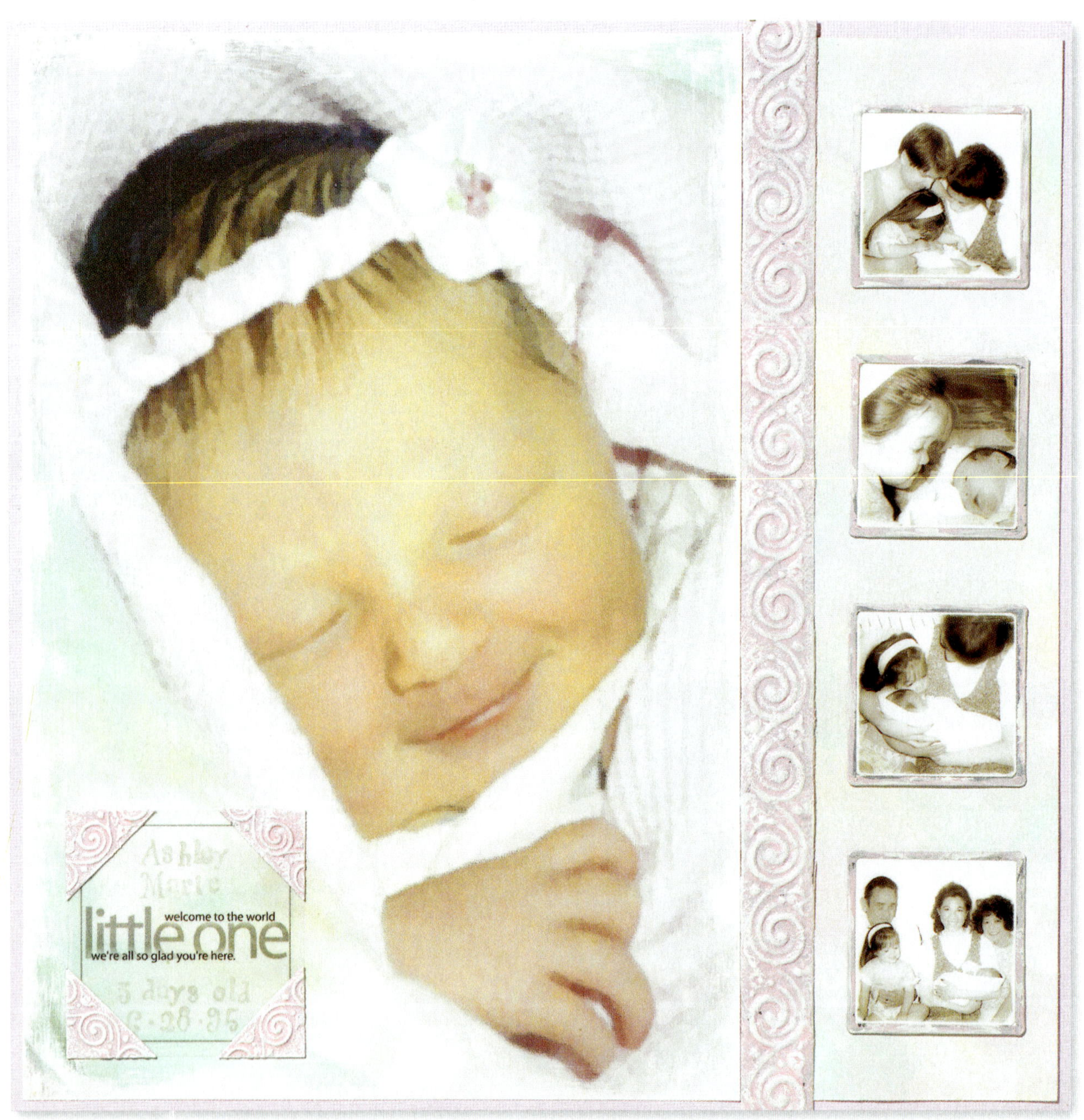

Little One *Supplies:* Lisa pink, ivory and tropic bay blue Ceramcoat acrylic paints, gesso (Delta); Spongeit tool (Loew-Cornell); metal molding strip, photo corners, square metal-rimmed tags (Making Memories); letter stamps (Hero Arts); VersaMagic chalk ink (Tsukineko); vellum quote (Memories Complete); all-purpose spray adhesive (Krylon); textured cardstock (Bazzill); stiff paintbrush

In traditional artistic circles, scumbling is usually referred to when a lighter color is dragged over a darker color, leaving some areas still exposed from the first layer. But my idea of scumbling is simply the act of scrubbing a layer of paint over and around another one so that they interact to create a softly distressed type of look. Layering color over a still-damp layer will drag and pull off some of the underlying paint for a rougher texture than when more color is applied over a dry layer. You can scumble colors over each other with a variety of tools such as a brush, sponge, or rag using either a scrubbing motion or rough strokes, and each way will result in a slightly different texture. Either way, it's a fast and fun process that will make you look and feel like a painting pro!

When using a lot of paint on a page background, I've found that base coating a thick, good-quality paper with a product called gesso can often make a difference in the finished result. Gesso is a type of artists primer used to prepare porous surfaces such as canvas, chipboard or cardstock so that the paint won't soak into it and warp it. White gesso is the most commonly used, but it also comes in black and clear versions as well.

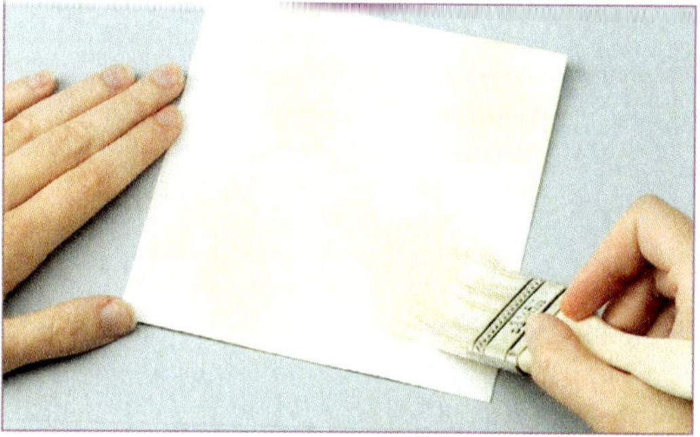

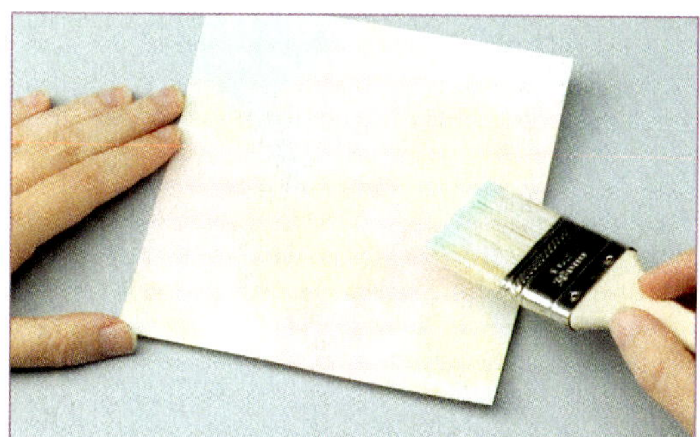

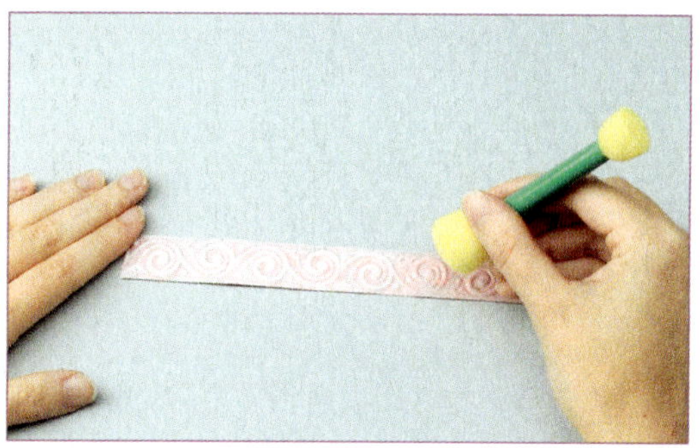

1

Prepare cardstock with a coat of gesso. Dip a large brush into ivory paint and blot off any excess onto a paper towel. Roughly scrub paint over background in random areas.

2

Mix pink and white to create a light pink tint; repeat Step 1 in unpainted areas, overlapping some of the ivory in places. Add a third layer of blue paint in the same manner.

3

With a light scrubbing motion, quickly apply pink paint over molding strip, concentrating on getting most of the paint in the grooves. Then daub white paint over the top to highlight the raised areas. If desired, lightly rub with sandpaper for a more distressed finish.

Tips & Tricks

- *Use an inexpensive brush for this technique so you don't ruin the nice ones that you will want to use for other painting techniques.*
- *If you want a smoother, more opaque finish on the metal embellishments, apply the paint with a regular brush instead of the sponge tool, which makes a rough, mottled texture.*
- *If needed, randomly scrub in a little white paint to blend edges of the various colors. You can also go back and add more paint to continue layering and softening the colors around each other until you achieve the desired effect.*

Other Ideas to Try . . .

1. Apply gesso and scumble paint over embossed or flat cardstock, then sand down to reveal parts of the gesso underneath.

2. Scumble a tinted glaze over a solid acrylic paint.

Glazed Transparency

This is a design where I wanted to use a lot of photographs featuring a wide variety of colors and textures on the same page. A large custom-printed transparency box painted with a rainbow of glazed colors became the central anchor that holds everything together on a simple, neutral background.

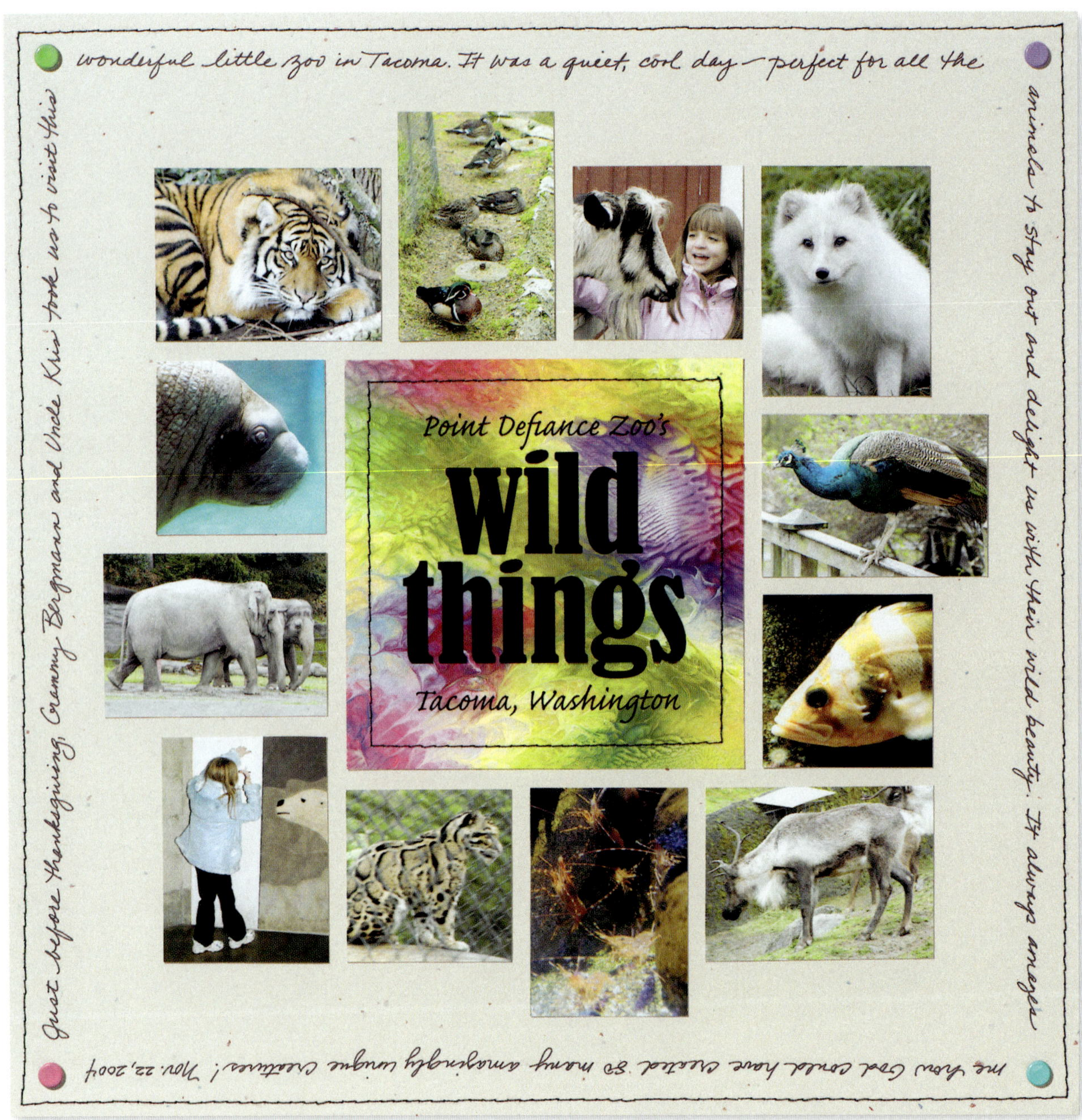

Wild Things **Supplies:** Butter yellow Ceramcoat acrylic paint (Delta); Hauser light green Americana acrylic paint (DecoArt); Quinacridone Magenta and Cerulean Blue Chromium Fluid Acrylics, Acrylic Glazing Liquid (Golden); transparency; Dura-Lar Wet-Media Film (Grafix); flat-top eyelets (Stamp Doctor); black sewing thread

One of the best things about acrylic paints is the fact that they dry so quickly, but sometimes you may need a little more time to work with them or want a sheer tint instead of an opaque one. If that's the case, you need a product called glazing medium. When mixed with acrylic paint, it thins the color down without dulling the finish and extends the drying time so you can do a variety of techniques, such as faux finishes. You can use a glaze anywhere you would use regular paint, but for this example I wanted to show one of my favorite techniques, using it behind a printed transparency to create a multicolored, textured effect. The bonus is you get two projects for the "price" of one!

Tips & Tricks

- *The ratio of paint to glazing liquid will affect the translucency of the color. The more paint you add, the stronger and more opaque the tint.*
- *If you can't find wet-media film, you could also try using a page protector or a sheet of acetate. (But don't use acetate in scrapbooks!)*

Other Ideas to Try . . .

1. Glaze "stamped" with bubble wrap.
2. Crumpled plastic bag or wrap pressed into glaze.
3. Dry foam stamp pressed into glaze and lifted out.
4. Wood-grain faux-finish tool used over glaze.

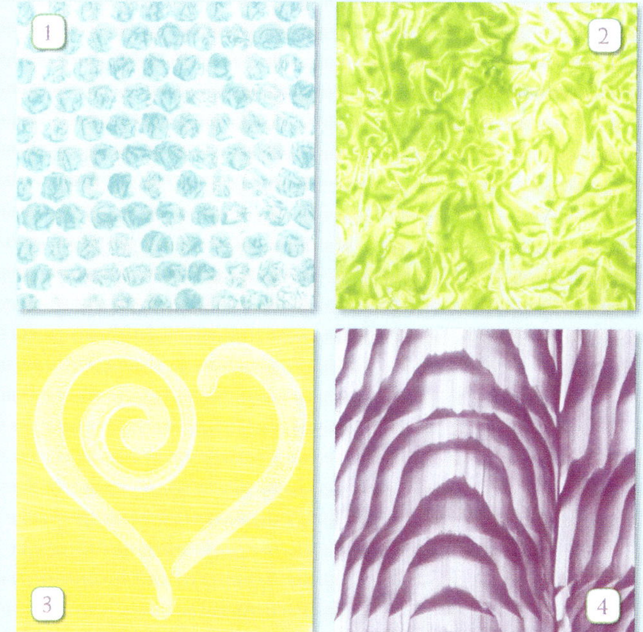

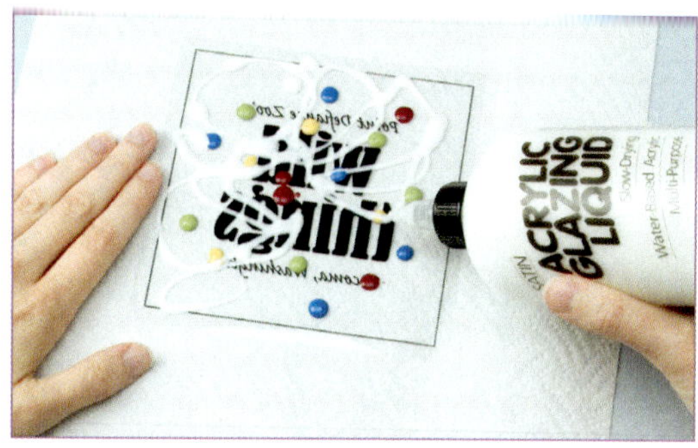

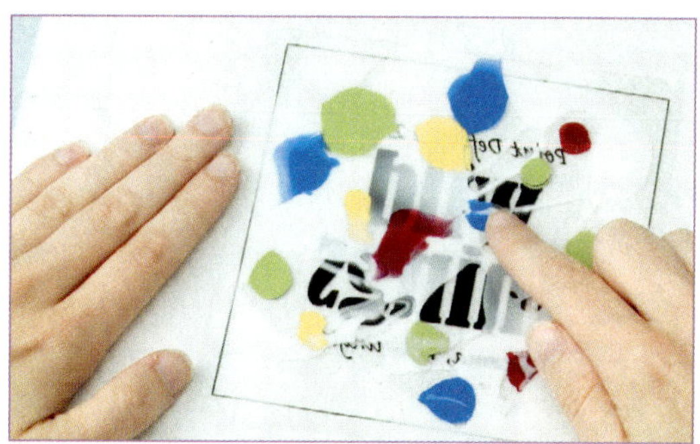

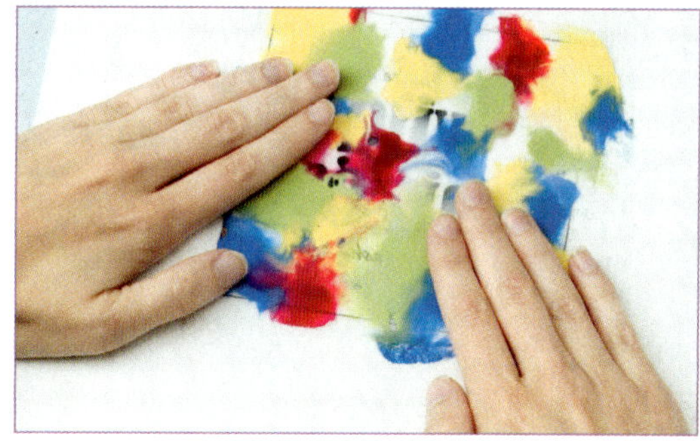

1

Place a couple of drops of each color onto the back of a printed transparency. Squirt glazing liquid in a swirly motion over the entire area.

2

Place a plain piece of wet-media film cut slightly larger than the transparency over the top and gently smooth and twist it down with your fingers to blend the paints together.

3

Continue until the colors have merged into a soft pattern (do not mix them too much or they will begin to look muddy or combine into a solid color). Then carefully lift up film, starting at one side or corner, slowly pulling to the opposite side. Once dry, attach to your background and use the extra piece of glazed film on another project!

Waxed & Stamped Backgrounds

It was almost impossible to find the perfect patterned papers to coordinate with my favorite jacket, so I decided to use two separate painting techniques to create my own unique background and accents. I also made a custom diamond stamp using a die-cutting machine and craft foam. Journaling is revealed on tags that pull out of the stamped library pockets.

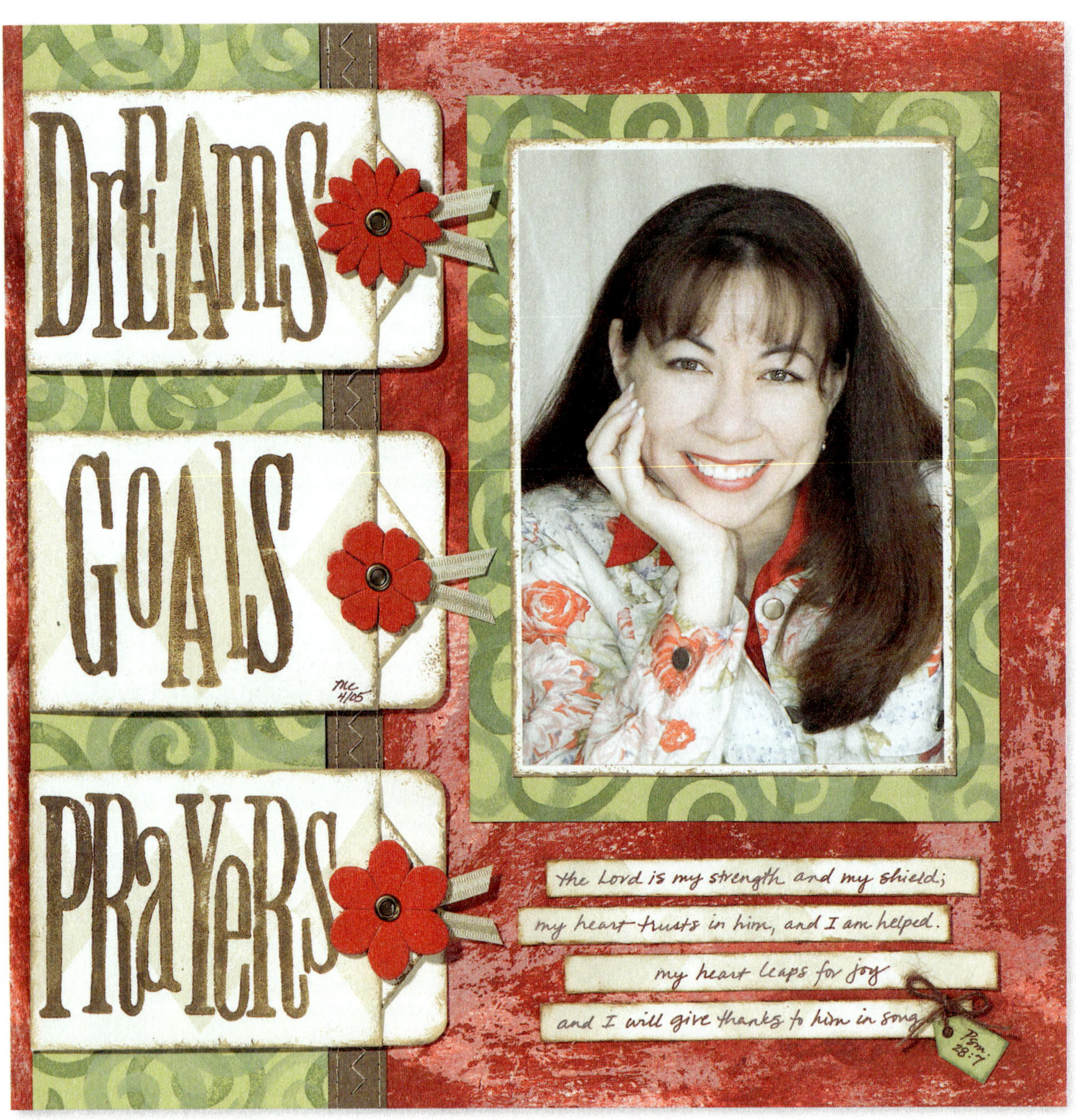

Dreams, Goals, Prayers

Supplies: 140 lb. cold-press watercolor paper (Strathmore); Dorland's Wax Medium (Jacquard Products); deep burgundy, French mauve and light avocado Americana acrylic paints (DecoArt); raw linen Ceramcoat acrylic paint, Paint & Toss Sponges (Delta); Burnt Umber Light Fluid Acrylics paint (Golden); swirl foam stamp (Rubber Stampede); foam letter stamps, ribbon (Making Memories); leather flowers (Prima); diamond and tag dies (Sizzix); die-cutting machine (Provo Craft); pocket template (Deluxe Designs); brown pen (Staedtler); glue dots (Glue Dots International); natural sponge (Loew-Cornell); stiff wide brush

Not feeling particularly artistic? Then here's two different techniques that will get you totally creative—and you won't even have to lift a brush! The first is basic stamping with paint. If you can apply liquid makeup to your face, then you already have the skill to create stamped designs on your layouts. Simply pat the paint onto the stamp, turn it over and press down. While you can use any kind of stamp, foam tends to be the best because the paint doesn't dry as quickly or smear as it can with rubber stamps.

The second technique uses a layer of wax to create a softly distressed, hand-rubbed finish. You can use different waxes such as candle or bowling alley wax, but I prefer a conservation wax because it's an archival medium used to help preserve fine paintings. Experiment with how long you let the second coat of paint sit before rubbing it off—you can achieve results ranging from a very soft tinted look to a more saturated, dramatic effect.

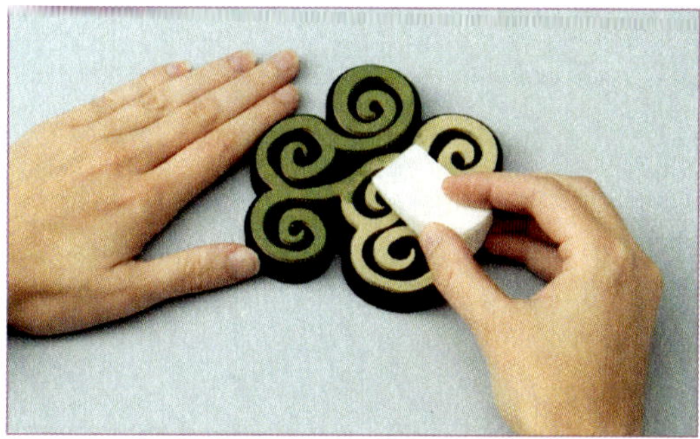

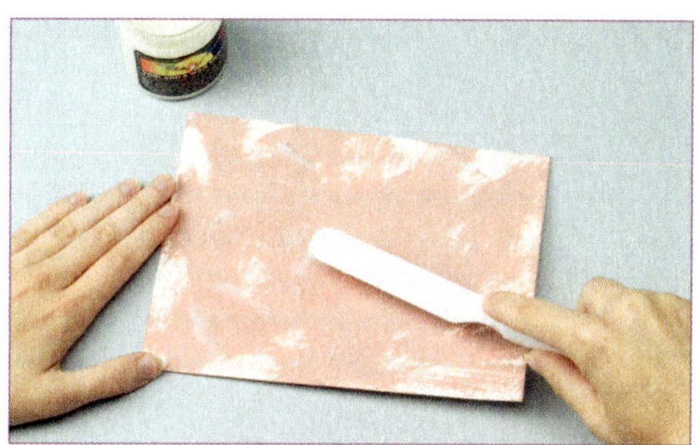

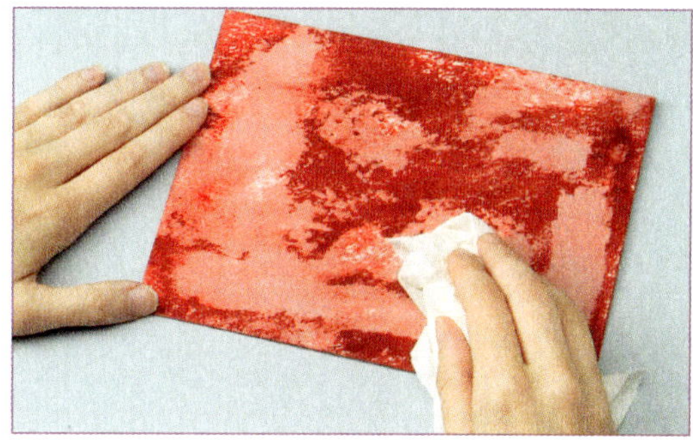

1

Using a foam wedge, pat an even coat of dark green paint onto stamp, then firmly press onto cardstock. Repeat process until entire background is covered. Add a second layer of the same stamped design using a lighter tint of green paint.

2

To create the waxed background, first paint watercolor paper with mauve paint, leaving some parts of the paper open. Once dry, scrape on a random layer of wax with a palette knife.

3

Brush burgundy paint over the entire surface. Wait a few seconds, then rub off paint and wax with a paper towel or rag to reveal the first paint layer underneath.

Tips & Tricks

- *The first time you apply the paint to a foam stamp, some of the paint will soak into the foam and may create a blotchy impression. Stamp a few test runs on scrap paper, reapplying paint after each impression, to make sure you get a consistent design on your actual project.*
- *To prevent paint from drying on your stamps before you have a chance to property wash them, keep a bowl of warm, soapy water nearby so that you can throw your dirty stamps into it as you work.*
- *Don't let the wax dry completely, or it will be very difficult to remove.*

Other Ideas to Try . . .

1. Experiment with applying the wax with different tools such as a sponge or stiff brush to create different kinds of rubbed textures.

2. Apply several colors to a stamp at the same time for a multi-tonal effect.

3. After applying paint to a stamp, remove some color by blotting with a crumpled paper towel or cheesecloth before stamping to create a distressed texture.

Dimensional Paint

Dimensional paint was the perfect medium to use on a layout celebrating the fun of a silly string war between my two daughters. I like how the same paints could be thinned down to create the softly tinted, flat border.

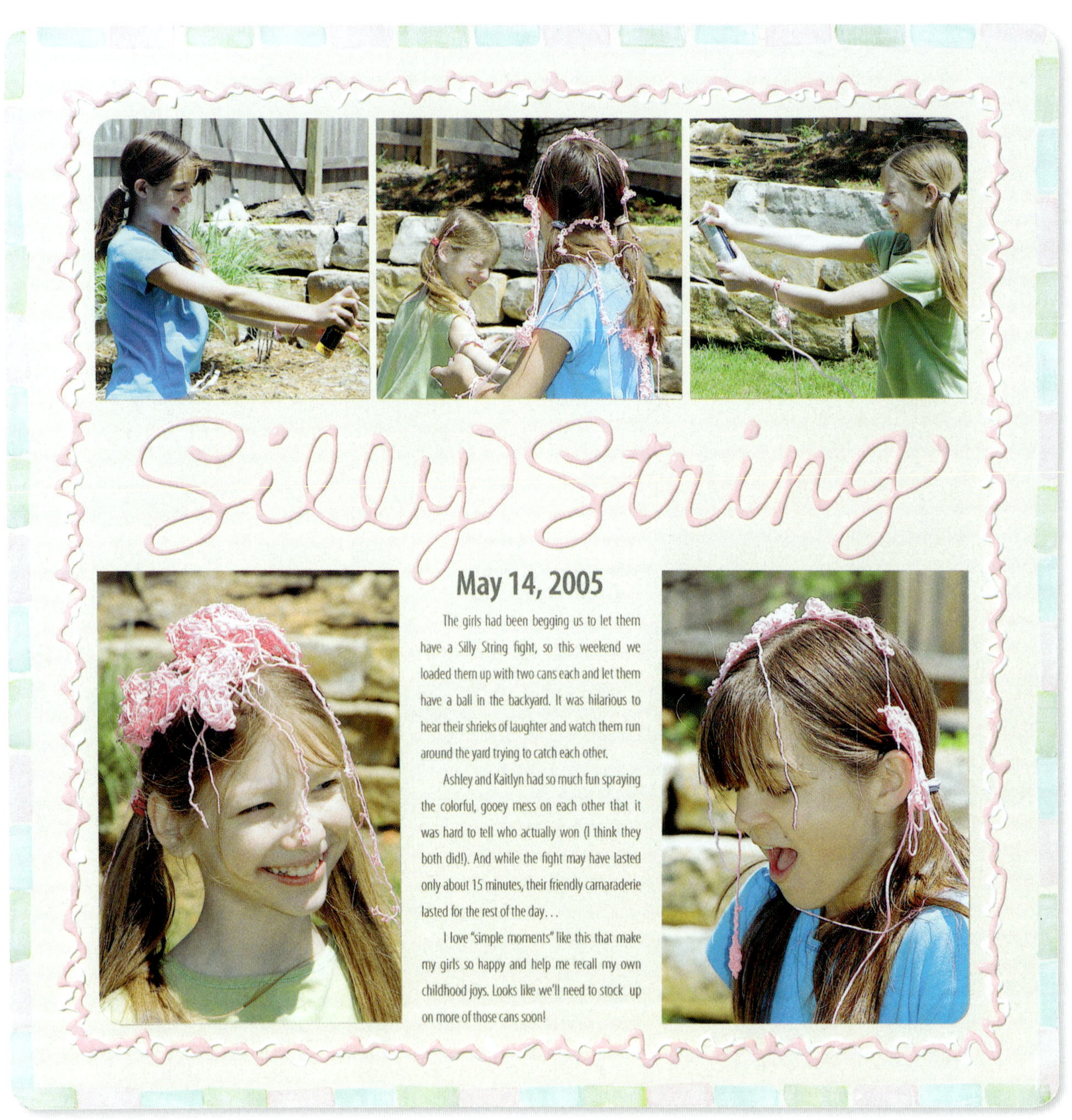

Silly String

Supplies: Baby pink, wicker white, fresh foliage and calypso sky Folk Art Papier paints, Flow Medium (Plaid); ¾" flat brush (Loew-Cornell); corner rounder (EK Success)

Dimensional paints are acrylics that come in a thicker version that will create a dimensional, raised effect to your design. You can use them to "draw" lines in various widths, depending on how much pressure you apply when squeezing the container, or you can brush them out with the help of thinning agents such as Flow Medium or water. Craft-quality dimensional paints are usually found in squeezable containers, while artist-quality "heavy body" paints come in jars or tubes and are applied with a tool such as a palette knife. Keep in mind that because of their higher density and thickness when applied, these paints take much longer to dry than their regular acrylic cousins. I recommend allowing them to dry at least 24 to 48 hours before placing a layout inside an album or page protector.

Tips & Tricks

- *To prevent air sputters, gently tap the tube two or three times so the paint drops towards the tip, and the air goes to the back.*
- *To create the smoothest lines, apply as much continuous pressure as possible in one long squeeze versus several shorter ones.*
- *Add embellishments such as buttons, fibers or charms to the paint while it's still wet to secure them into place without glue.*

Other Ideas to Try . . .

Dream Matchbook

Dimensional paints are also available in other unique formulas, such as glitter, gel and metallic colors. I used one that turns into a texture resembling velvet when heated to create an elegant butterfly image on this small matchbook cover.

Supplies: Volume Touch dimensional paint (Pebeo); PureColor stamp ink (Delta); stamp (Stampendous!); matchbook (EK Success); heat tool (Wagner)

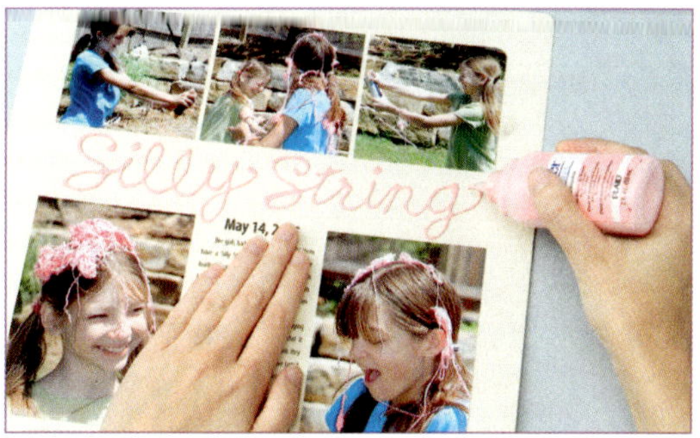

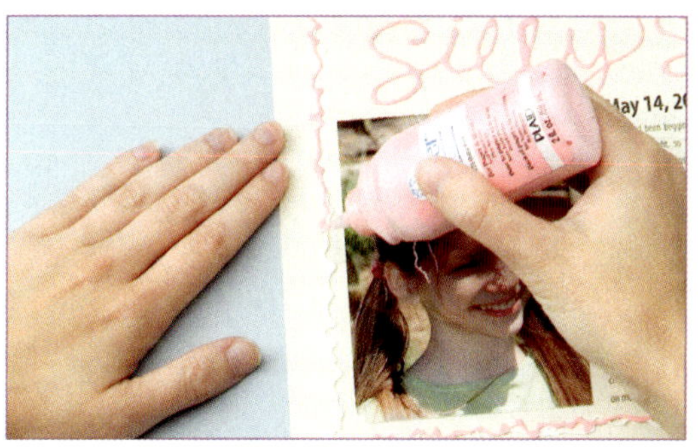

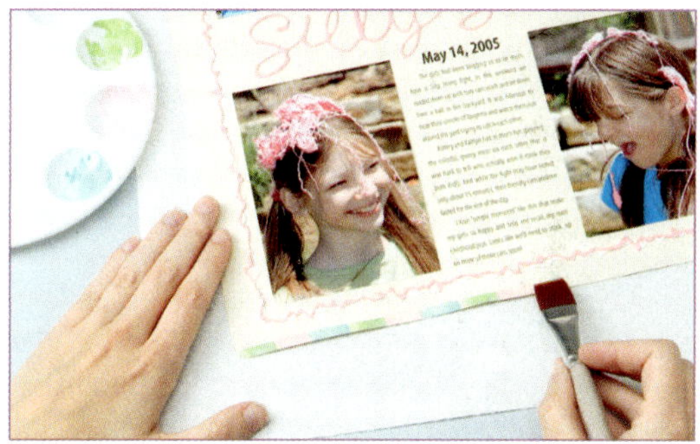

1

Trim and adhere all photos to the layout background. Holding the pink paint tube so that the tip is about ½" from the paper, squeeze and spell out the title.

2

Create the first layer of the inside border by holding the white paint tip about 4" from the layout. Squeeze and let the paint loosely drizzle out as you slowly wiggle your hand down the border. Repeat this process using the pink paint.

3

Mix equal parts of pink, green and blue paints with Flow Medium to thin them down into sheer glazes. Use the top edge of a flat brush to create the striped border using alternating colors.

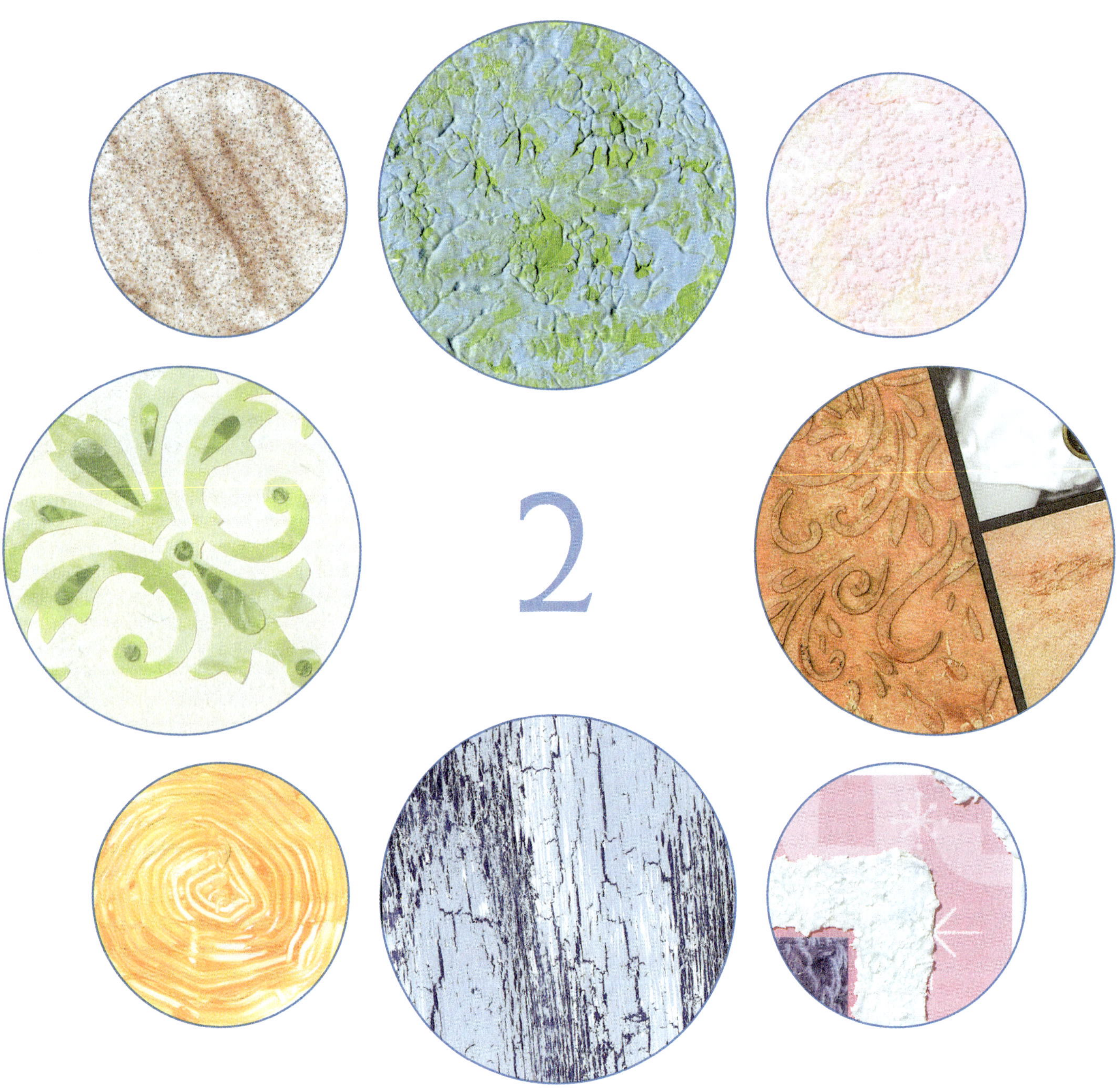

2

Artist Mediums

Now that you've become familiar with using acrylic paints, it's time to bring it up a notch and add something extra to the mix! That extra punch comes in the form of a group of products called artist mediums, which are unpigmented mediums used primarily to enhance the texture, flow and finish of regular paint. There are different kinds of mediums made for specific types of paint and colorants, but in this chapter we will be dealing only with acrylic-based mediums that can be used alone or mixed with acrylic paints.

Since mediums will add some amount of extra bulk and moisture to regular paint, keep in mind that they will take longer to dry, usually around one to several hours. Although the surface may feel dry to the touch, some can even take up to a few days to completely "cure," depending on how thick the medium was applied and what type you used (always read the label to see what the manufacturer recommends). To be on the safe side, don't put your finished artwork inside a page protector or album for at least 24 to 48 hours after it is dry to the touch. I also like to create several large "textured papers" in various colors whenever I'm playing around with a medium technique so that I can have completely cured sheets to work with on future projects, which is especially useful when I need to finish a project quickly.

Artist mediums are some of my favorite products to work with because they are so versatile and fun to use. They can bulk up or thin down paint, add an interesting texture or create a matte to super-glossy finish—all without compromising the integrity of the paint. So with just a handful of basic artist mediums, you can jazz up your regular paints in a wide variety of ways. The mediums and techniques I'll show you in this chapter are only a small sampling of the wonderful effects you can achieve, so I encourage you to also explore the Web sites of artist supply companies listed on pages 93-94. They can be great resources for ideas, and even though some may be geared more for the "fine artiste," you can easily take just a few elements and simplify them to suit your needs.

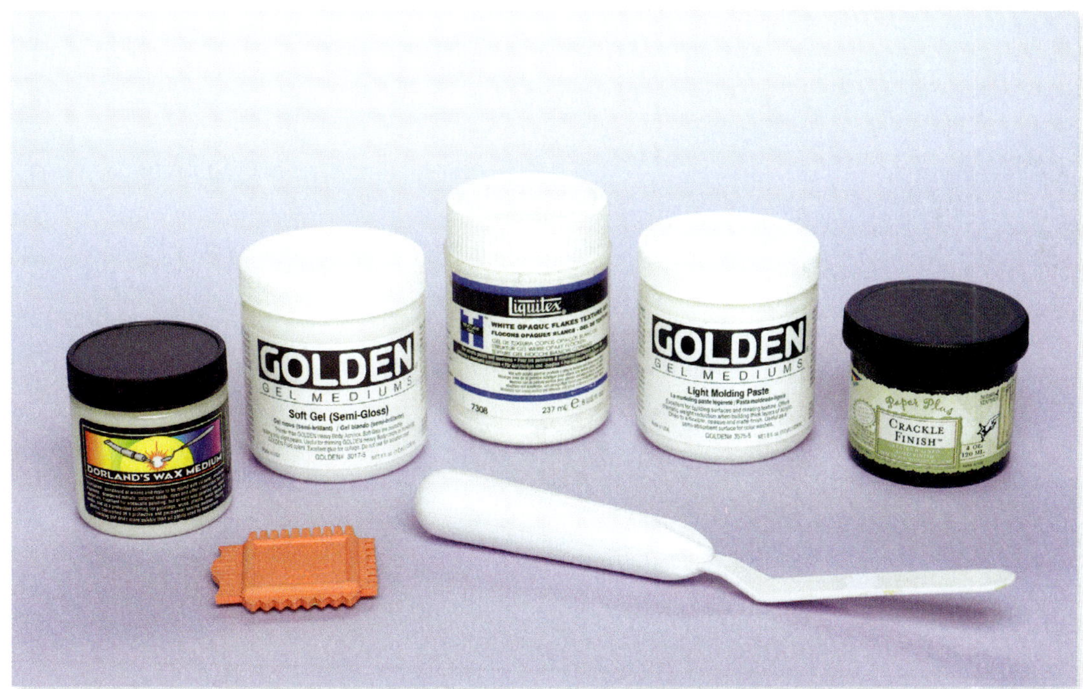

Featured Supplies

Wax Medium

Soft Gel

Texture Mediums

Light Modeling Paste

Crackle Medium

Texture Comb

Palette Knife

Soft Gel Mediums

Designer Allison Strine created this dynamic layout using a variety of soft gel mediums and tools. Once the designs were dry, she cut circle shapes from the best parts of each sample and machine-stitched them to her layout.

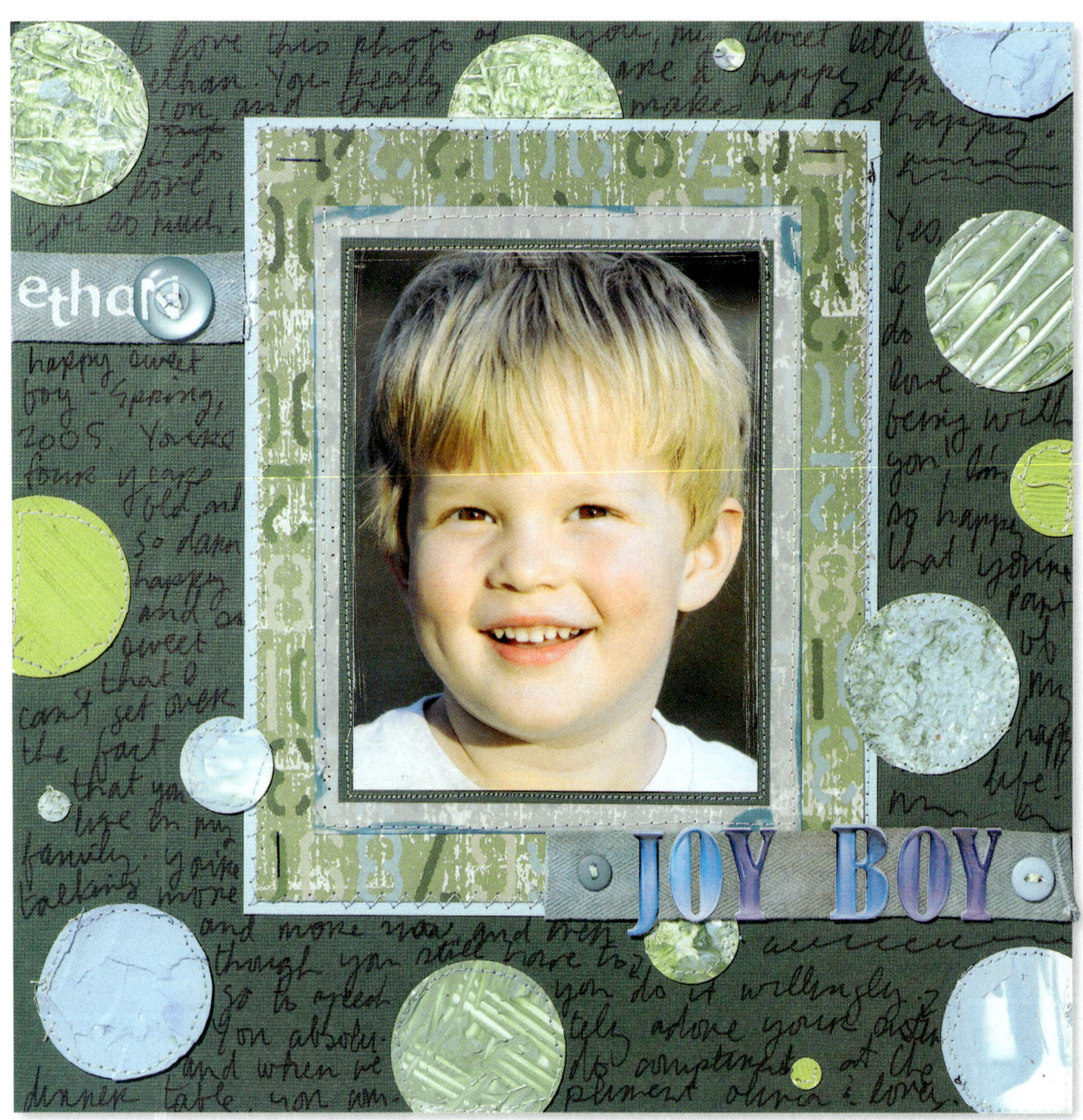

Joy Boy *Supplies:* Semi-Gloss, Gloss and Matte Soft Gels (Golden); baby blue and Hauser light green Americana acrylic paint (DecoArt); natural sea sponge (Loew-Cornell); comb tool (Plaid); patterned paper, rub-on letters, epoxy stickers (Creative Imaginations); fibers (Carma); pen (Tombow)

Allison Strine, Roswell, Georgia

Soft gels are thick, creamy, white mediums that dry to a flexible finish and can be either transparent or translucent, depending on the specific medium type. They are used primarily to thicken acrylic paints for dimensional effects, come in a variety of sheens ranging from matte to high gloss, and you can use the same techniques with any variety. Regular and heavy gels are essentially the same products, but are stiffer and heavier, so are not as practical for use on layouts. Another feature of these versatile mediums is that they have great adhesive qualities, making them ideal for collage and altered-art techniques.

Tips & Tricks

- *Some glossy mediums will remain tacky even after they've completely dried. A little wax rubbed over the finished design will prevent it from sticking to the page protector.*
- *Be extra careful when cleaning up gel mediums because once they dry on your tools or table, they'll probably be there forever!*

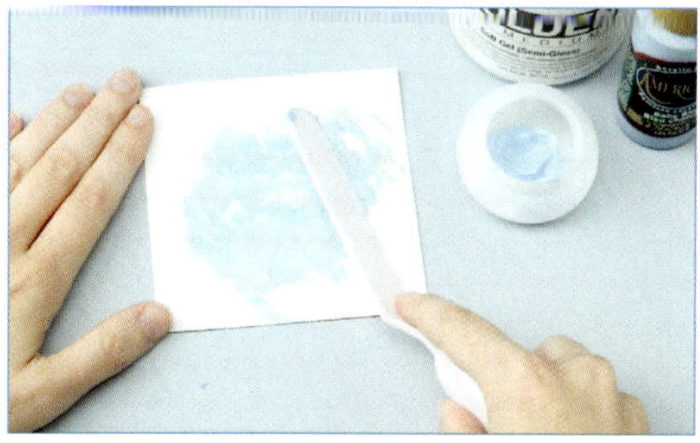

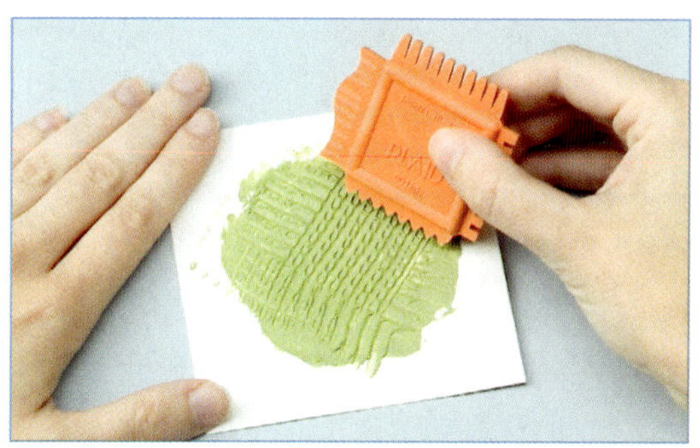

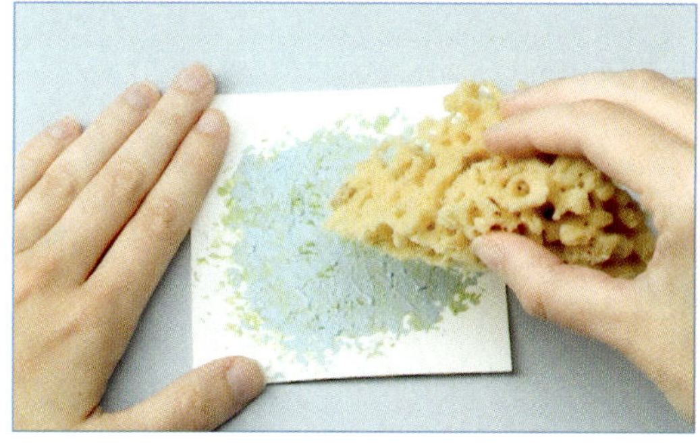

1

Mix Semi-Gloss Soft Gel with blue paint and spread a thick layer onto watercolor paper with a palette knife, just like you would spread butter.

2

Mix Matte Soft Gel with green paint and apply a thick layer to watercolor paper with a palette knife. Create a woven texture with the comb tool by dragging it first in one direction through the gel, then again in the opposite direction.

3

Mix Gloss Soft Gel with green and blue paints to create two different colored gels. Using a dabbing motion and one color at a time, apply each to the watercolor paper with a natural sea sponge.

Other Ideas to Try . . .

1. Matte Soft Gel textured with a palette knife.
2. Gloss Soft Gel with comb tool dragged in a circle.
3. Semi-Gloss Gel textured with a regular sponge.
4. Semi-Gloss Gel rubbed on with fingers.

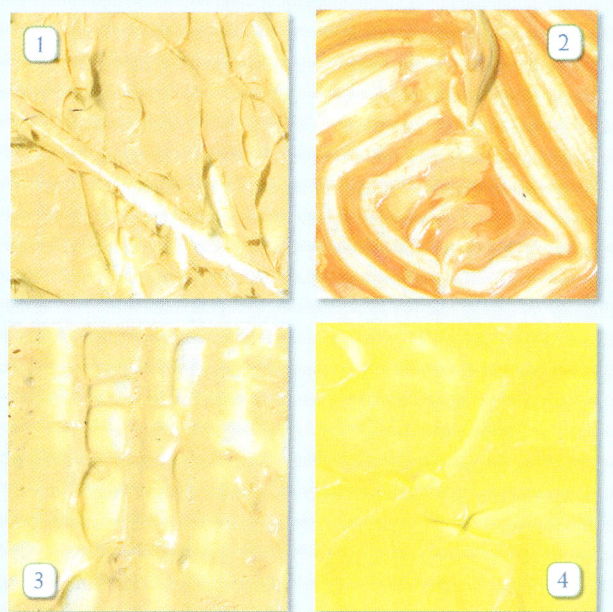

What could be more fun than spending a day outdoors in the snow? Staying inside with a cup of hot chocolate and doing something creative with the photographs is more my style! I had so much fun making a frame that looks as if it's made of fluffy snow but will never melt in my album!

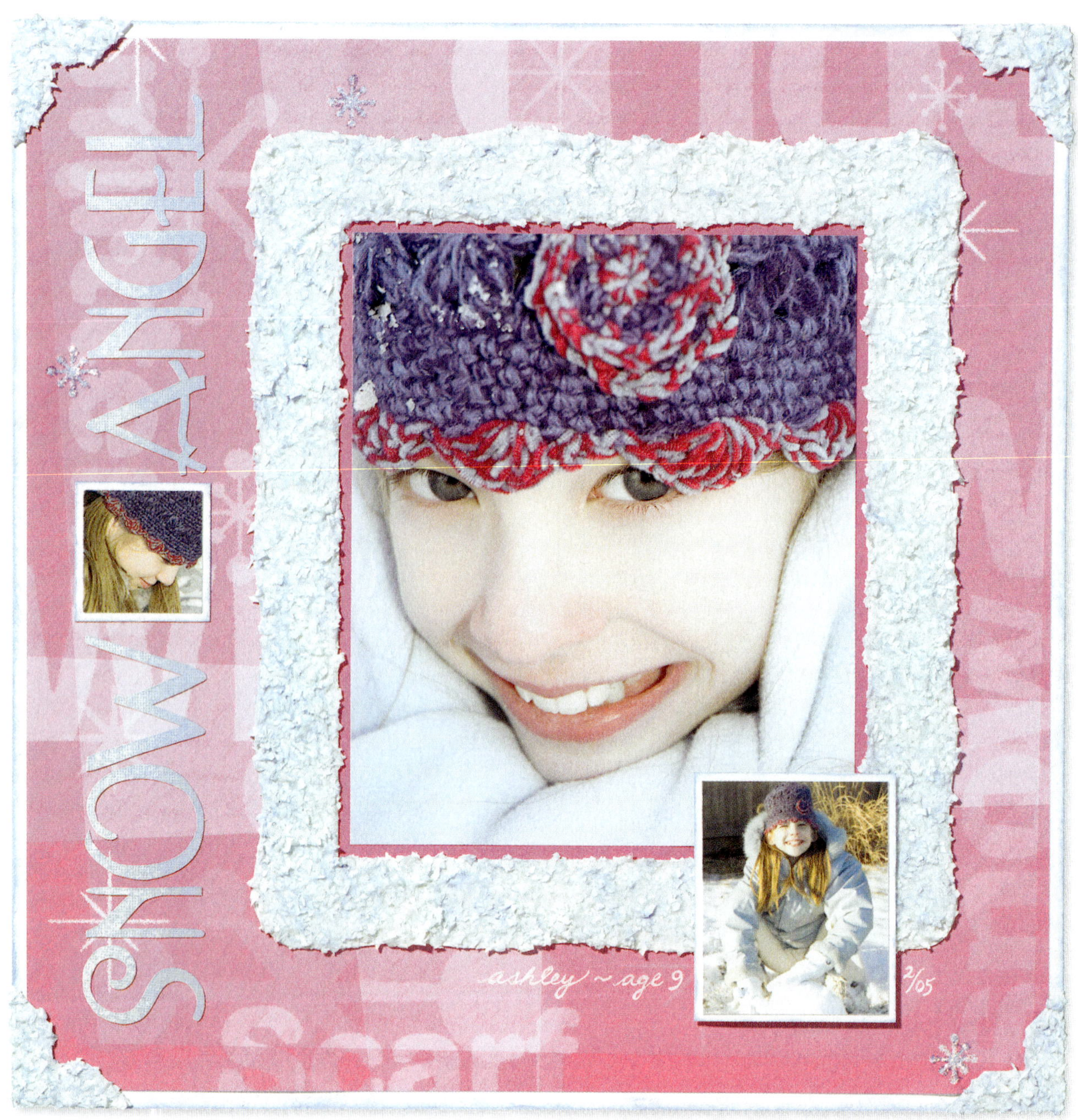

Snow Angel *Supplies:* Periwinkle blue, chambray blue and white Ceramcoat acrylic paint (Delta); White Opaque Flakes Texture Gel (Liquitex); textured cardstock (DieCuts with a View); patterned paper (Daisy D's); Stickles glitter paint (Ranger); notched corner punch (EK Success); square punches (McGill); gel pen (Sanford); Spongit Stick (Loew-Cornell); chipboard

Texture mediums are soft gel mediums with a fun twist—they have different elements like fibers or crushed pumice added to them to help create unique textural and dimensional effects. In addition to the ones shown here, there is a wide variety of other textures available that you can use straight out of the jar or tint with acrylic paint. You can also make your own by adding materials like glitter or sand to plain soft gel medium, but keep in mind that whatever you add may not have a good reaction with the product, so always do a test swatch before using it on your layout.

Tips & Tricks

- *Most gels will dry clear in places if not mixed with enough paint, so use a background that will blend in with the desired effect. You can also paint surfaces before adding the gel.*
- *Texture mediums can be heavy and are very moist before applying, so use extra thick cardstock, high quality 140+ lb. watercolor paper or acid-free chipboard as a base.*

Other Ideas to Try . . .

1. Garnet Gel Medium (untinted)
2. Resin Sand Texture Gel (untinted)
3. Blended Fibers Texture Gel (tinted)
4. Glass Beads Texture Gel (tinted)

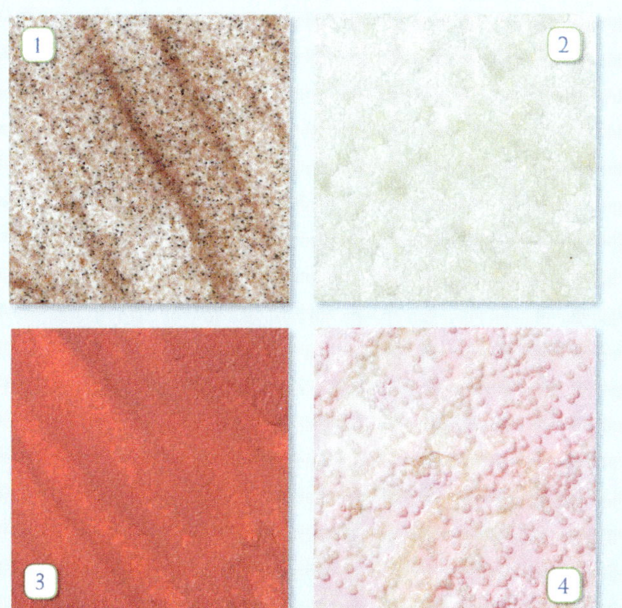

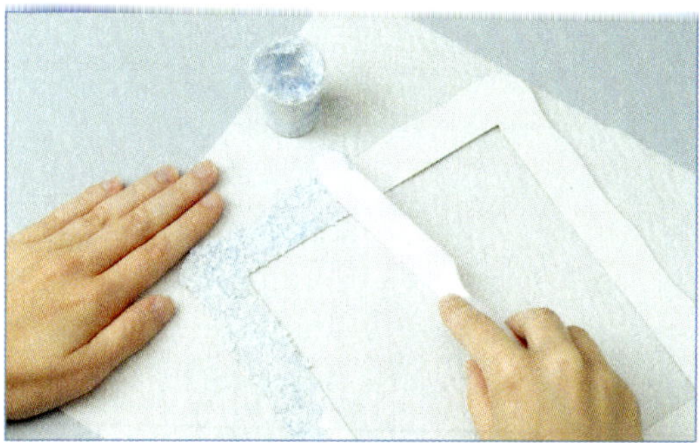

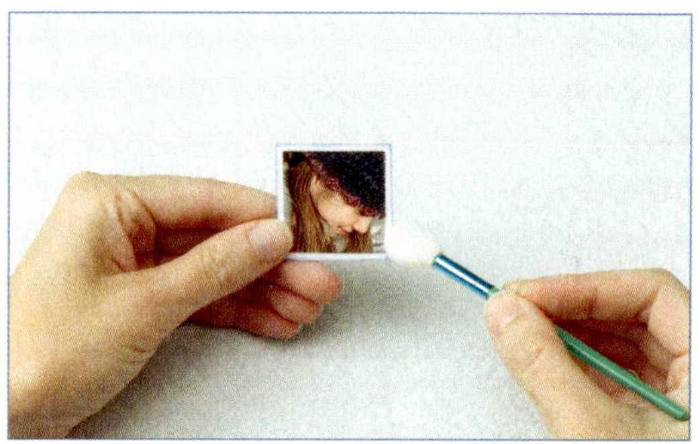

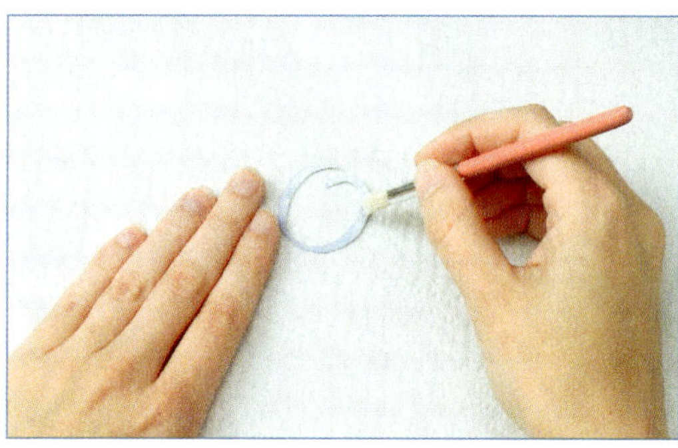

1

Cut out frame and punch large corners from chipboard. Add 4 to 6 drops blue paint to a few teaspoons of White Flakes Texture Gel and mix gently until just barely blended (or mix well for a solid tint). Apply to frame and corners with a palette knife; allow to dry for a few hours or overnight.

2

Rub edges of layout background and small photo mats with blue paint and a foam applicator.

3

Stipple blue and white paint over the top of each title letter, concentrating more paint at the top and lessening pressure as you move toward the middle for a graduated effect.

Light Molding Paste

This is one of my favorite photos of my daughters with their cute cousin, Jaguar. Because I wanted to make sure there was an equal emphasis on all of them, I used a combination of "faux stucco" and glazed scrollwork in rich, earthy tones to give this layout a balance of feminine and masculine design. Journaling is printed on a custom tab that pulls up out of the top of the photograph.

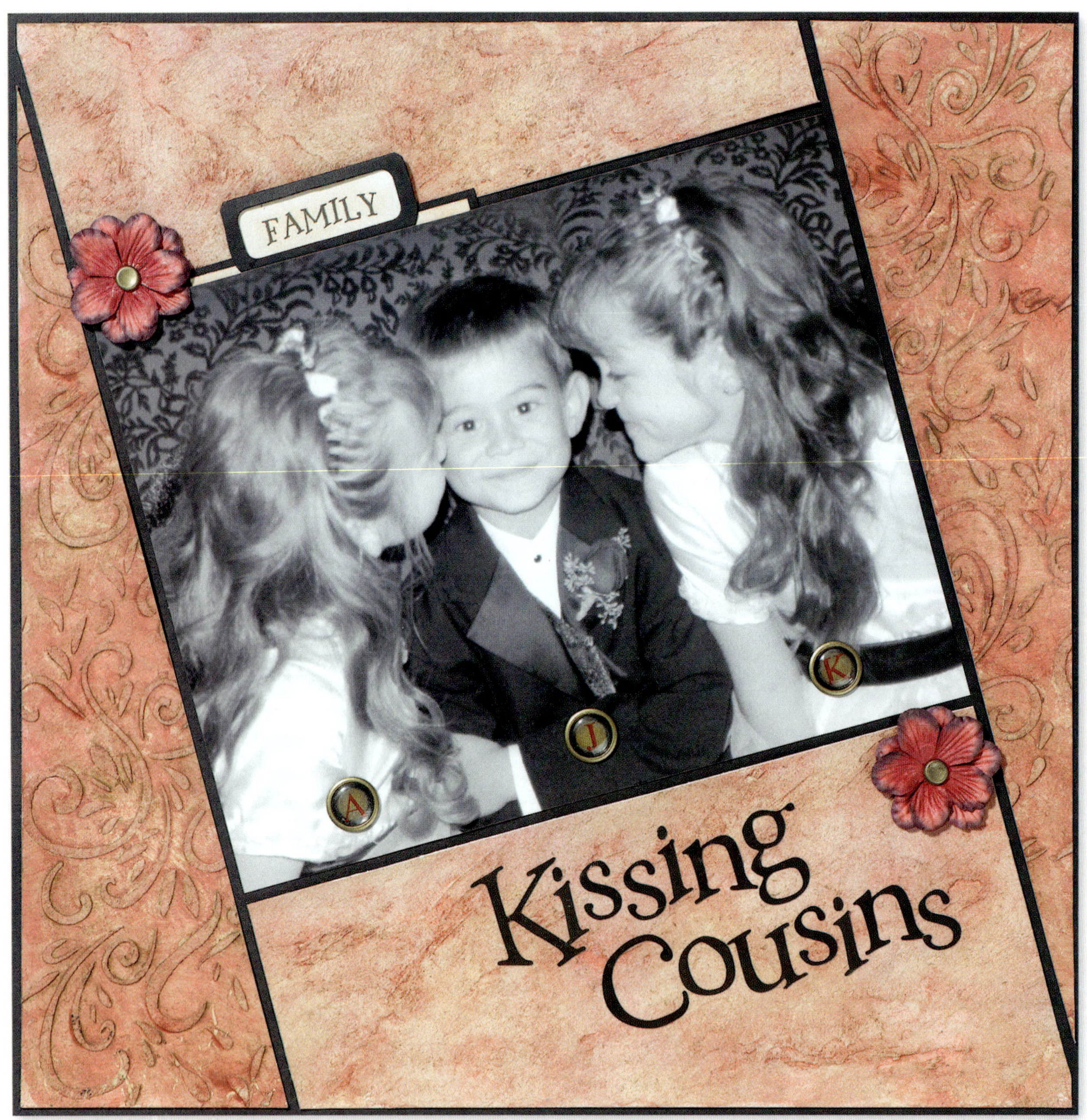

Kissing Cousins

Supplies: Light molding paste (Golden); Ceramcoat acrylic paint, Sheer Color Finish glaze medium, Scroll stencil (Delta); 1" American Traditional wash brush (Loew-Cornell); Bristol paper (Strathmore); letter stickers (Creative Imaginations); epoxy letters, metal discs (K & Company); tab die (Sizzix, Provo Craft); paper flowers (Prima); snaps (Making Memories)

Light molding paste is a very lightweight, opaque white medium that dries to a matte, flexible finish and will accept a variety of different paints, inks and dyes. Because of its slightly spongy and absorbent texture (similar to craft foam), it's perfect for applying a painted finish or design after it's dry, or you can mix in paint to color it before applying to a surface.

Because this is a stiff, dimensional medium, it can be applied and textured with a palette knife and also works well over stencils or other interesting items such as mesh. I love to use glazes or color washes over dried molding paste because it gives a soft, mottled effect that looks similar to a faded fresco.

Both types of molding paste backgrounds used on this layout use the exact same glazing technique and colors over the top, but have two different looks because the "stucco" sections have glaze rubbed over pure paste, while the stenciled sections have glaze also brushed over an exposed paper surface, which absorbs the glaze differently. (To create a glaze, see page 19.)

Tips & Tricks

Light molding paste is also handy to use underneath embossed metal and paper designs to help give support without adding extra weight.

Other Ideas to Try . . .

Field of Flowers Accent

Thin acrylic paint with water, and paint a design over a dried molding paste for a soft, watercolored effect.

Supplies: Light molding paste (Golden); acrylic paint, metal frame (Making Memories)

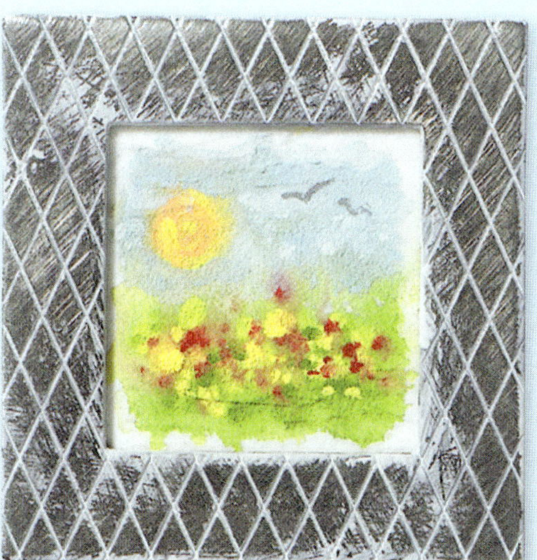

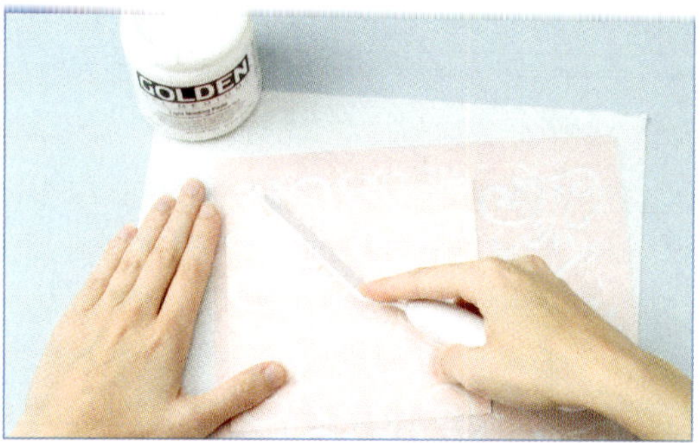

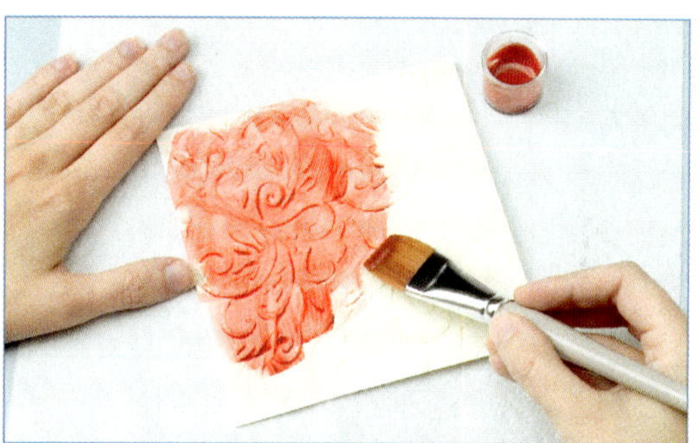

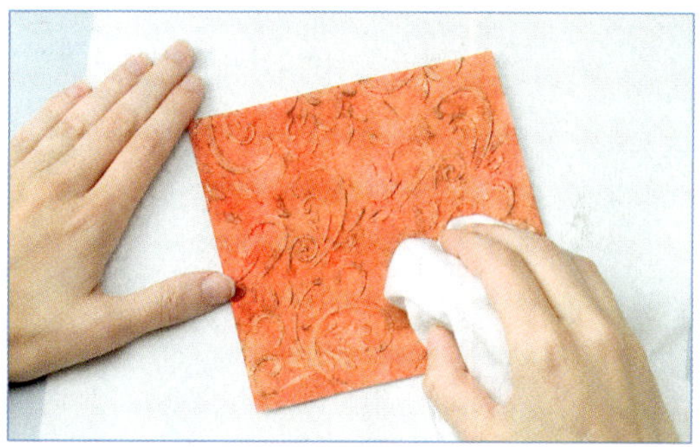

1

For the side pieces, apply paste over the stencil with a palette knife. For the top and bottom pieces, apply paste directly over the entire surface, pushing it around to create high and low areas.

2

When paste is dry, brush cream glaze over the entire background; allow to dry. Brush maroon glaze over random areas and blend in with a damp rag. Leave some areas darker than others for a soft, mottled effect and allow to dry.

3

Brush dark brown glaze over entire background, concentrating around the raised and pitted areas so more glaze collects in the crevices. Use a rag to remove most of the glaze around the flat areas.

Crackle Medium

Crackled custom frames were created to work with patterned paper that already had a weathered feeling. A touch of ink around the journaling box and a metal accent strung on ribbon were all that was needed to give this layout its warm, rustic appeal.

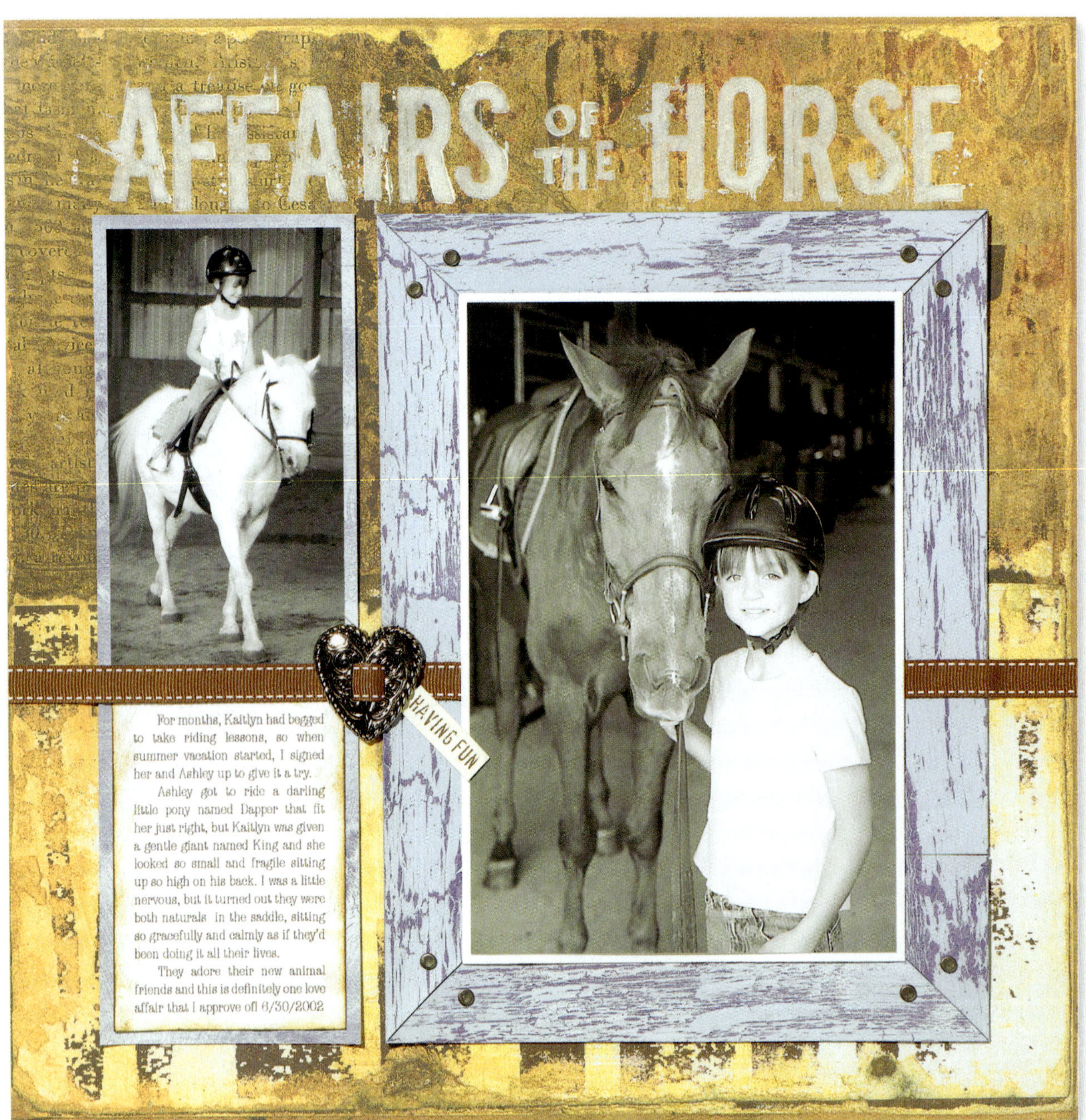

Affairs of the Horse

Supplies: Paper Plus Crackle Medium, lavendar lace and white Ceramcoat acrylic paint (Delta); patterned paper (Paper Loft); flat-head eyelets, tag (Making Memories); ribbon (Morex); heart concho (Tandy Leather Company); letter stamps (Purple Onion Designs); Distress Ink (Ranger)

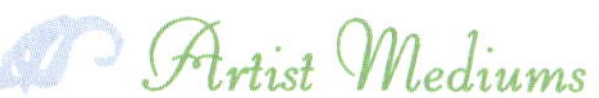

Crackle medium is such a fun product to play with because it's very unpredictable and every time you use it, you'll get a completely different result. It works by causing a reaction underneath acrylic paint to create random cracks in the upper painted layer and reveals the lower surface, which can be almost anything, such as a painted watercolor paper, plain cardstock or a metal bookplate. The size, direction and type of the cracks depends largely on how thick the medium is first applied and how the acrylic paint is brushed on afterward.

The trickiest part about using this unique medium is understanding the timing of when to add the top layer of paint—it will smear and break down if the medium is still too wet, and if it's allowed to get too dry, it won't crackle at all. How the paint is applied is critical as well and should be done with a minimum of overbrushing. But once you get the hang of it, it's a very easy process and creates a beautifully weathered pattern that looks as if it took years to happen.

Tips & Tricks

- *A thin layer of crackle medium will result in finer cracks, while a thick layer will produce larger, more dramatic cracks.*
- *Not all crackle mediums are acid-free, so be sure to check the label before using it on scrapbook pages.*
- *Speed up crackle medium drying time by using a mini hand fan.*

Other Ideas to Try . . .

1. Experiment by brushing in different directions when you paint on the top layer of color—the crackles will go in the direction of the strokes.

2. Purposefully apply the top coat of paint a little too early to create another type of interesting pattern that resembles a wood-grain texture.

3. Paint a base layer with a contrasting color of paint and allow it to dry before applying the crackle medium (this first layer will not crackle).

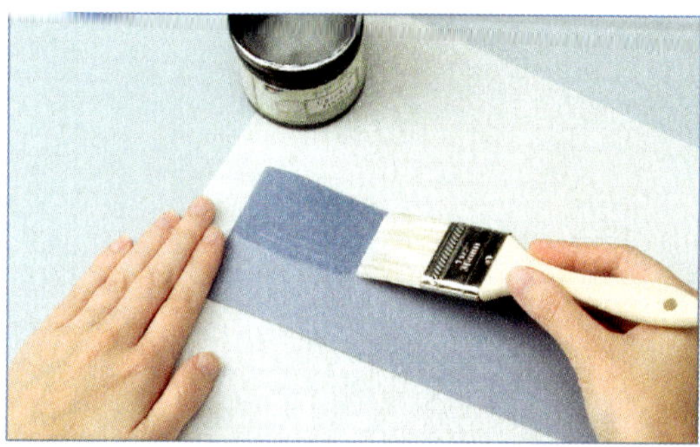

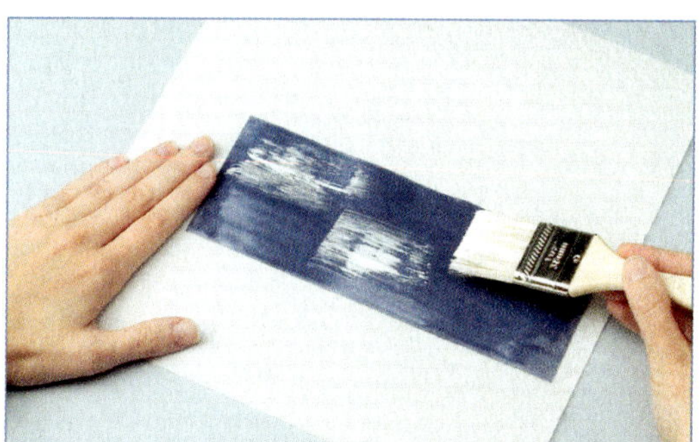

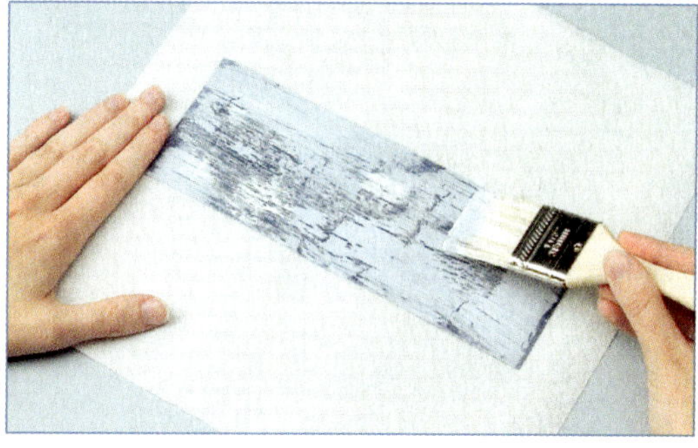

1

Brush on crackle medium using firm strokes to apply an even layer of medium over dark blue cardstock. Allow to dry until tacky, or about 15 to 30 minutes, depending on humidity and the thickness of the layer.

2

Lightly brush on white paint in random areas, being careful not to brush over the same spot more than once to avoid smearing the medium.

3

Quickly brush on lavender paint over most of the background, leaving some areas with the white paint alone. Do not overbrush paint—just wait for the magic of the crackle to happen in a few minutes!

Acrylic Gel Sheet

Several shades of green-tinted medium were swirled together to create a gel sheet that I handcut into a fleur-de-lis design (using a stamp as my pattern) and embellished with darker punched gel shapes. I like how the finished accent gives a smooth, subtle dimension without adding a lot of weight.

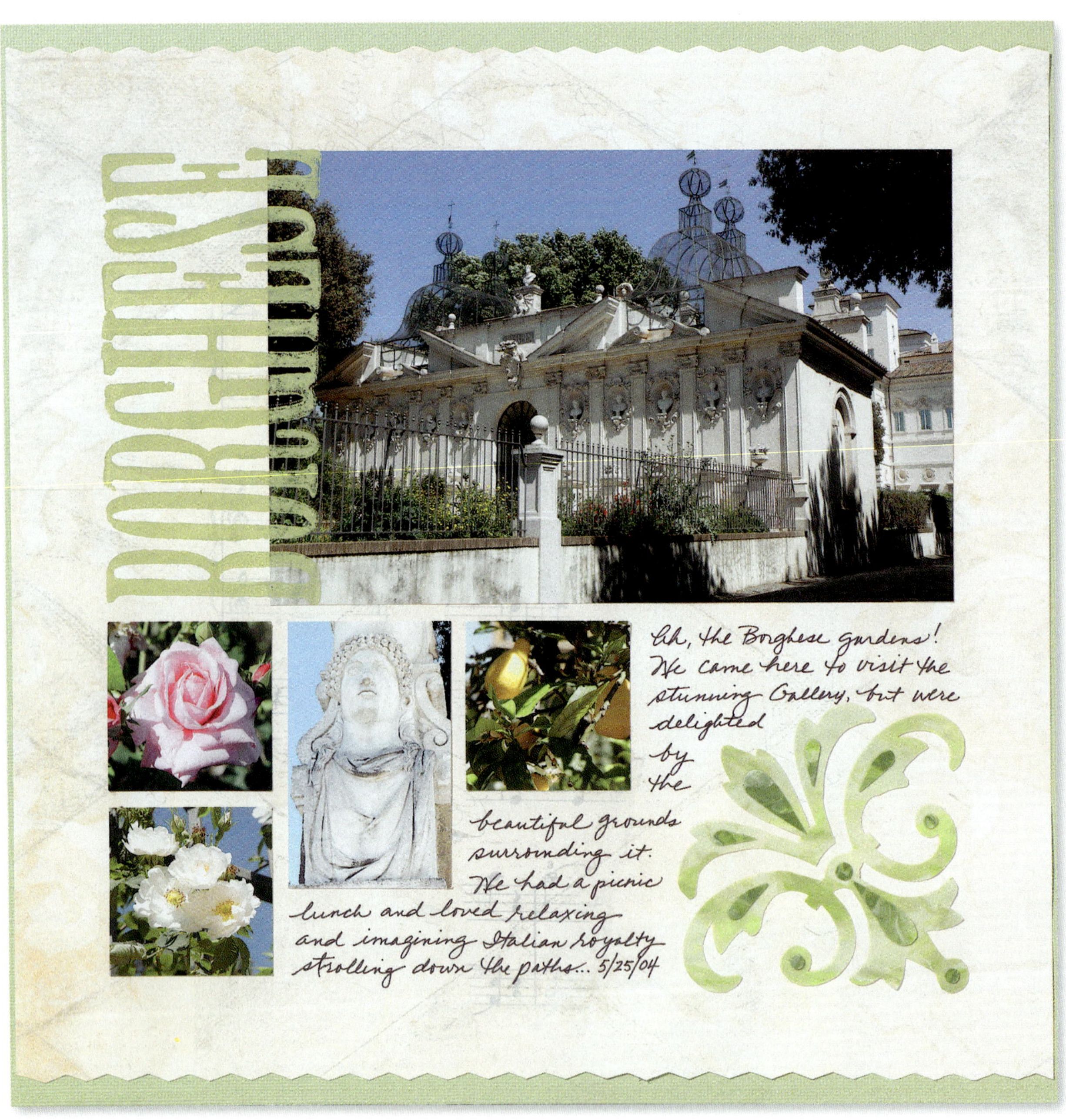

Borghese Gardens *Supplies:* Semi-Gloss Soft Gel Medium (Golden); green tea, light foliage green and wedgewood green Ceramcoat acrylic paint, palette knife (Delta); rectangle die (Sizzix, Provo Craft); decorative stamp (Rubber Stampede); foam letter stamps (Making Memories); decorative scissors (Fiskars); heart and circle punches (EK Success); nonstick craft sheet (Ranger); painters tape (Henkel Consumer Adhesives)

Did you know that you can make sheets of paint that can be handled and embellished just like a piece of heavy handmade paper? They are called acrylic sheets and are created by spreading a thick, uniform layer of acrylic medium inside a frame to help keep its shape until it has cured and dried. These sheets can be made with different types of mediums, but I prefer the soft gel varieties for scrapbooking projects because they make very strong, flexible sheets that can be die cut, punched or freehand cut into any shape.

All types of acrylic sheets will dry to a translucent or transparent finish, depending on the type of medium used. For example, a gloss medium will dry to a clearly transparent sheet, while a matte medium will have a slightly milky look. You can paint over plain acrylic sheets or mix in paint before spreading it in the frame to cure, or even both!

Tips & Tricks

- *Mix colored gels in air-tight containers so that you can save and store any leftover gel for another project.*
- *Make sure your work surface is perfectly clean and smooth, as any dirt or creases will be transfered to the back of the gel sheet.*
- *I love to use my nonstick craft sheet underneath all my projects using artist mediums because they won't stick and the sheets are easily removed once dry.*

Other Ideas to Try . . .

1. Die cut a simple shape like a large leaf, heart or flower instead of a square to create a frame for the acrylic sheet.
2. Instead of a swirled effect, try creating something like a striped or dotted pattern.
3. Use a texture medium instead of soft gel to create a highly textured, dimensional sheet.
4. Add a transparent paint to the gel or embellish a plain acrylic sheet with tinted glaze to create a stained-glass effect.

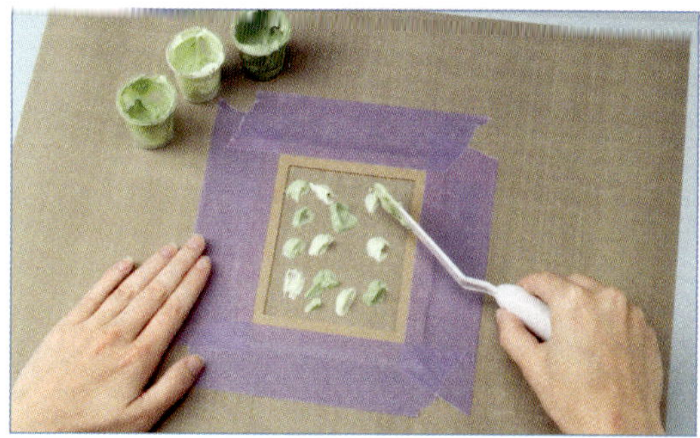

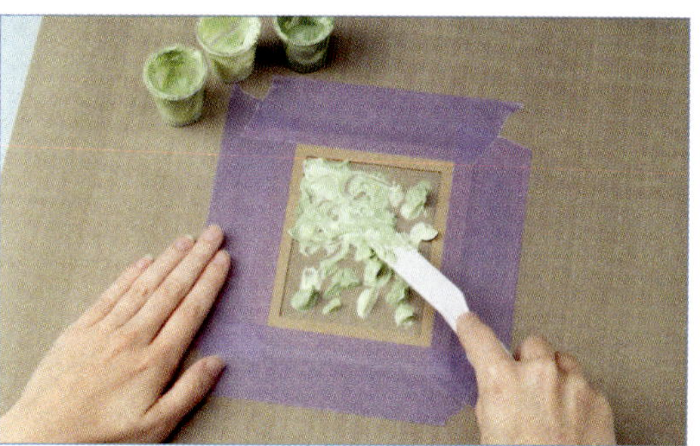

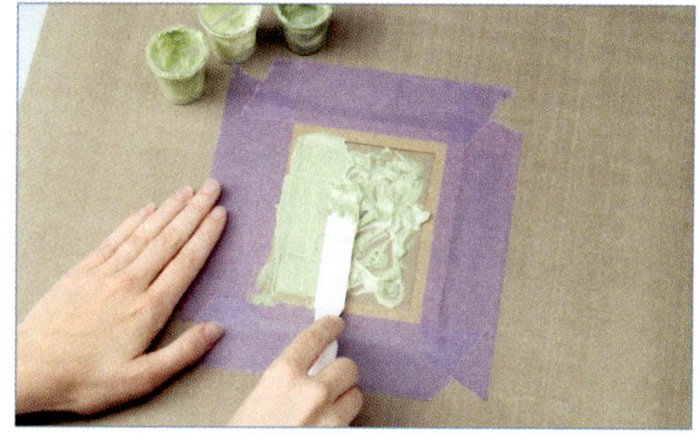

1

Die cut (or handcut) frame from chipboard, tape to nonstick craft sheet (or a piece of glass) with painter's tape to hold in place. Mix green paints and soft gel medium into three separate shades and randomly drop into frame opening.

2

Lightly swirl colors together with the tip of the palette knife, but be careful not to overmix or the colors will combine into one solid color.

3

Gently smooth gel mixture so it completely covers the opening and is flush with edges of chipboard. Set aside to dry for 24 to 48 hours (depending on the thickness). Remove from nonstick surface and then cut sheet away from frame with a craft knife to reveal the swirled pattern on the underside.

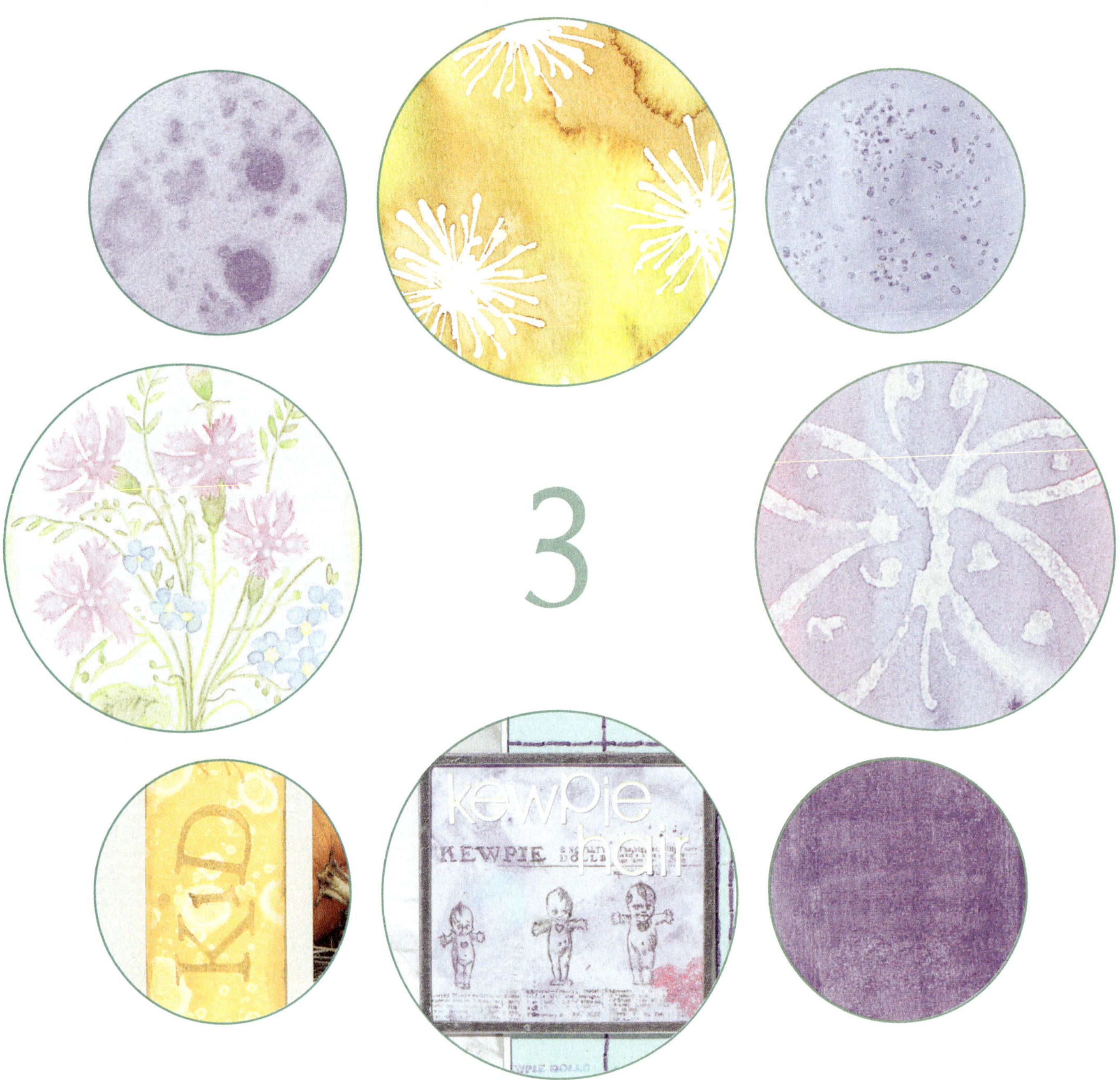

3

Watercolors

Watercolor paints, one of my favorite mediums to work with, are valued for their transparent, free-spirited beauty. One of the best (and sometimes frustrating!) qualities about them is that you can never create the exact same design more than once. Although you can control a technique in order to achieve certain effects, the way the colors will blend together is always a unique process. Knowing this fact frees up the perfectionist in me and allows me to have fun just letting the medium work its magic!

Another nice thing is that watercolors come in a variety of forms: moist tubes, dry pans or cakes, crayons, pencils, pens and liquid. They all create the same paint, but depending on your own individual style and budget, you may find you like working with some types more than others. Like acrylic paints, watercolors are available in two levels of quality: artist and student (these do not include the kind you buy for children). A good quality student paint can certainly work well for scrapbooking applications, but may not be as lightfast or vibrant as artist grade paints.

There are three paper groups made specifically for use with watercolors: hot-pressed, cold-pressed and rough. Hot-pressed is the smoothest, while rough has a heavily textured surface. I like to use the lightly textured cold-pressed paper in 140 lb. weight or heavier because it's easy to paint on and doesn't warp as much as lighter weights.

When painting large areas, it's a good idea to prepare the paper with a process called "stretching," which will minimize any warping. Completely saturate the paper with water, and then either staple it to a stretcher board or tape it to a nonabsorbent surface like masonite. Allow to dry (I find overnight works best) before painting. Another option is to use a watercolor block, which is a stack of watercolor papers held together by a layer of glue around all the edges. The strength of the combined papers act as sort of a stretcher board, so you can paint on the topmost sheet, allow to dry and then simply cut away the perfectly flat painting from the rest of the block. You can also paint on cardstock and vellum, but these papers tend to warp quite a bit more so I'd suggest reserving them for techniques that use very little water.

In addition to traditional brushes, there are brushes with water reservoirs built right into them, so you don't have to worry about spills or drips, which is especially useful while working at your scrapbook table or at a crop. Now that you're prepared, let's go discover some fun new techniques!

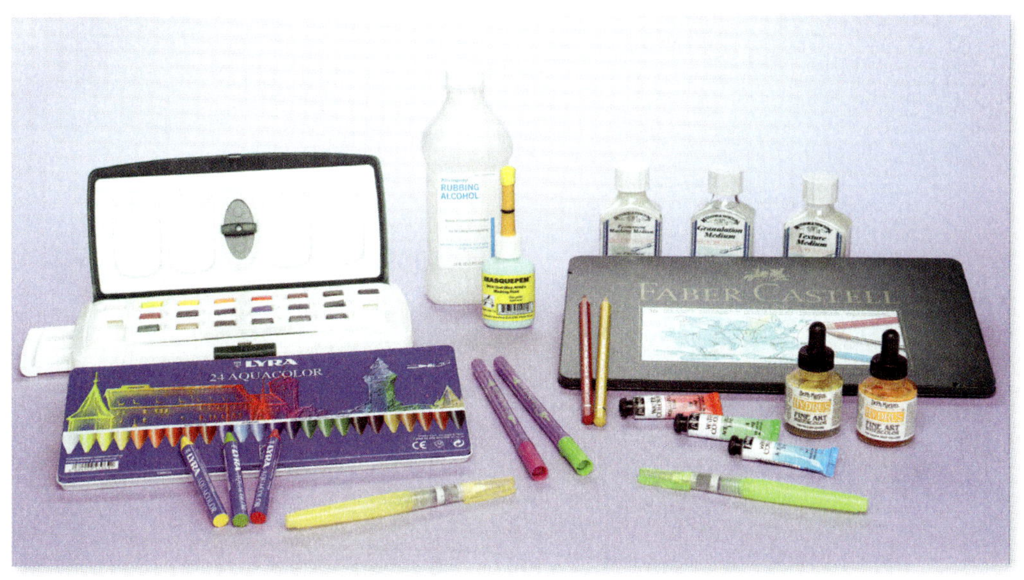

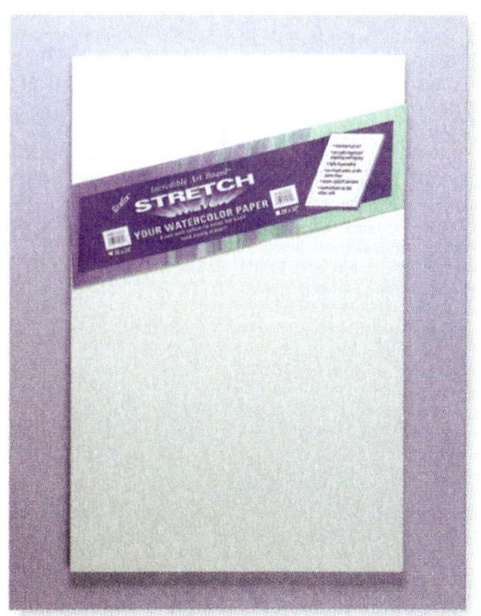

Featured Supplies

- Watercolor Crayons
- Watercolor Pencils
- Pan Watercolors
- Tube Watercolors
- Concentrated Liquid Watercolors
- Watercolor Brush Pens
- Watercolor Mediums
- Masking Fluid
- Stretching Board

Wash & Splatter Technique

A watercolored background was the obvious choice for this layout recalling a special family reunion weekend by the beach. Golden specks give realistic sparkle to the sandy "beach" and sand dollar photos over real mesh add a touch of dimension.

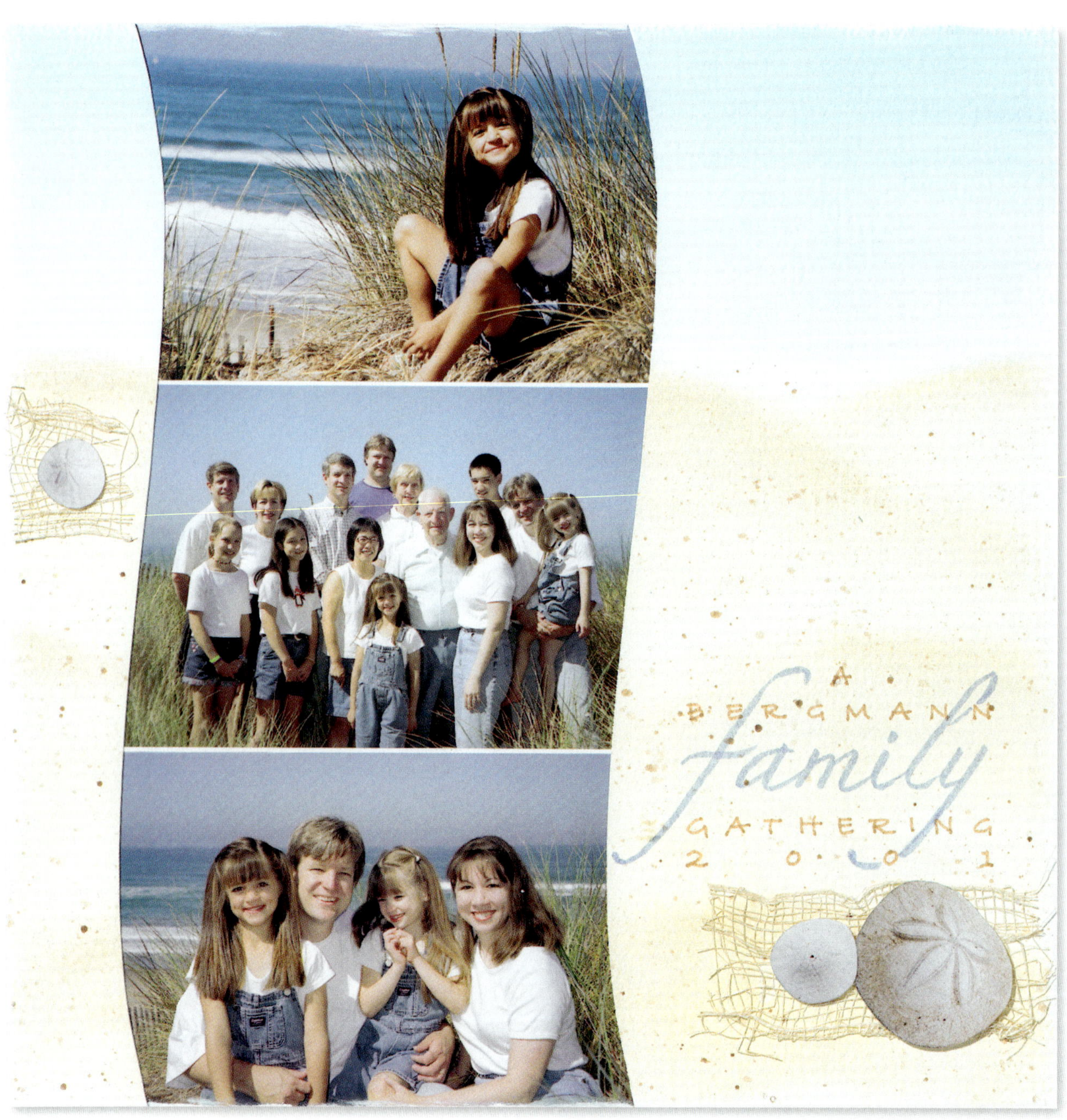

A Bergmann Family Gathering

Supplies: 140 lb. cold press watercolor paper (Strathmore); Artists' WaterColours (Daler-Rowney); American Painter ¾" wash brush, #5 Round Golden Taklon brush (Loew-Cornell); Zig brush pens (EK Success); Incredible Art Board (Grafix)

One of the easiest and most common ways to use watercolors is with a technique called a "wash" where the paint is quickly applied to—or washed over—the surface to add softly blended color to a background or other large areas in a design.

There are two kinds of wash applications that you can use alone or combined with other techniques. A basic wash is an overall solid-looking area of color, while a graded wash is where one end goes from dark to light or where several colors are blended into each other. The key is to use a large, flat brush, pre-moisten your paper with a damp sponge or brush, and make sure the paper stays damp at all times to create seamless blends and avoid any lines as the paint dries.

Another popular technique is splattering paint to create a randomly speckled texture that can mimic the look of sand, dirt, snow, age or just add general interest to a design. The shade and size of your specks will vary by the amount of water you add to the brush, how high above the paper you are holding it, and how hard you tap it off.

Tips & Tricks

- *Keep a small mist bottle of water at hand, and mist paper often to keep it moist as you work on large areas.*
- *If you find the wash is too light (while still wet, or even after it's dried), you can repeat the process over the existing wash until you get the shade you want.*
- *A toothbrush is also a great tool for splattering color, and will create a finer speckle than with the paintbrush. Just dip the toothbrush into the paint and rub over the bristles with your fingernail.*

Other Ideas to Try . . .

1. Layer several different colors over a basic wash using the splatter technique.
2. Add stamped or rub-on designs over a dried wash.
3. Splatter metallic ink over a dark wash for an elegant, dramatic effect.
4. Watercolor paper sands easily and will reveal an interesting texture through the paint.

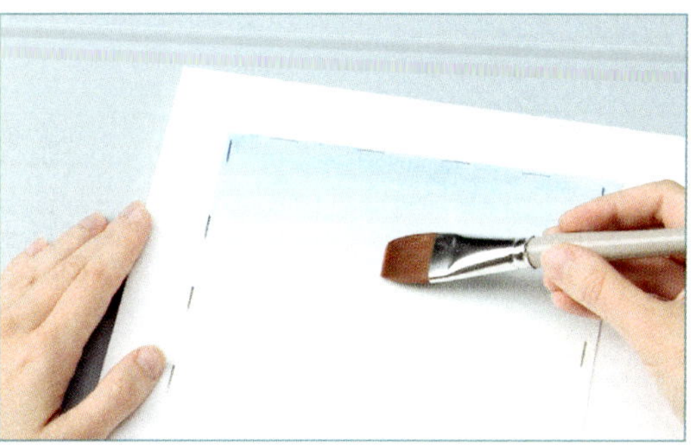

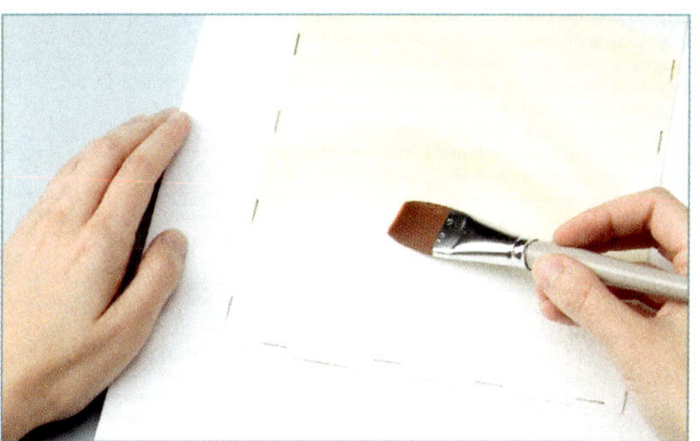

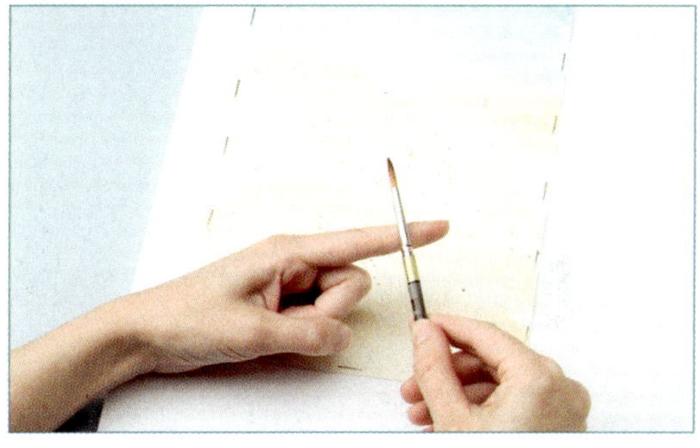

1

To create the "sky," mist paper with water and starting at the top, apply a horizontal line of blue paint with a wide wash brush. Dip brush into water and add another line below the first one, slightly overlapping it. Continue process until the color fades into nothing at the bottom edge.

2

For the "sand dune" wash, use same technique as for the sky, applying yellow ochre in random curvy lines. While wash is still damp, go back and add just a light tint of burnt umber at the tops of the dunes and fade down for added definition.

3

Create a "sandy" texture over the dried wash by loading a round brush with brown or gold paints and gently tapping it over your finger as you hold it over the paper.

Masking Fluid Resist

My wish to be able to create fluffy white dandelions for this painted background was easily granted by using simple strokes of masking fluid. Watercolor paint also adds a delicate touch to the edges of the mats and ribbon.

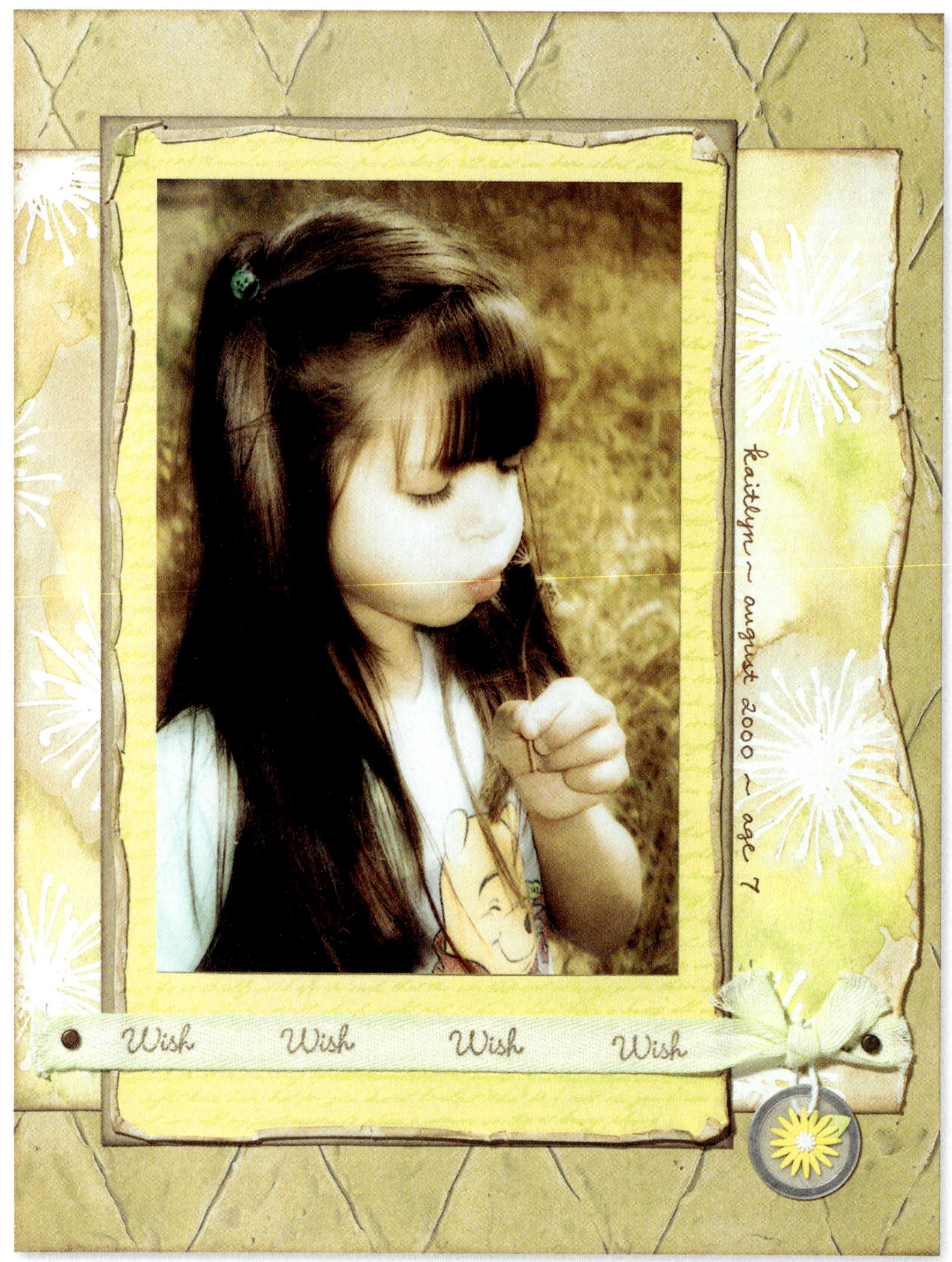

Wish . . . *Supplies:* 90 lb. cold press Montval Aquarelle watercolor paper (Canson); Aquarelle Fine tube watercolors (Pebeo); Masquepen (Cruddas Innovations); American Painter 1" wash brush, #5 Round Golden Taklon brush (Loew-Cornell); patterned paper (Daisy D's, Mustard Moon); stamp (Delta); Staz-On solvent ink (Tsukineko); Fluid Chalk Ink (Clearsnap); circle tag (K & Company); ribbon (Creek Bank Creations); flower sticker, pen (EK Success); mini brads (Limited Edition Rubberstamps); Incredible Art Board (Grafix)

Although there are several ways to mask out shapes so that they resist paint, masking fluid (also known as liquid frisket) is one of the most traditional and easiest tools to use with watercolors because it's completely waterproof and rubs off easily without damaging plain paper or a previously painted design underneath. It can also be used with dyes and acrylics.

For this layout, I used tube watercolors, which are already moist and can be used straight out of the tube or thinned with water before painting. To create the harder blended edges between each color, apply paints over dry paper instead of pre-moistening it as you would for a wash. This keeps the colors from blending too much into each other, but make sure to work while the paint is still damp or the edges will not blend at all.

Tips & Tricks

- *If your paints are drying too quickly before you are able to add the next colors, lightly mist paper with water before adding more paint.*
- *Sometimes the paint will not dry as quickly over the resist as it does on the paper. Make sure all areas are completely dry, or the paint may smear when you remove the masking fluid.*
- *Using watercolor along the edges of photo mats or cardstock also softens them for easier tearing and curling effects.*

Other Ideas to Try . . .

Butterfly Tag

There is another type of liquid masking fluid that is permanent and cannot be removed once it is dry. To create this butterfly tag, it was brushed onto a stamp that was pressed onto the paper before painting.

Supplies: 140lb. cold press watercolor paper (Strathmore); Aquarelle Fine tube watercolors (Pebeo); Permanent Masking Medium (Winsor & Newton); metal-rimmed tag, chain (Making Memories)

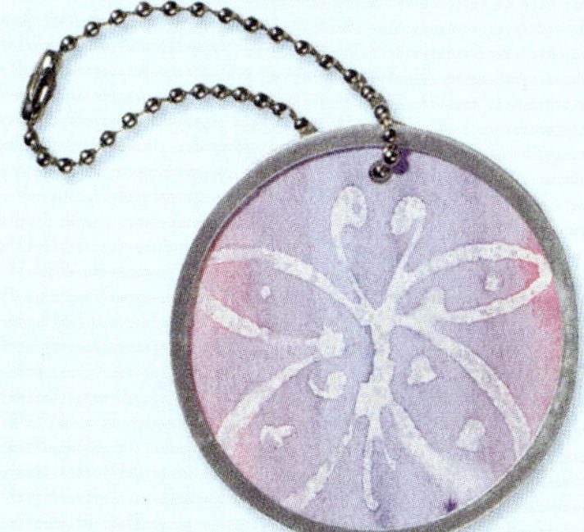

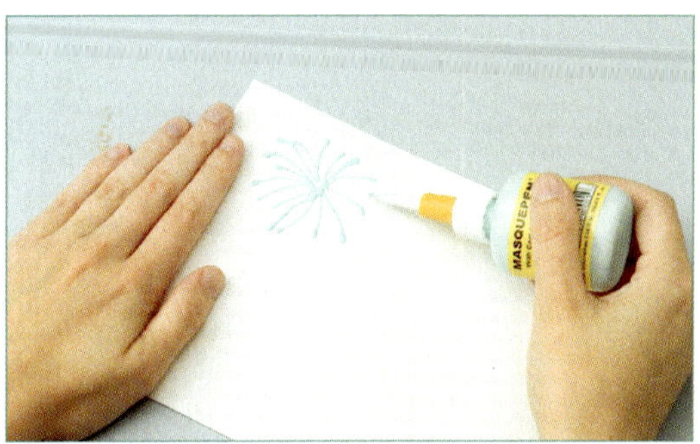

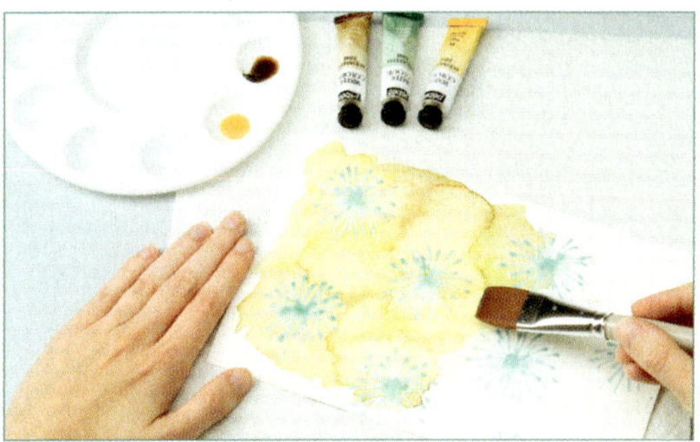

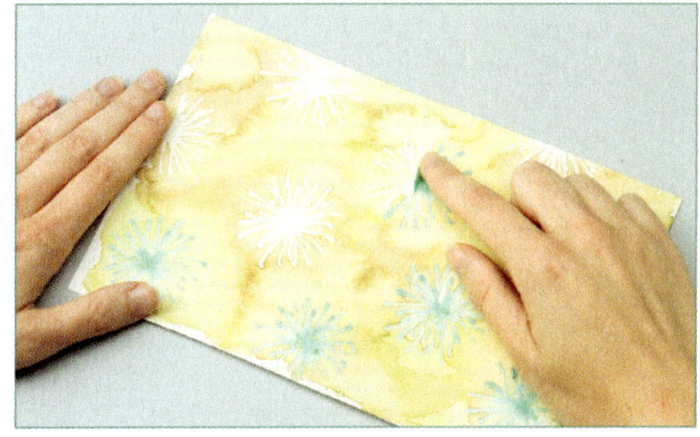

1

Stretch watercolor paper, if needed. Draw dandelion designs with Masquepen masking fluid in a random pattern over entire surface of paper; allow to dry.

2

Prepare all three colors in advance by mixing with water. Start with the lightest color, and apply in random patches. Quickly repeat process with the other colors, allowing wet edges to overlap until entire background is covered.

3

After painted background is completely dry, remove masking fluid by gently rubbing over it with your fingers or use an adhesive remover tool. Add brown paint to edges of photo mat and torn background paper before curling for a dimensional effect.

Designer Nicole Gartland created a sweet background for this layout featuring her own little doll of a daughter by using stamps and a hand-stitched floss border.

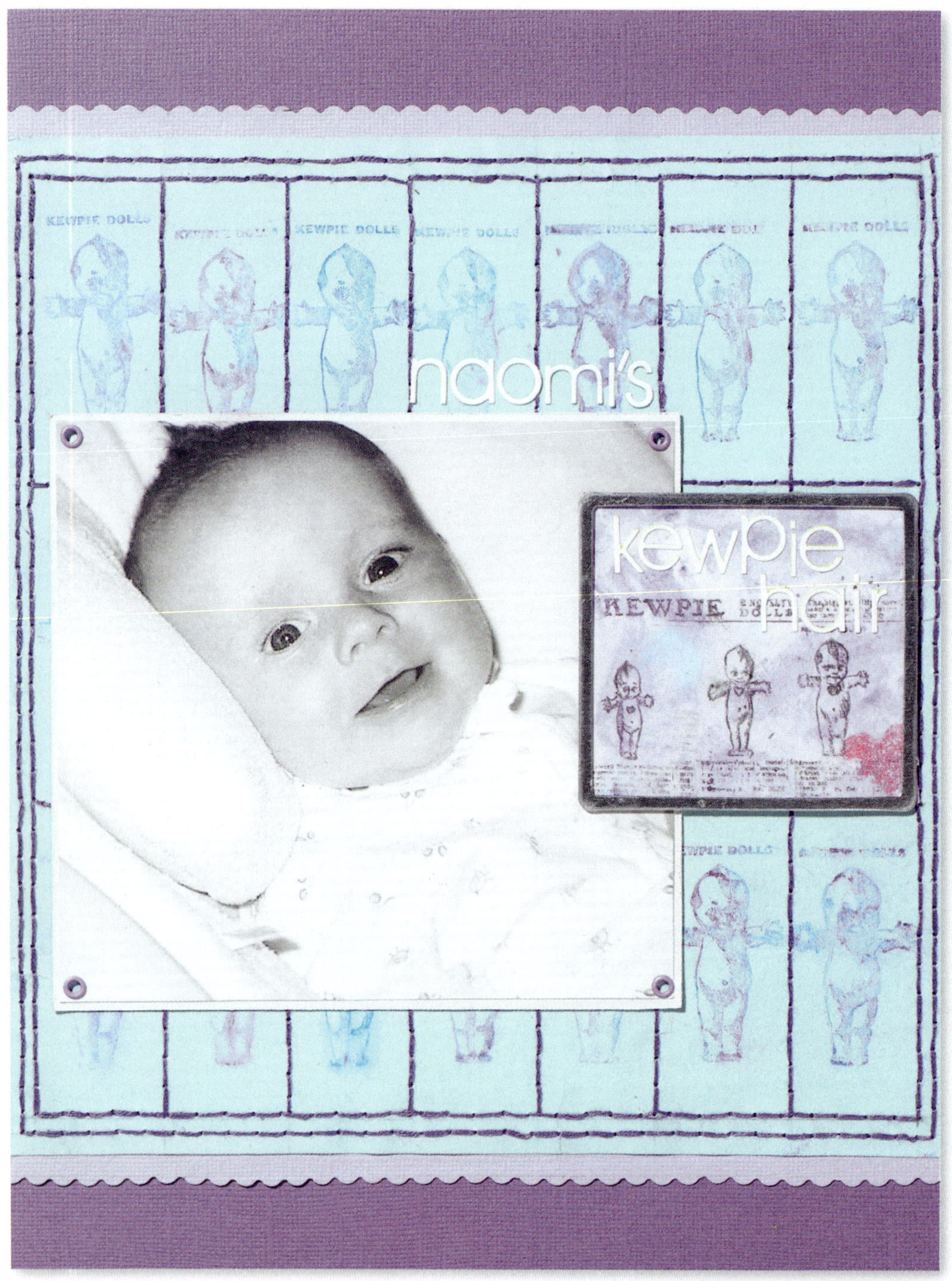

Naomi's Kewpie Hair

Supplies: Kewpie doll stamps (Hampton Art Stamps); watercolor crayons (Lyra); eyelets, metal-rimmed tag (Making Memories); letter stickers (Deluxe Designs); Staz-On solvent ink (Tsukineko); floss (DMC); textured cardstock (Bazzill)

Nicole Gartland, Portland, Oregon

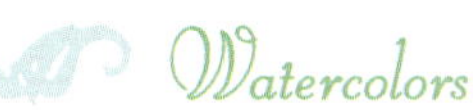

Did you know there is a quick and easy way to achieve beautifully painted designs without even picking up a paintbrush? Well, there is and it's so simple, even a child can do it!

The key to these two techniques is using watercolor crayons, which contain the same paint pigments as other forms of watercolors, but in a solid stick that can be used just as you would regular crayons. Find a stamp to use (simple, bold designs work the best) and a bottle of mist water, and you'll be amazed at the soft, pretty images you can "paint" onto your layouts.

Tips & Tricks

- *If the water causes the cardstock to warp a bit, stitch a grid over it through the background layer to get it to lie flat. Or you can press the still-damp paper between paper towels and place under some heavy books until dry.*
- *Stamps made out of firm rubber instead of foam work best with this technique because it allows the paint to stay on the surface as you rub the crayons over the top.*
- *Nicole misted her paper first, but you can also try misting the stamp after coloring it with the crayons, then stamp onto dry paper.*

Other Ideas to Try . . .

Sweetheart Frame

To create this pretty slide holder frame, Nicole cut out a custom heart shape from a compressed sponge, expanded and dipped it into several colors, then pressed it onto the painted frame.

Supplies: Compressed sponge (Loew-Cornell); watercolor crayons (Lyra); buttons (Making Memories)

Nicole Gartland, Portland, Oregon

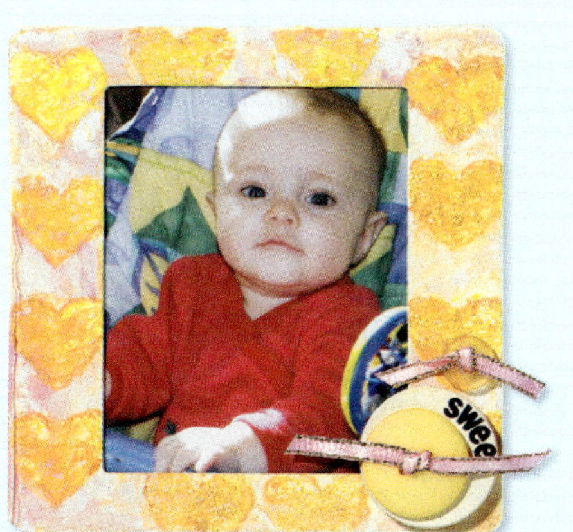

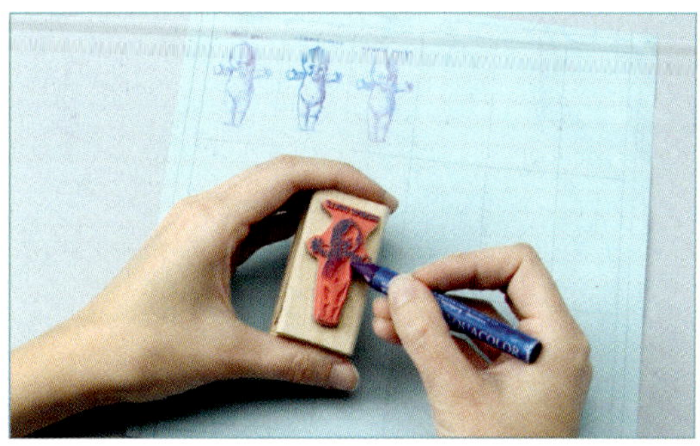

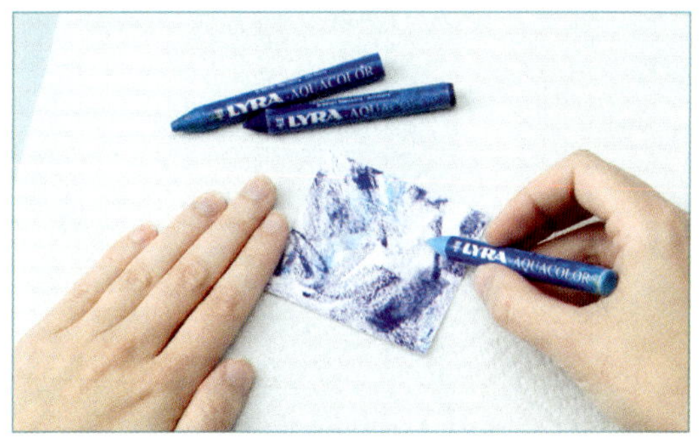

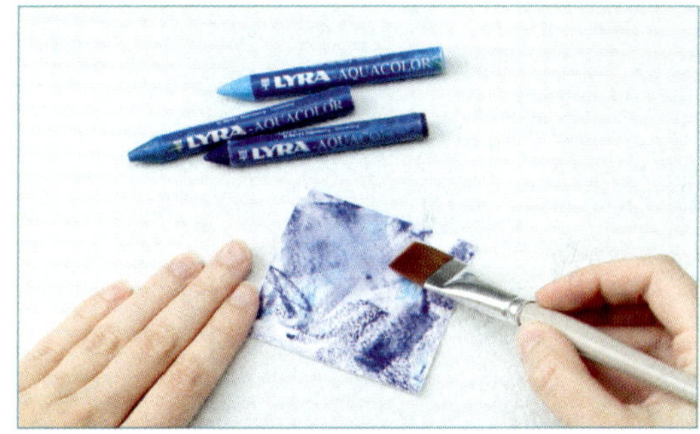

1

Draw a grid onto a piece of cardstock with a pencil and very lightly mist the cardstock with water. Color directly onto the rubber on the stamp with the crayons and stamp onto each square of the grid. When paper is dry, stitch around the grid lines with floss.

2

Lightly mist a plain white tag with water and randomly rub several colors of watercolor crayon over it.

3

Blend colors together with a wet brush; allow to dry. Stamp design with black ink and add letter stickers.

Shading With Pencils

A fresh-picked bouquet of watercolored flowers works especially well with the patterned paper and dimensional floss accents. The title was also painted with pencils, then journaling was added over the top to create layers of text.

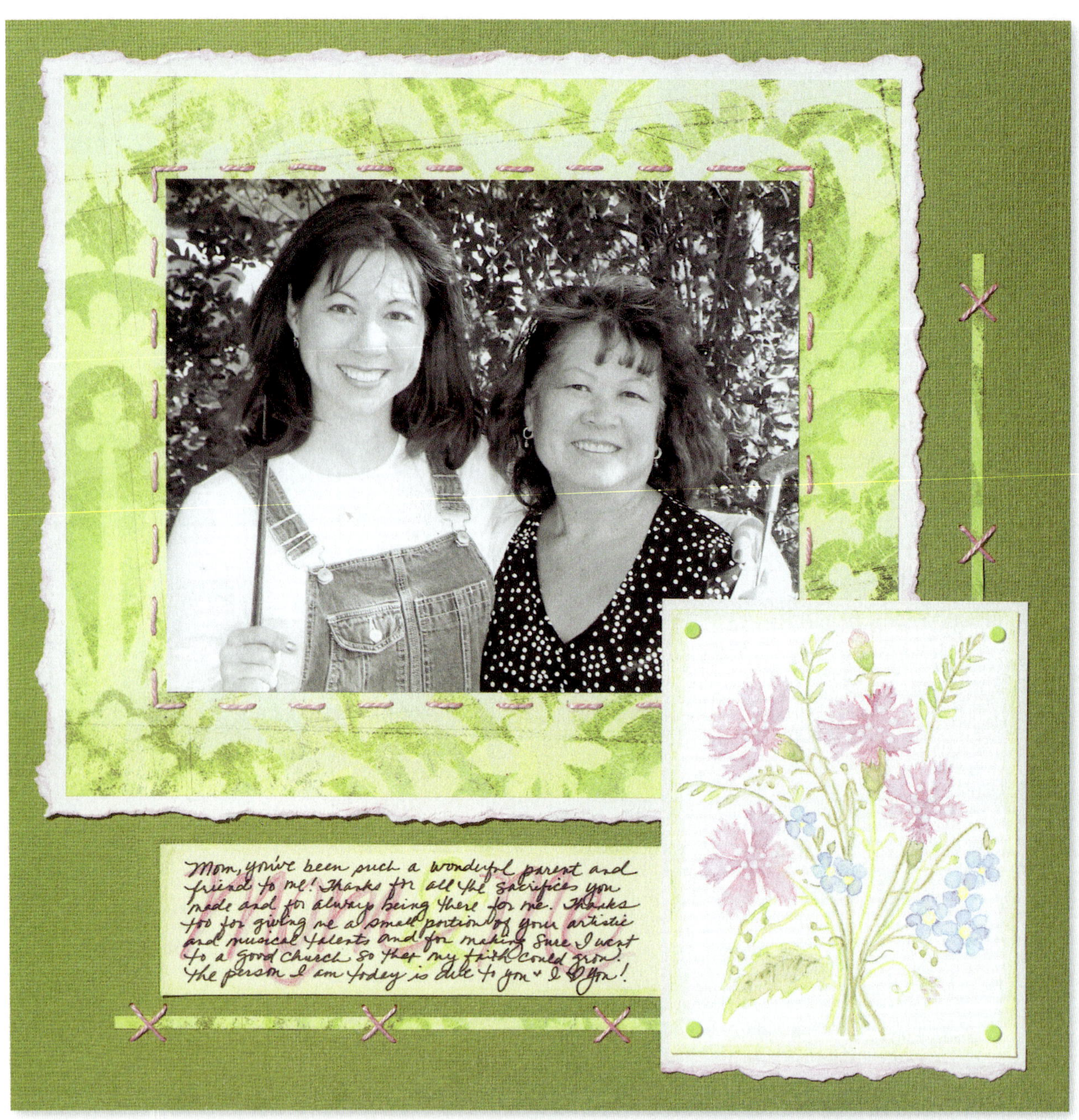

Mom & Me *Supplies:* 90 lb. cold press watercolor paper (Canson); Albrecht Durer watercolor pencils (Faber-Castell); Art-Kure water sketch brush (Sunday International); stencil (American Traditional Designs); patterned paper (Daisy D's); flathead eyelets (Making Memories); Fineliner pen (Staedtler); textured cardstock (Bazzill)

I love using watercolor pencils because they are so versatile. I can draw a design just like I would with regular colored pencils and then add water, or touch a wet brush directly to the tip to form paint, which is very useful on small touch-up jobs.

If you're not comfortable drawing freehand, there are plenty of different stencil products that can take the guesswork out of what color goes where and can help you create a design that will fool everyone into thinking you painted it all by yourself. The embellishment on this layout is a great example of this—by using a three-step stencil, I was able to create overlapping and shaded shapes that blend together to form a realistic still life.

You can use straight lines, even lines, doodled lines or scratchy lines—it doesn't really matter because once the water hits them, they will magically melt into paint! The trick is to leave the penciled outlines darker by starting with the wet brush tip on the outline and then pulling it toward the center and blend the color in to create lighter areas with visual dimension. If you want to add more color or deeper shadows, you can draw over specific areas or use the wet-brush-to-tip method and repeat the blending process.

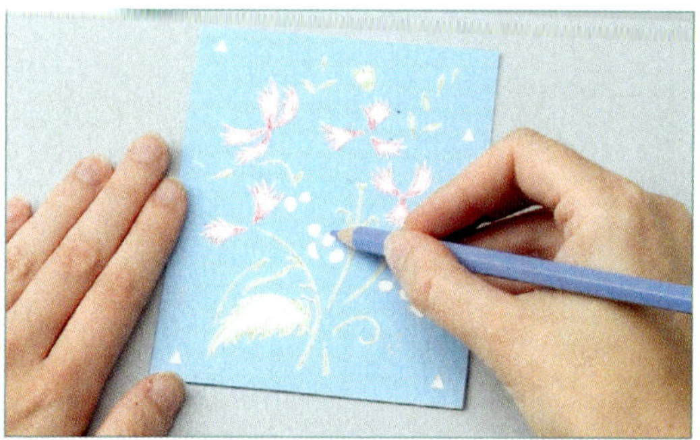

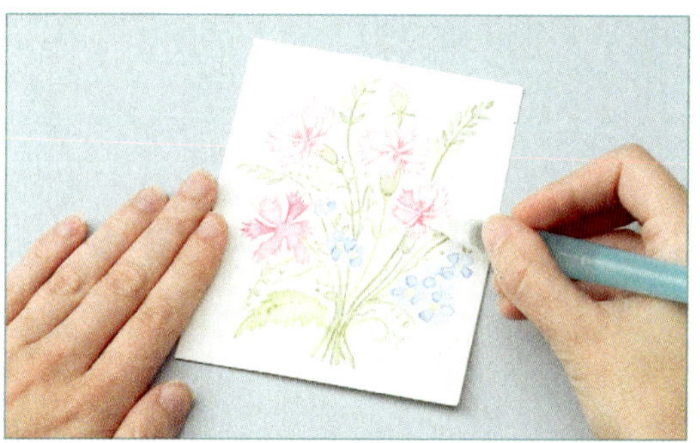

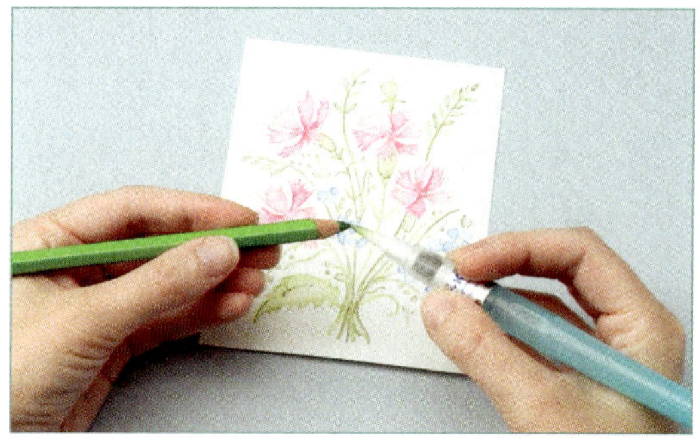

1

Trace the outline of each stencil shape with watercolor pencils, shading darker in areas where you want a stronger color.

2

With water sketch brush, moisten pencil marks to "melt" them into a paint and rub with brush tip to pull the color into the center of each shape until it is completely filled in.

3

Pick up concentrated paint color by rubbing wet brush against tip of pencil, then go back and reapply paint to areas of the design that may need a little extra shading or another color.

Tips & Tricks

- *You can also mist your paper with water first, then rub over it with the pencils to draw and blend the paint at the same time.*
- *Use a slightly dull pencil tip, as a sharp one may create indentations in your paper and will show up when you try to blend out the paint.*
- *Use a lighter touch when drawing with these soft pencils to avoid any harsh lines and to get the best blend of color when water is added.*

Other Ideas to Try . . .

1. Trace an image from a child's coloring book to create a design that looks like stained glass.
2. Fill in wide bands of different colors and blend together with a brush for a fast and easy graded wash.
3. Mist paper and draw a design freeform and let the paint bleed over the surface.

Mixed Reactions

I think the alcohol ring background on this title block looks great with the colors of the pumpkins and my nephew's shirt. I used a hot press watercolor paper with a smoother texture to help get the clearest stamped impressions.

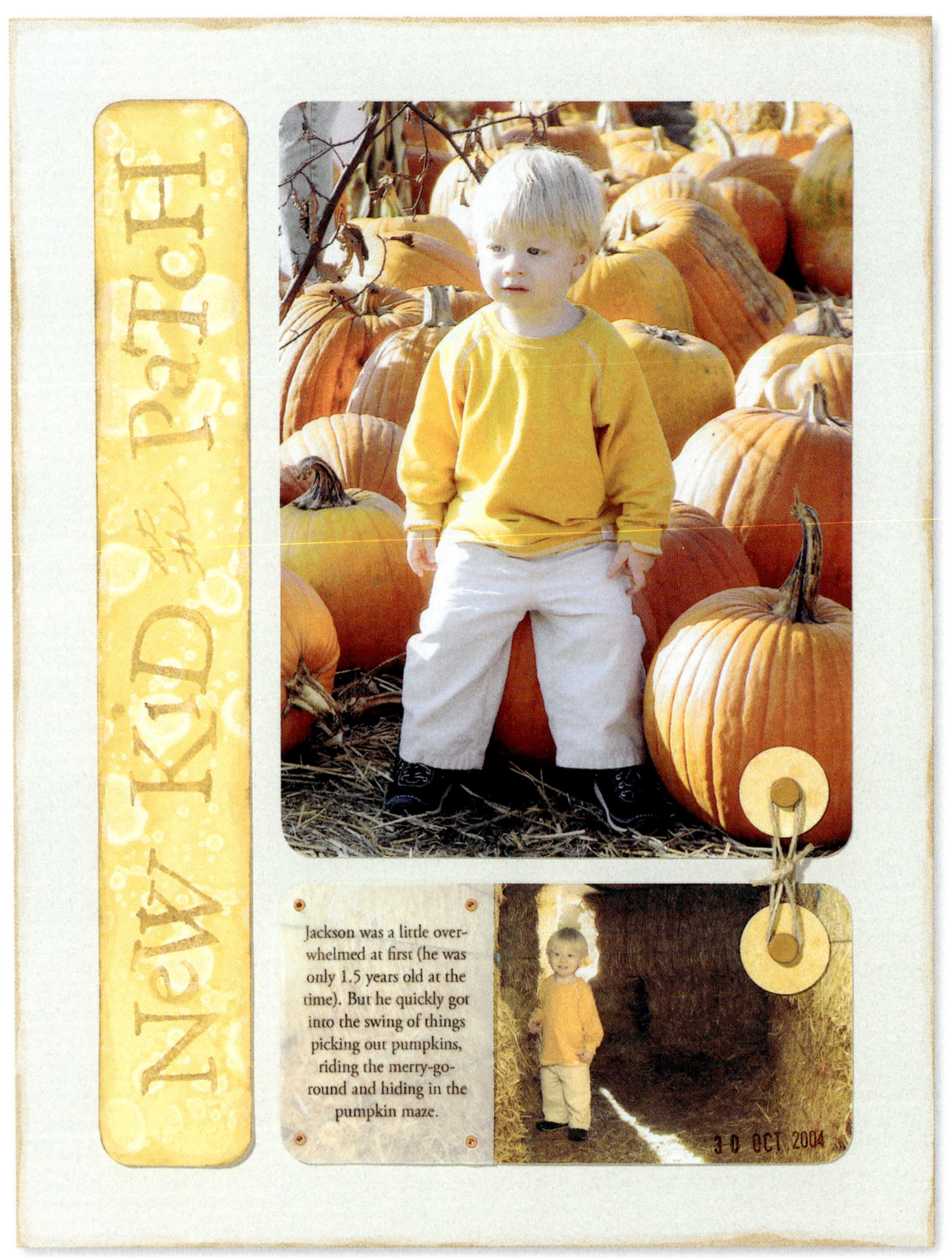

New Kid at the Patch

Supplies: 140 lb. hot press Arches watercolor paper (Canson); Dr. Ph. Martin's Hydrus watercolors (Salis International); ColorBrush Twin watercolor pen (EK Success); 1½" American Painter Big Brush, Round Golden Taklon brush (Loew-Cornell); letter stamps (Purple Onion Designs); circle punch (McGill); corner rounder (Marvy); flattop eyelets (Stamp Doctor); eyelets (Making Memories); vellum; rubbing alcohol

One of the easiest ways to create an interesting visual texture with watercolors is to add products that will cause a reaction with the paint while it's wet, such as rubbing alcohol. When added at precisely the right time, it causes the paint to separate into abstract rings and splotches of lighter color. There are several types of household and watercolor-specific products that can cause other kinds of reactions, such as different types of salt and special texture mediums.

You can use any type, but for this layout I used bottled liquid watercolors. These also work very well with calligraphy and other pens for lettering or detail work such as fine outlining or texturing applications.

Tips & Tricks

• Richer, deeper colors will usually show a reaction pattern better than pastel shades.

• The trickiest part is knowing when to add the alcohol—you won't get much of a reaction if the paint is too wet or too dry.

Other Ideas to Try . . .

1. Second wash of paint over alcohol splatter.
2. Granulation Medium, mixed with paint, no water.
3. Epsom salt in wet paint, brushed off when dry.
4. Texture Medium, applied to paper before paint.

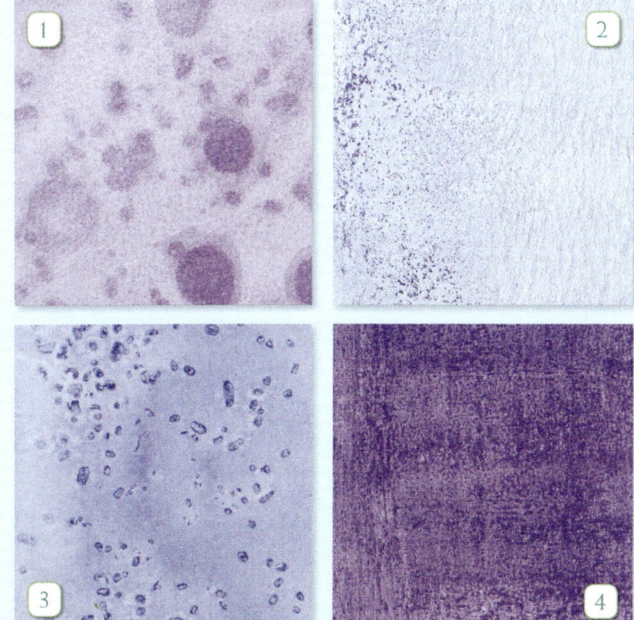

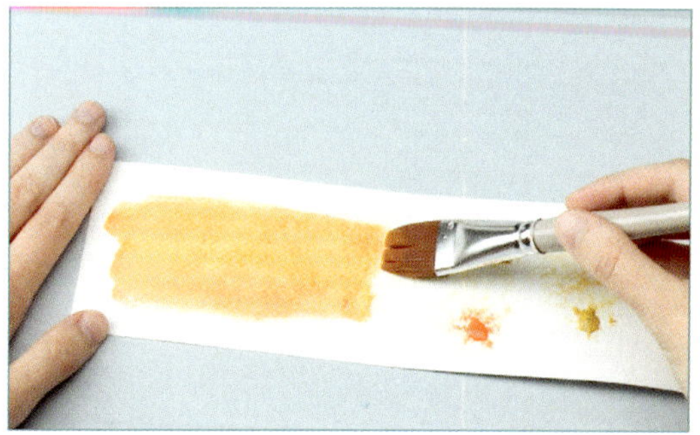

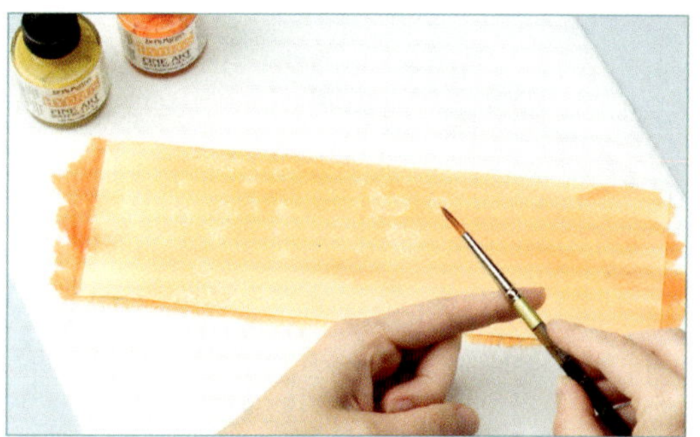

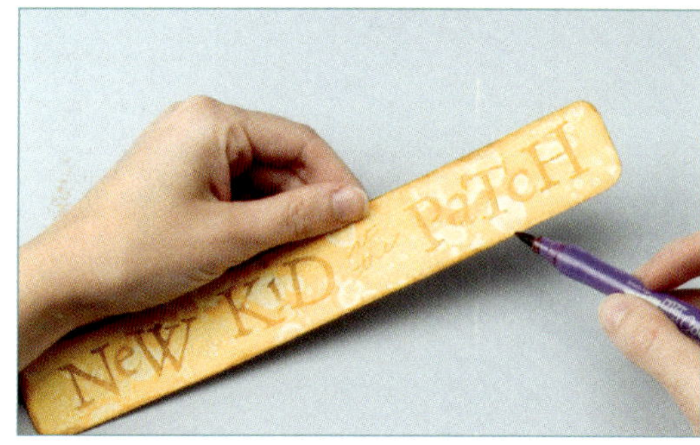

1

Lightly mist paper with water and add about 4 to 5 drops of yellow ochre and Hansa deep yellow in random areas, then quickly spread paint with a big brush and blend out over the background.

2

Working quickly, dip round brush into rubbing alcohol and let drip onto wet paint to create larger rings. Tap gently over a finger to create finer rings and splotches.

3

After the paint has dried, rub a brown watercolor brush pen over stamps and press them onto the painted paper to create the title. Rub edges of title strip and cardstock background with more brown color and soften lines with a wet brush.

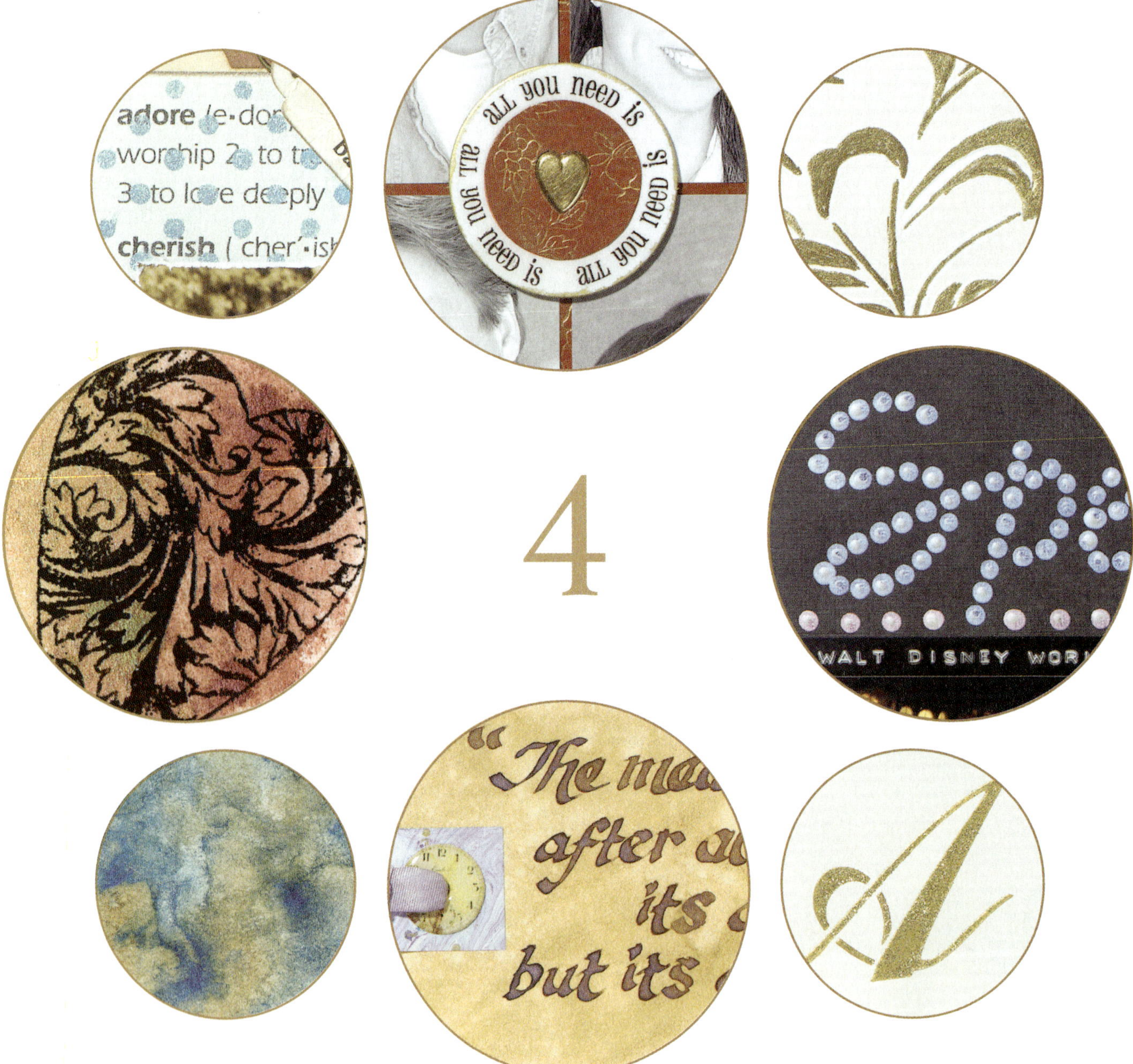

adore
worship 2 to
3 to love deeply
cherish
all you need is
all you need is
all you need is
WALT DISNEY
"The
after
its
but its

4

Shimmer Effects

Sometimes a layout just cries out for a big dose of glitz and glamour to make it really stand out from the crowd. Other times, all a page might need is a just little touch of classic elegance—like putting on a special piece of jewelry to finish off that nice outfit. Fortunately, there is a sparkling variety of shimmery paints that can come to the rescue and instantly add the Midas touch to your scrapbook pages!

The paints in this chapter vary by type—such as acrylics, powders, stains and inks—but all have extra luminous colors that can really draw attention with their rich effects. Some create bright and bold finishes, while others have a more demure and dreamy quality. Some reflect light like a shiny new copper penny (and may even have actual metal particles in it), while others refract light like the magically changing colors on a soap bubble or the inside of an abalone shell. As with other paints, you can usually create your own custom mixes to suit your needs or combine them with another medium such as a glaze. So depending on the look you want, there are many of these glowing products and techniques for you to choose from. I've included some of my favorites in this chapter and I think you will love them all as much as I do!

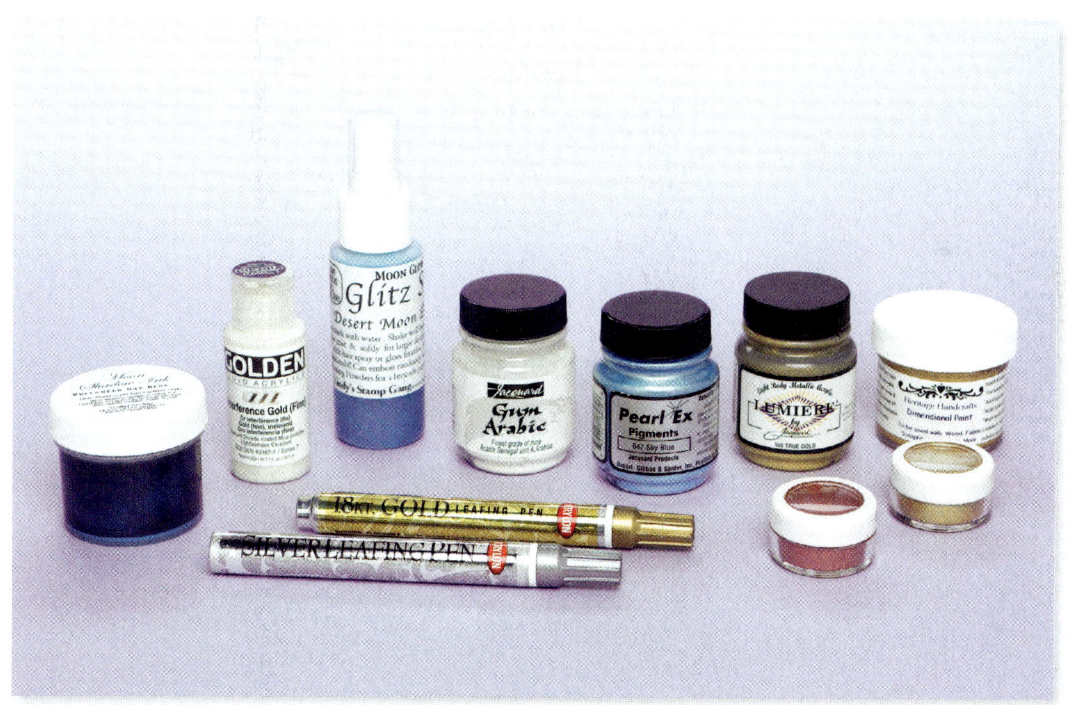

Featured Supplies

- Shimmery Sprays & Inks
- Interference Paints
- Mica Powders & Gum Arabic
- Iridescent/Metallic Paints
- Dimensional Paints
- Perfect Pearls Powder Paints
- Metallic Leafing Pens

Interference Paints

I can still recall that magical night I spent watching this parade for the first time with my family—the night was pitch black and a procession of ever-changing lights gracefully passed us by. A combination of one- and two-tone interference paints mimic the light's effects dramatically on black cardstock, especially when the page is moved.

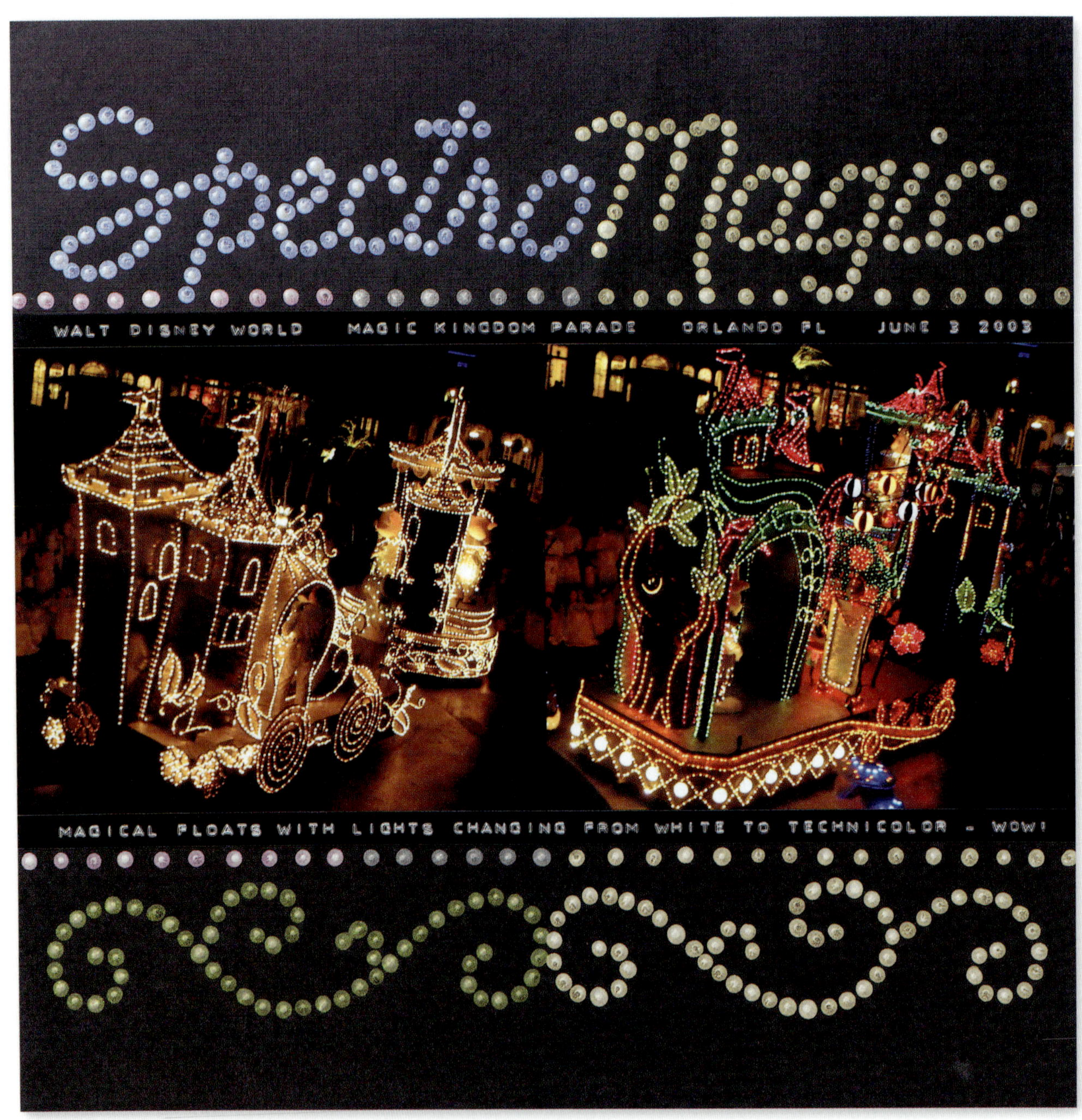

Spectromagic *Supplies:* Fluid Interference paint (Golden), Round Style Stix, #5 Golden Taklon round brush (Loew-Cornell), label maker (Dymo), wax-free tracing paper (Prym-Dritz)

Interference paints, also known as opalescent paints, are sneaky little guys—they look colorless and unassuming in the bottle, but once they hit the right surface, the bolder side of their personality shines through! Some can be two-tone and others are only one color, but they all have a beautiful sheen much like what you see when looking at an oil slick. These unique paints don't actually have a colored pigment in them like regular paint, but are made with fine mica particles that reflect and refract light that changes depending on the angle you're looking at it.

Interference paints can be mixed with a variety of other paints and mediums to enhance them and create different effects, but they show their best features when used on darker papers and surfaces. The two-tone varieties are some of my favorites, as they may look to be a certain color at one angle, but will change to a totally different one when viewed in another way.

Tips & Tricks

- *Thin layers of these paints are more dramatic than thicker ones.*
- *Adding glossy or translucent colors will result in more luminous effects, while matte or opaque colors tend to dull them.*
- *Mixing two interference colors together will result in a shimmery pearl color.*

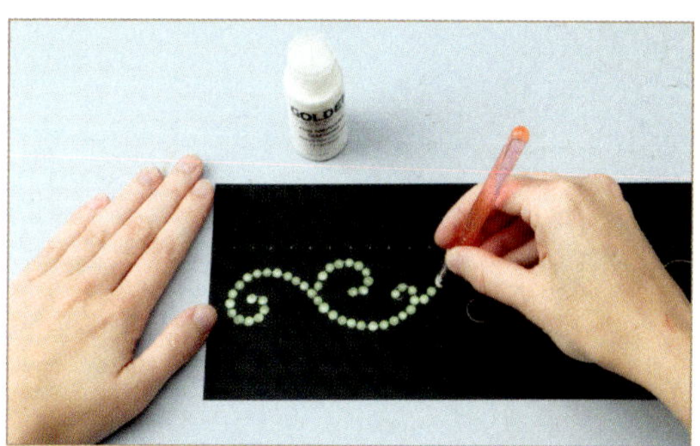

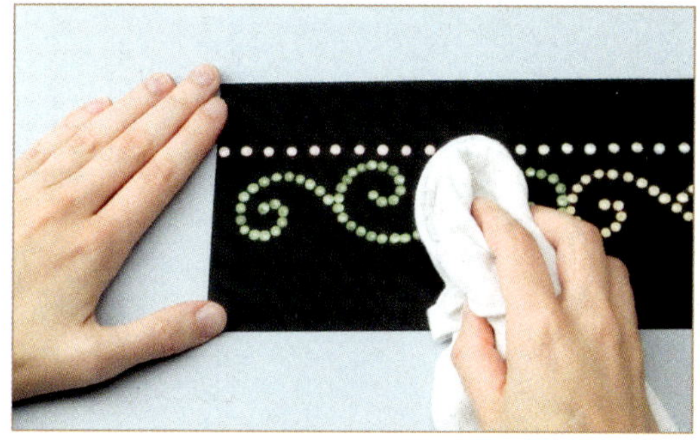

1

Trace the design onto dark cardstock using a pattern and wax-free tracing paper.

2

Dip round Style Stix tool into paint and apply over traced design using a straight up and down motion to create a uniform dot.

3

Once the paint is completely dry, gently rub off the tracing marks with your finger or a soft cloth.

Other Ideas to Try . . .

1. Mix a tiny bit of black paint into any interference paint to give it more of a visual pop.
2. Layer an interference paint over its complementary color, such as blue over an opaque orange for a more solid effect.
3. Interference paints over lighter papers will result in a more mother-of-pearl kind of effect.
4. Experiment with different color combinations of interference glazes over regular paint colors—you may be pleasantly surprised at some of the unexpected results.

Iridescent Paints

I used metallic paint to enhance faux-leather embossed paper for a rich but subtle effect. For additional charm, I applied the same paint to the edges of the patterned paper background and a plain chipboard embellishment. The perfect touch to celebrate a solid gold relationship!

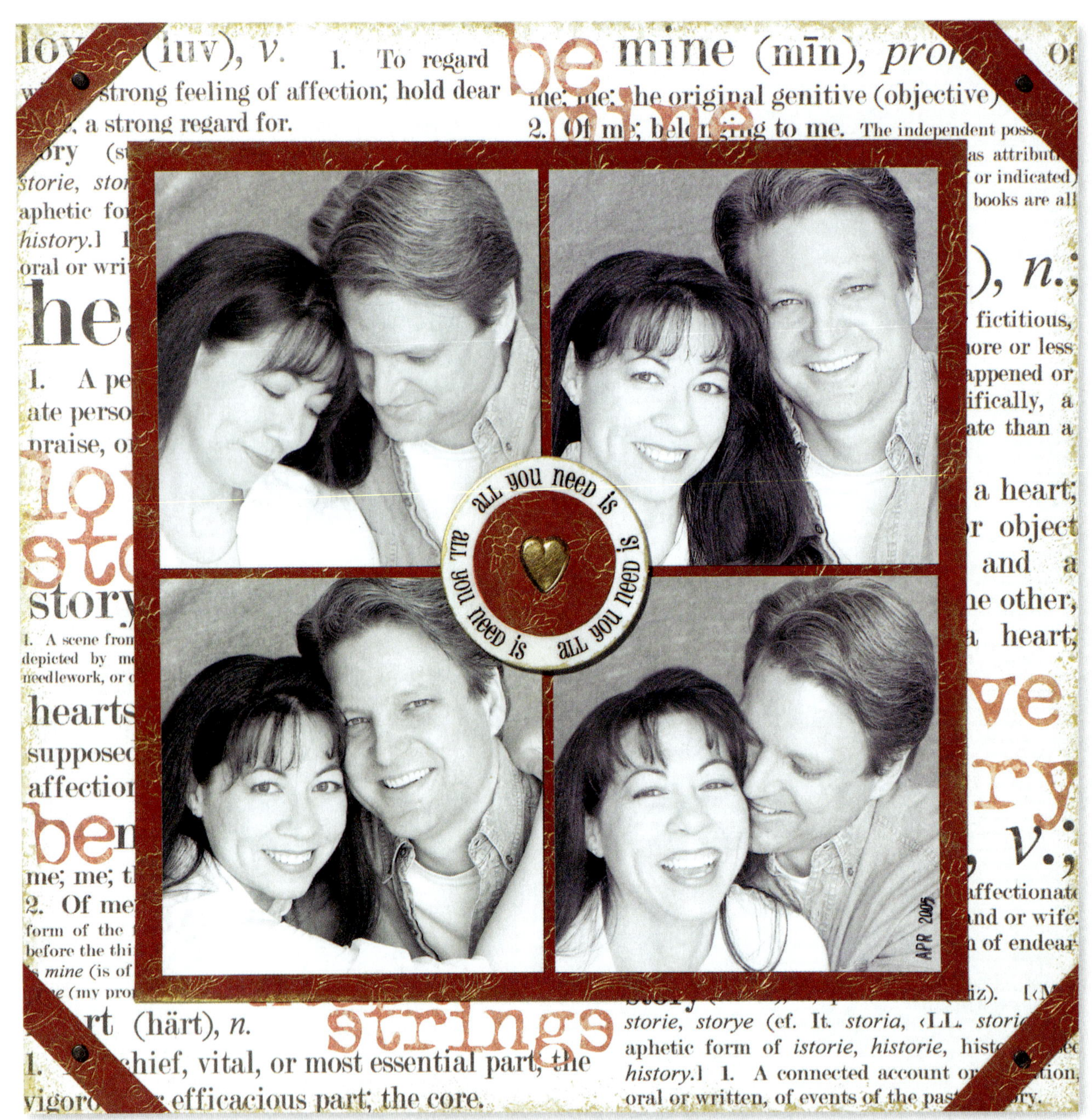

All You Need Is . . .

Supplies: Lumiere metallic paint (Jacquard Products); sea sponge, SpongIt applicator (Loew-Cornell); embossed paper (K & Company); patterned paper (Carolee's Creations); chipboard coaster (Li'l Davis Designs); Staz-On solvent ink (Tsukineko); brads (Limited Edition Rubberstamps); heart nailhead (JewelCraft)

Although closely related, there is a distinct difference between interference and iridescent paints. Iridescents—also referred to as "special effects," metallic or pearlescent paints—have an iron oxide coating in addition to the mica particles, which gives them a more dense, shimmery quality that does not change with various viewing angles.

In addition to realistic metal finishes such as gold, silver, and copper, iridescent paints also come in gorgeous pearlescent jewel and pastel colors. These paints can also be mixed with various glazes, mediums and acrylic paints to create different effects and custom colors.

Tips & Tricks

- *Mixing a glossy medium to these paints or adding a clear layer over the top will give them a more lustrous appearance.*
- *For a perfectly even border every time, cut a tiny notch in your paint pen so that it will line up in the same place as you run it along the edge of the paper.*

Other Ideas to Try . . .

Love Frame

For another rich effect, reverse the technique and decorate raised embossed designs. For this project, a gold metallic leafing pen was used to highlight the raised pattern on the paper to create a beautiful frame. It's a more time-consuming process, but definitely worth the effort for those extra-special projects.

Supplies: Embossed paper (K & Company), 18kt Gold Leafing Pen (Krylon); textured cardstock (DieCuts with a View)

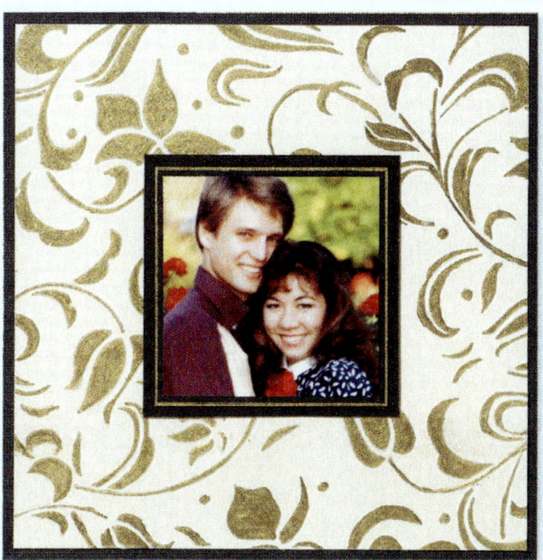

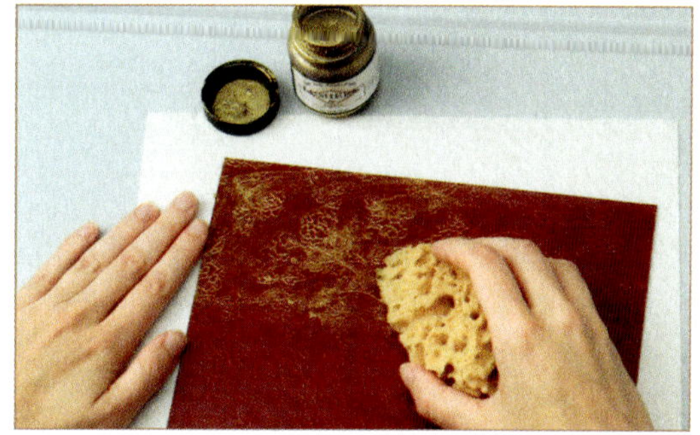

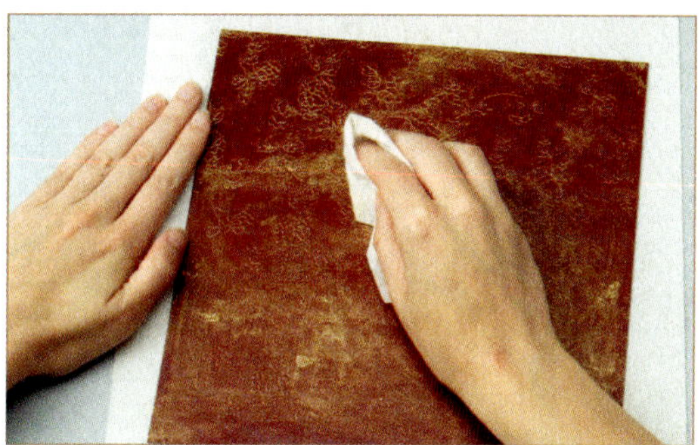

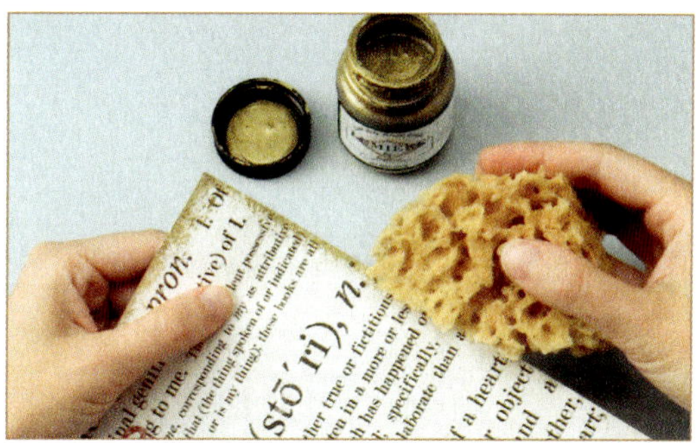

1

Dip a damp natural sea sponge into gold paint and rub it over the embossed paper, making sure the paint gets into all the little grooves of the design.

2

Lightly rub off excess paint with a paper towel or alcohol-free baby wipe, leaving most of the gold in the grooves. Repeat process if too much paint was rubbed off.

3

Apply gold paint to the edges of the layout with a natural sponge. Use a sponge tool to apply paint around the edges of the coaster accent, and glue a circle of the painted embossed paper to the center.

Designer Allison Strine's children's faces are not the only things glowing on this layout! She combined mica paints and stamping techniques to create luminous effects on the title, dimensional photo mat, and a series of multicolor heart accents.

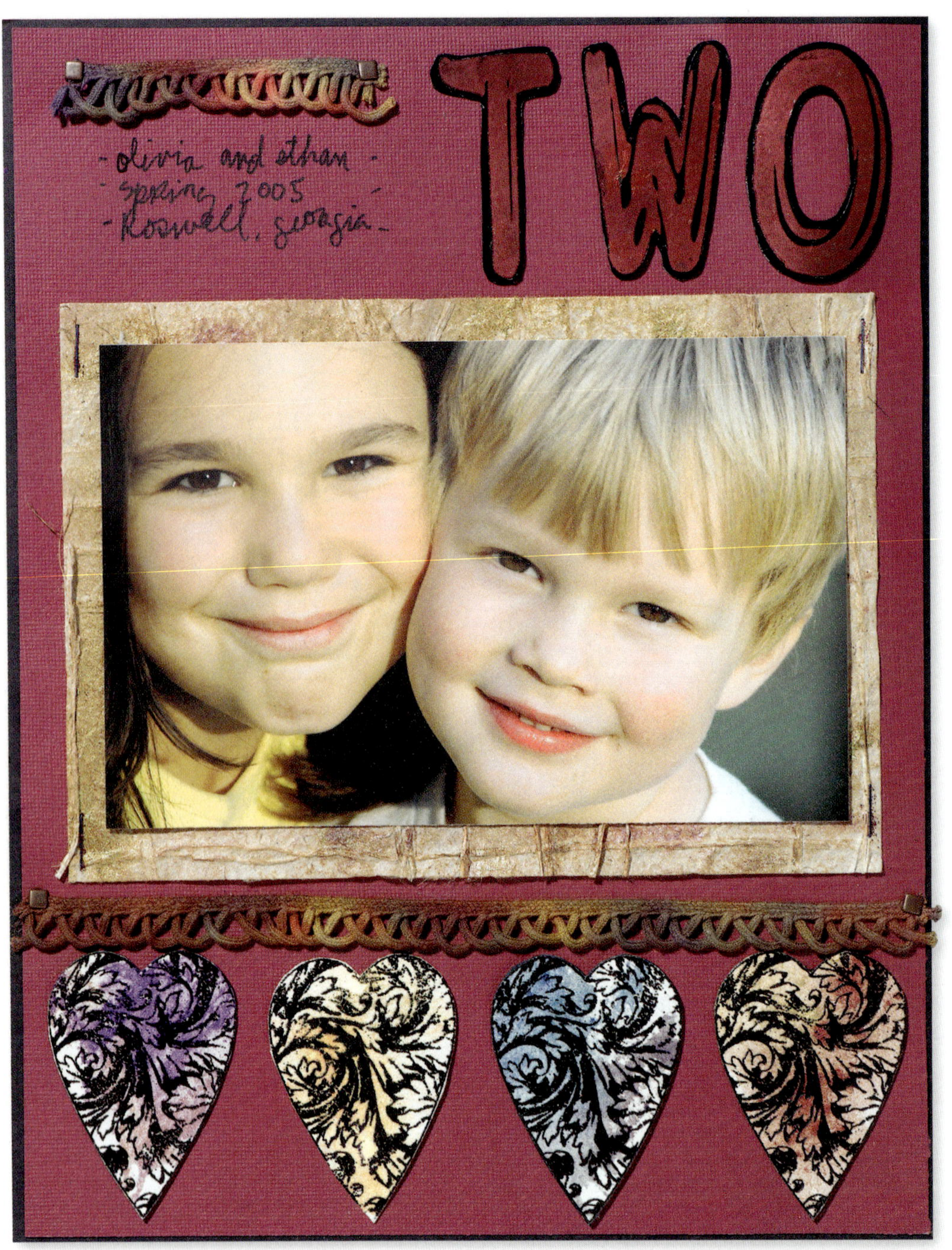

Two *Supplies:* 140 lb. cold press Arches watercolor paper (Canson); Perfect Pearls embossing powder (Ranger); letter stamps (Technique Tuesday); heart stamp (Stewart Gill); pigment ink (Tsukineko); patterned paper (Creative Imaginations); blue fiber (Carma); pen (Tombow); brads (Karen Foster Design)

Allison Strine, Roswell, Georgia

If you would like a more translucent, shimmery effect, there are a couple of different brands of products to choose from. My favorite is one that comes in a little container filled with what appears to be ordinary mica powder, but when you add a few drops of water, you can create a creamy, luminous watercolor to paint with. The difference between this powder/paint is that it already has a special binder in it that allows it to bond with paper—regular mica powder would easily rub off when the water evaporated. You can also use mica powders dry for other fun techniques such as with stamping or clay projects, or you can mix it with acrylic paints, glazes, mediums or inks.

Tips & Tricks

- *Using a higher quality watercolor paper will achieve better results than a less expensive, thinner brand.*
- *Do not create the paint in the original container! Pick up a small amount of powder with the tip of your brush and mix it with water on a palette.*

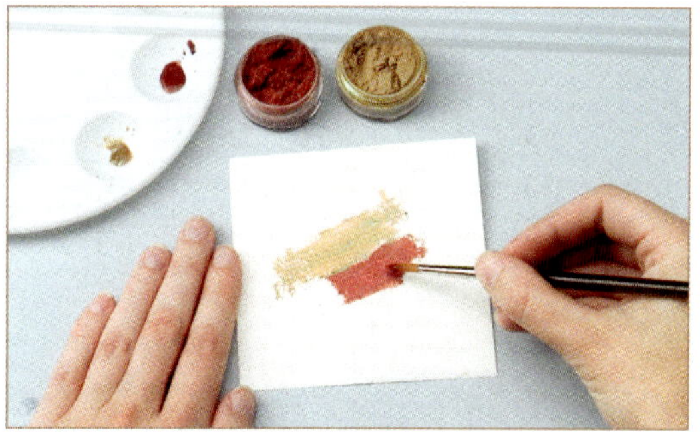

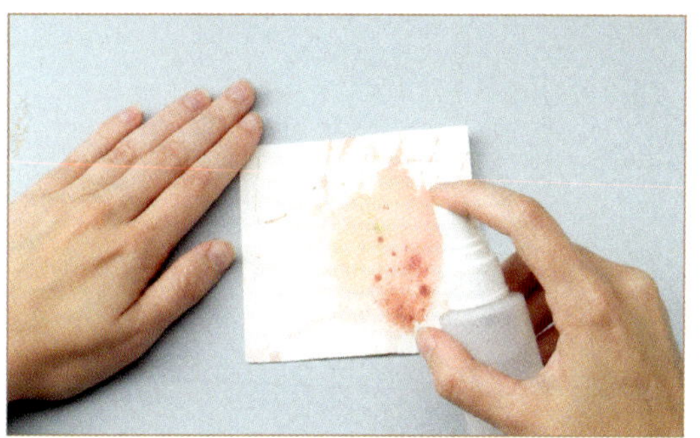

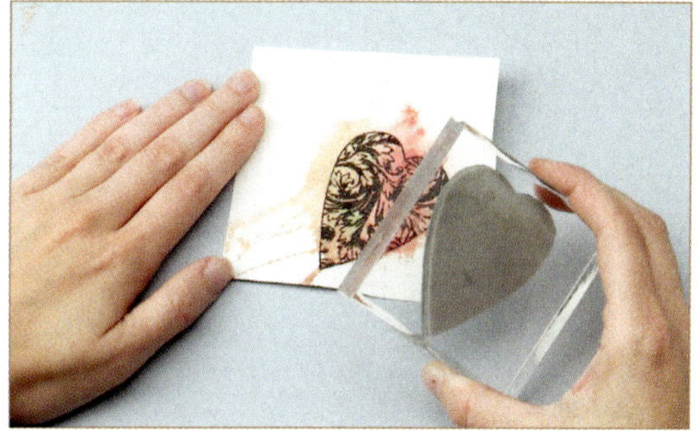

1

Mix mica powders with water to create two different creamy paints. Apply to watercolor paper with a brush.

2

Use a mister bottle and spray over paints with several hard bursts of water until they begin to mingle and spread out over the paper.

3

After paints are completely dry, stamp over the best section with black ink and emboss with black powder to create a raised outline. Cut out shape and repeat process with three more hearts.

Other Ideas to Try . . .

Baby Tag

If you already have regular mica powders in your supply stash, you can mix them with a product called Gum Arabic to create your own custom paints. The mixing ratio is about 4 parts powder to 1 part Gum Arabic. For this tag, designer Patina Campbell used a luminous blue powder to alter the flower and nailhead embellishments, and used it with a stamp to create the background on her tag.

Supplies: Large tag (Avery); flower, rub-on words, brads, sticker, mini tags (Making Memories); stamp (Technique Tuesday); Ancient Page stamping ink (Clearsnap); ribbon (source unknown)

Patina Campbell, Billings, Missouri

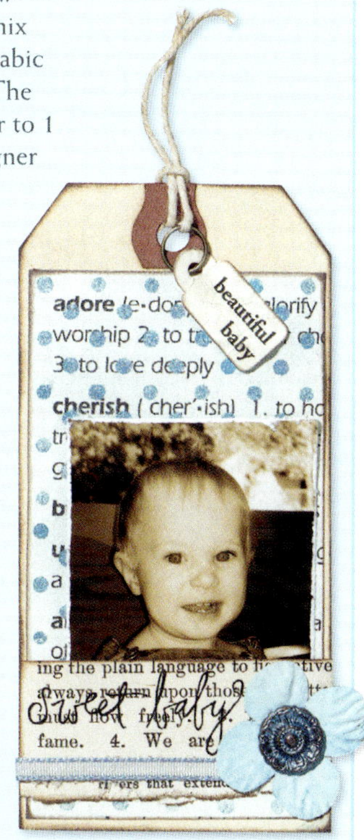

Dimensional Sparkle

"A" is for my own little angel, Ashley, dressed in her sparkling Halloween costume and ready to score some candy! The glittery monogram mimics all the gold elements in the photograph and pulls the whole layout together.

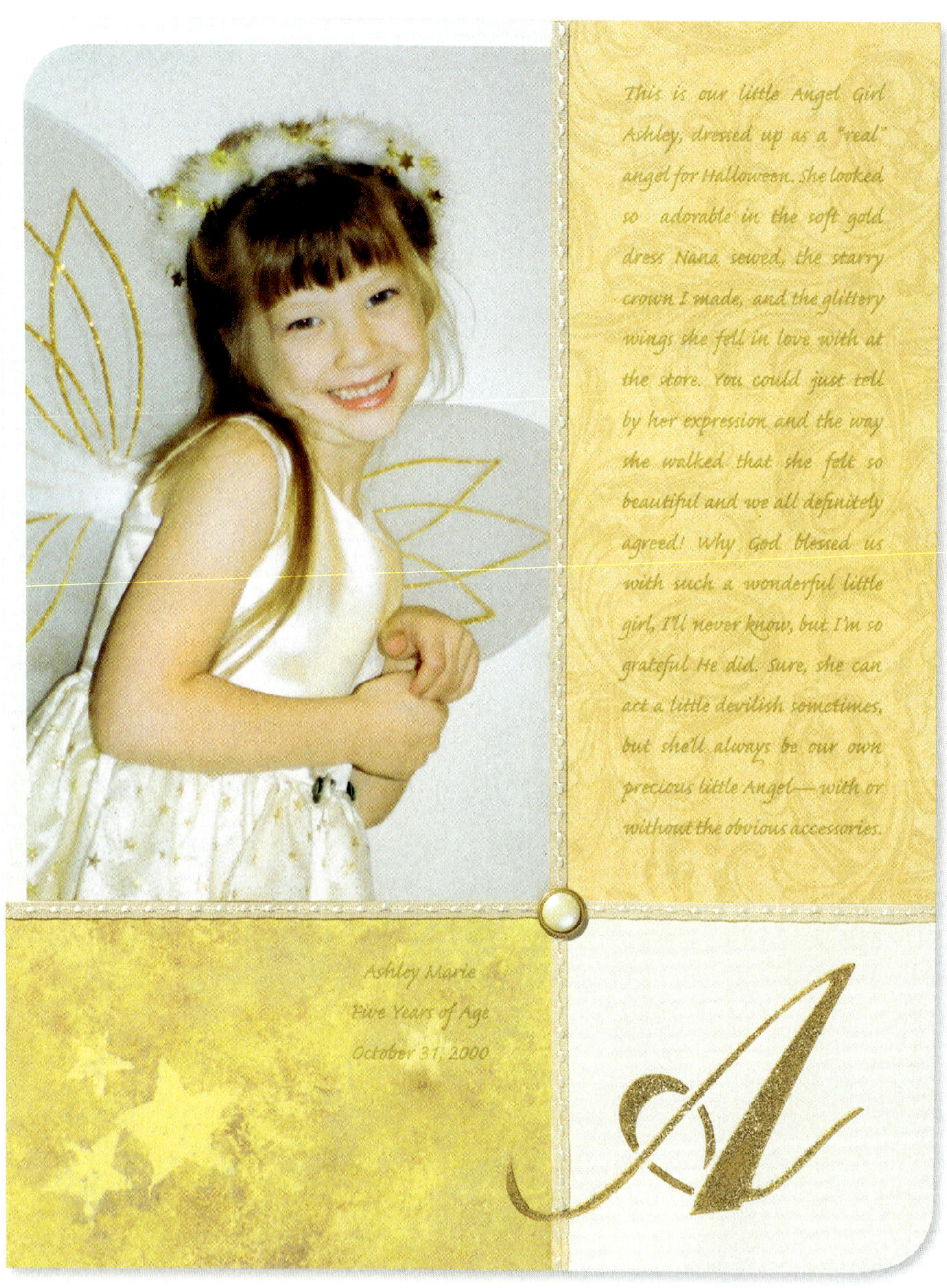

A *Supplies:* Dimensional paint (Heritage Handcrafts); patterned papers (K & Company, Provo Craft); stencil (One Heart, One Mind); micro glitter (Magic Scraps); ribbon (Making Memories); pearl brad (K & Company); adhesive dots (Therm O Web)

This unique dimensional paint has a thick, gluelike density with a rich shimmer to it. I love to use it with stencils, but you can also apply it with a palette knife or add texture with tools such as a faux finish comb in a similar manner as with any gel medium (see examples on page 27).

Because it is tacky when wet, it is also a wonderful base medium for creating glitzy effects by sprinkling on other items such as glitter or micro glass beads. Another way this specialty paint can be used is to heat it with a heat tool while the paint is still wet, which gives it even more dimension and a bubbly, weathered texture.

If you do not have access to this particular type of paint product, you can also try mixing iridescent acrylic paints or mica powders with a regular or heavy gel medium to create a similar look. But you should not use the heat tool technique with this kind of mixture.

Tips & Tricks

- *The glitter will grab instantly to the paint, so you can rub a very light sprinkling of it between your fingers for a subtle glisten or pour a larger amount over the top for a more festive look.*
- *The White Pearl version of this paint can be tinted with just a tiny drop of ink or acrylic paint to create a delicate pastel tint.*
- *This paint will retain the thickness of whatever stencil you use, so the thicker embossing kind like those made of brass will create the most dimensional designs.*

Other Ideas to Try . . .

1. Squeegee several different paint colors over a stencil for a pretty marbled effect.
2. Add a row of tiny rhinestones into the wet paint for a glamorous look.
3. There are other brands of shimmery dimensional paints that come out of squeeze bottles you may also want to try with the techniques shown on page 23.

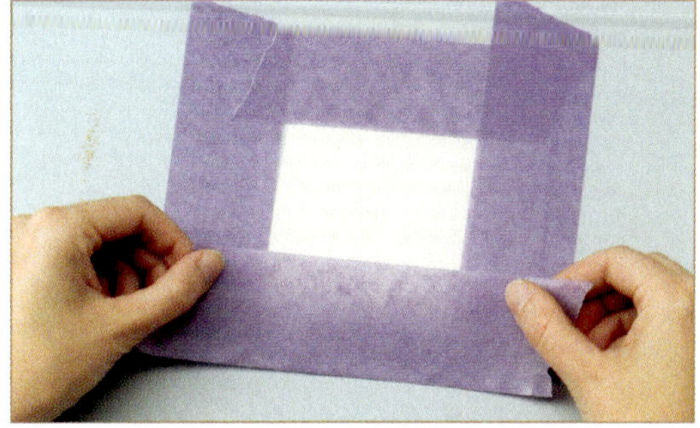

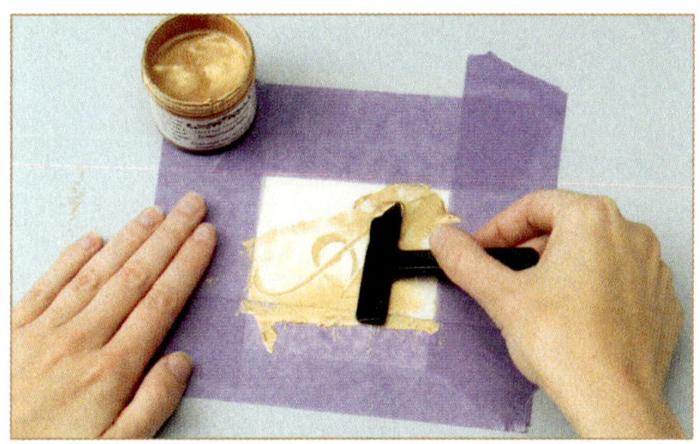

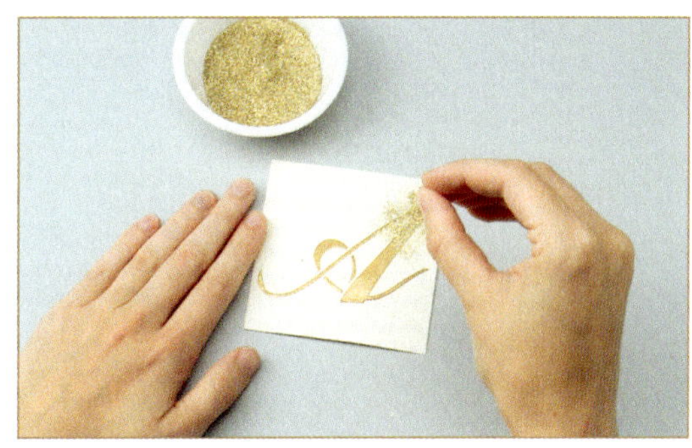

1

Spray back of stencil with stencil adhesive and position on cardstock. Mask off any open areas that you do not want the paint to get into, as well as all around the edges of the stencil to protect your paper.

2

Apply a large dab of gold dimensional paint at one edge of the stencil and spread out the paint with the mini squeegee until the letter has been filled in.

3

After carefully removing the stencil, sprinkle gold micro glitter over the wet paint, allow it to dry, and shake or brush off any excess glitter.

Shimmery Sprays & Inks

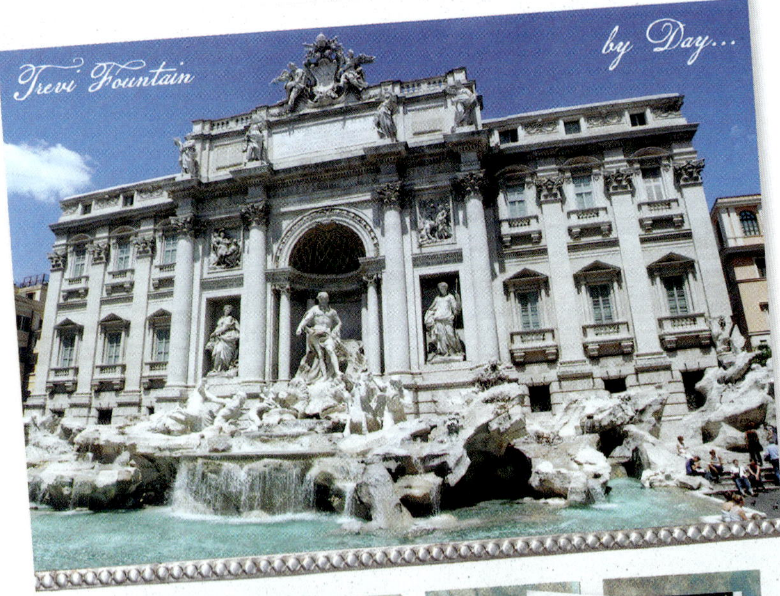

Ah, nothing says "romance" like a night in Rome! When my husband and I visited there, I was awed by the beauty of this famous fountain and determined to create a layout that would do it justice. The shimmery stains I used to create the small frames pull in the colors of the day and night scenes, and impart a feeling of movement as if we were still gazing into the water, making our wish to return again someday! More journaling about our magical visit is hidden behind the last photograph.

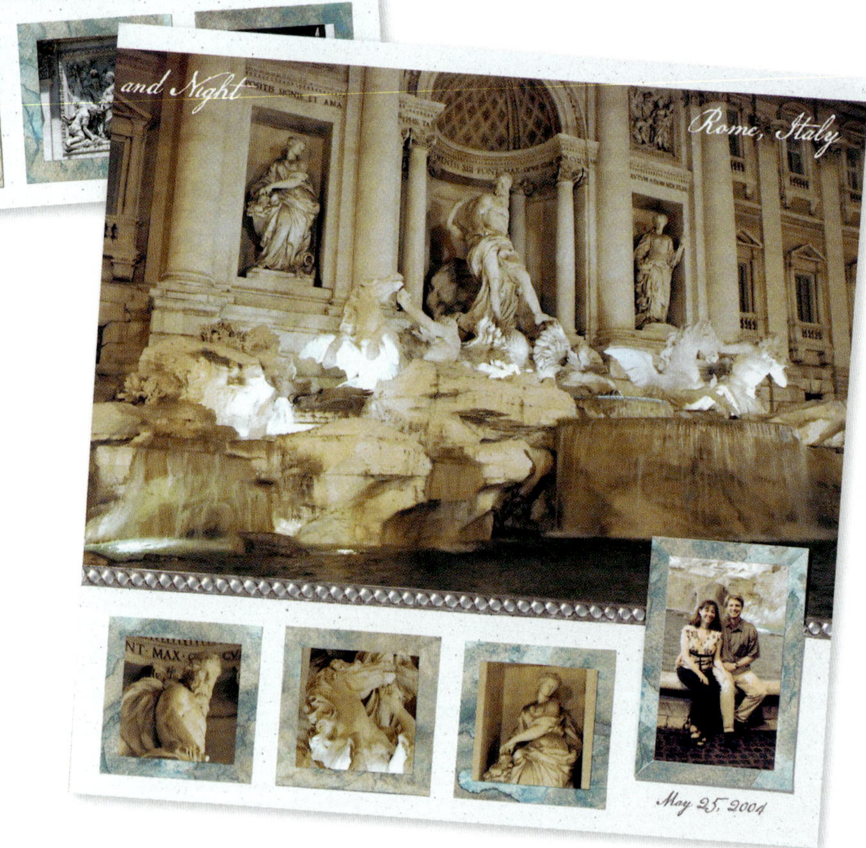

Trevi Fountain . . .

Supplies: Moon Shadow Mist, Glitz Spritz, Moon Shadow Ink (Lindy's Stamp Gang); Rub 'n Buff pigment powder (AMACO); American Painter 1" wash brush (Loew-Cornell); Bristol paper (Strathmore); bookplate (Li'l Davis Designs); molding strip (Making Memories); square punch (McGill); Milwaukee heat tool (Wagner); craft iron (Clover Needlecraft)

When I first discovered this particular line of luminous inks and sprays, I was immediately impressed by their sheer beauty and wealth of technique options. Although these were created with the stamper in mind, I think they have some wonderful "painterly" qualities that can be used for scrapbooking purposes as well.

These products are divided into three basic categories: single-color sprays, multitonal inks in jars, and sprays that have a unique blend of mica powder and walnut ink dye. While any of these used alone are very pretty, it is when they are combined in layers over each other that they make the most stunning background effects. And the best part is, all you have to do is pump a spray bottle or zap a puddle of ink with a heat tool and they naturally create beautiful abstract designs practically all by themselves!

Tips & Tricks

• Stir or shake these products well and often, especially the two-tone varieties, as the mica powder tends to sink to the bottom.

• Use a good quality, heavy watercolor or Bristol paper to avoid warping on large background areas.

• To speed up the drying process, wait until the paper is still damp (but not dripping wet) and apply a craft iron on the back side until it is dry and flat.

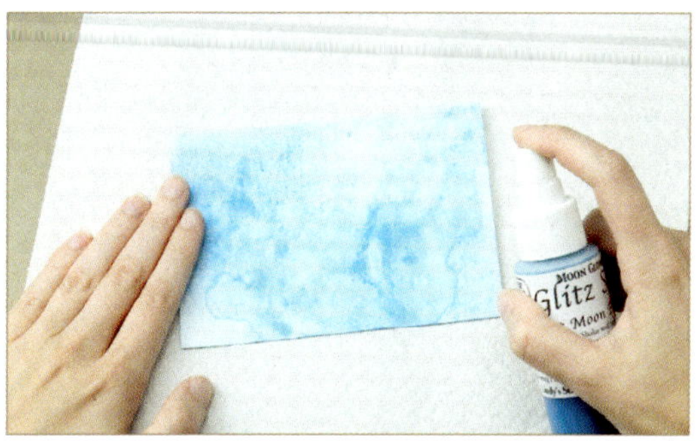

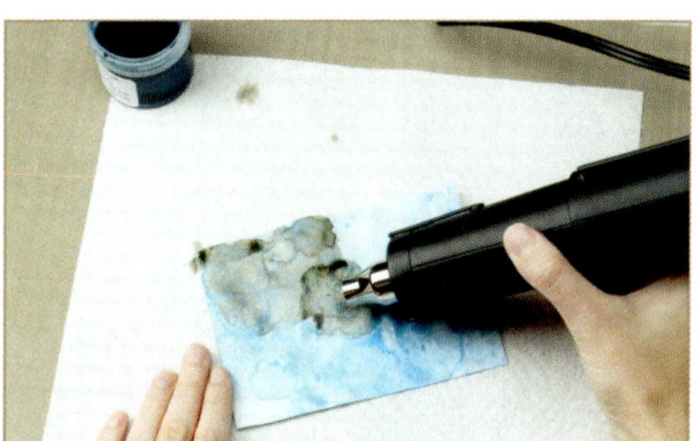

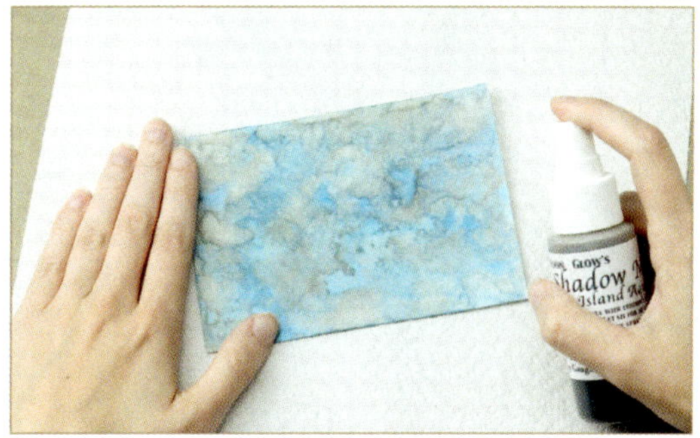

1

Spray sky blue Glitz Spritz liberally over entire background paper.

2

Working in small sections, randomly brush on darker blue Shadow Ink in large patches and immediately hit with heat tool and hold for a few seconds over wet ink to create loose rings and swirls of color. Continue working from one section into another to make a seamless background effect.

3

Lightly spray on aqua Shadow Mist over background to add another color layer and create the pitted effect as the wet ink interacts with the dried layers.

Other Ideas to Try . . .

Quote Tag

Dip a calligraphy pen into one of the inks and as you write, it will magically separate so that the stain color moves toward the center and the walnut dye concentrates around the edges of each letter.

Supplies: Moon Shadow Mist, Moon Shadow Ink (Lindy's Stamp Gang); calligraphy pen set (Speedball); American Painter 1" wash brush (Loew-Cornell); epoxy accent (EK Success); square punch (McGill); ribbon (Offray)

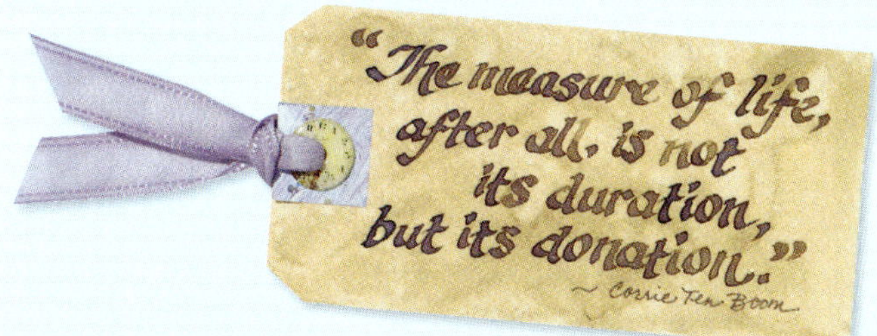

5

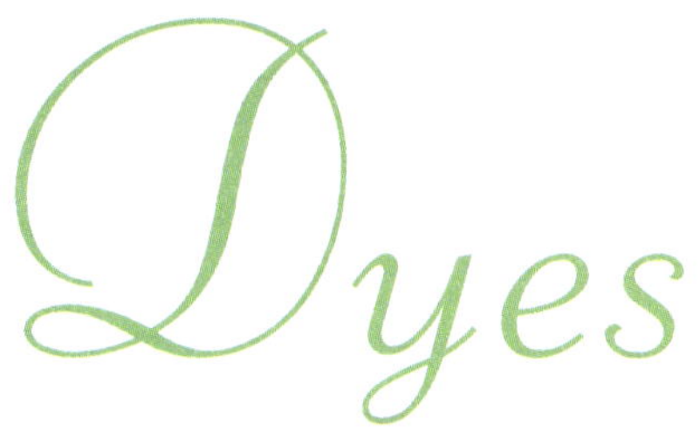

These days, dyes do not have to be used with fancy silk painting techniques to be considered a painting medium. There is now a wide variety of dyes and dyelike products available that can be used to color and embellish porous materials such paper, canvas and more common types of washable fabrics. And while silk painting is a stunning art form, for the purposes of this book, I will be demonstrating simpler but still very effective methods to use on your pages.

With the help of a simple dye bath process, you can convert a "not-quite-there" paper or fabric accent to that perfect shade, age it with brown colors for heritage layouts, or tone down those too-bright patterns we all seem to have at the bottom of our stash. Or you can paint on designs freehand, try your hand at some groovy tie-dying projects or create your own stamped wax batik backgrounds. The common ingredient all these techniques share is that dyes allow you to very quickly alter the overall color of something with very little effort or fuss compared to other painting methods. Most dyes will also need to be heat set in order to make them permanent, which you can do in just a few minutes with a craft iron or a heat tool.

In addition to dyes specifically labeled as being safe for scrapbooking use, I like to use household fabric dyes because they have a wide range of colors and are easy to find in my local grocery and craft stores. After a bit of research, I discovered that although these particular dyes are not considered acid-free, they score around 7 to 8 on the pH scale (keeping in mind that a score of 7 is considered pH neutral). So I figure that if it is good enough to be recommended for use on delicate silk fabrics, then it should be safe enough on my layouts, especially if I never use it next to precious original photographs or memorabilia. If you are still concerned about the acid issue however, stick with brands specifically tested to be safe for scrapbooking, as are all of the other products used in this chapter.

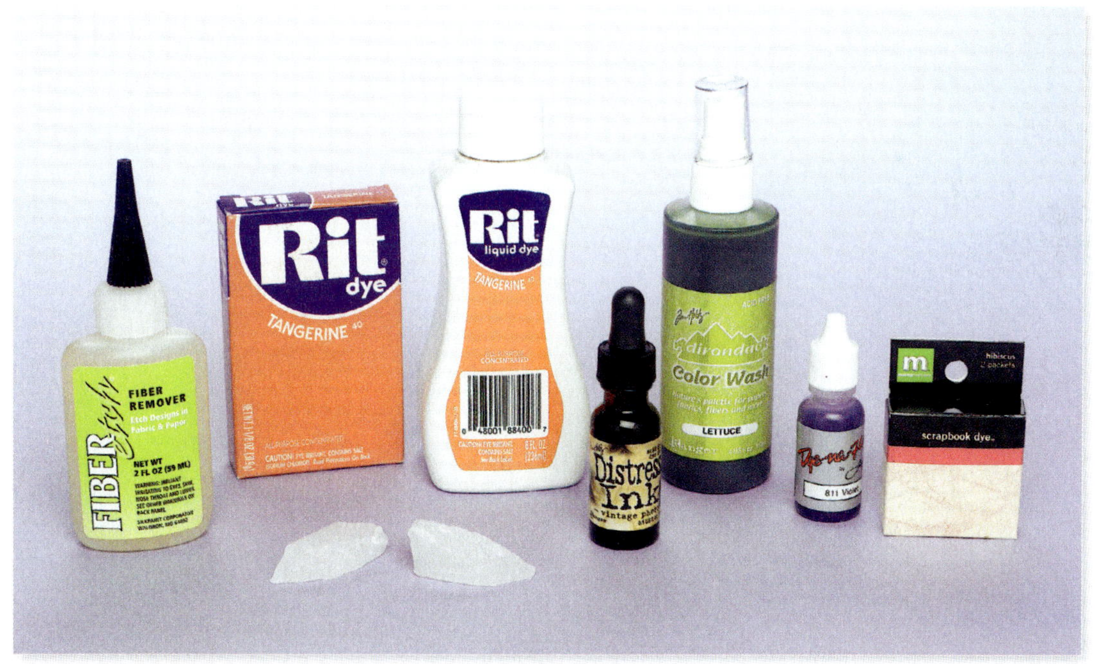

Featured Supplies

- Fiber Etch
- Fabric Dyes (powder and liquid)
- Distress Ink Refill Bottles
- Color Wash Dyes
- Textile Paints
- Scrapbook Dyes
- Candle Wax Blocks

Dip & Distress Technique

The floral patterned paper was too bright so I dyed and distressed both the paper and the cream lace trim so they would coordinate better with the other elements on the page. In doing so, I gave the layout a soft, homey feeling. More photographs and journaling are tucked away inside the mini book in the top right-hand corner.

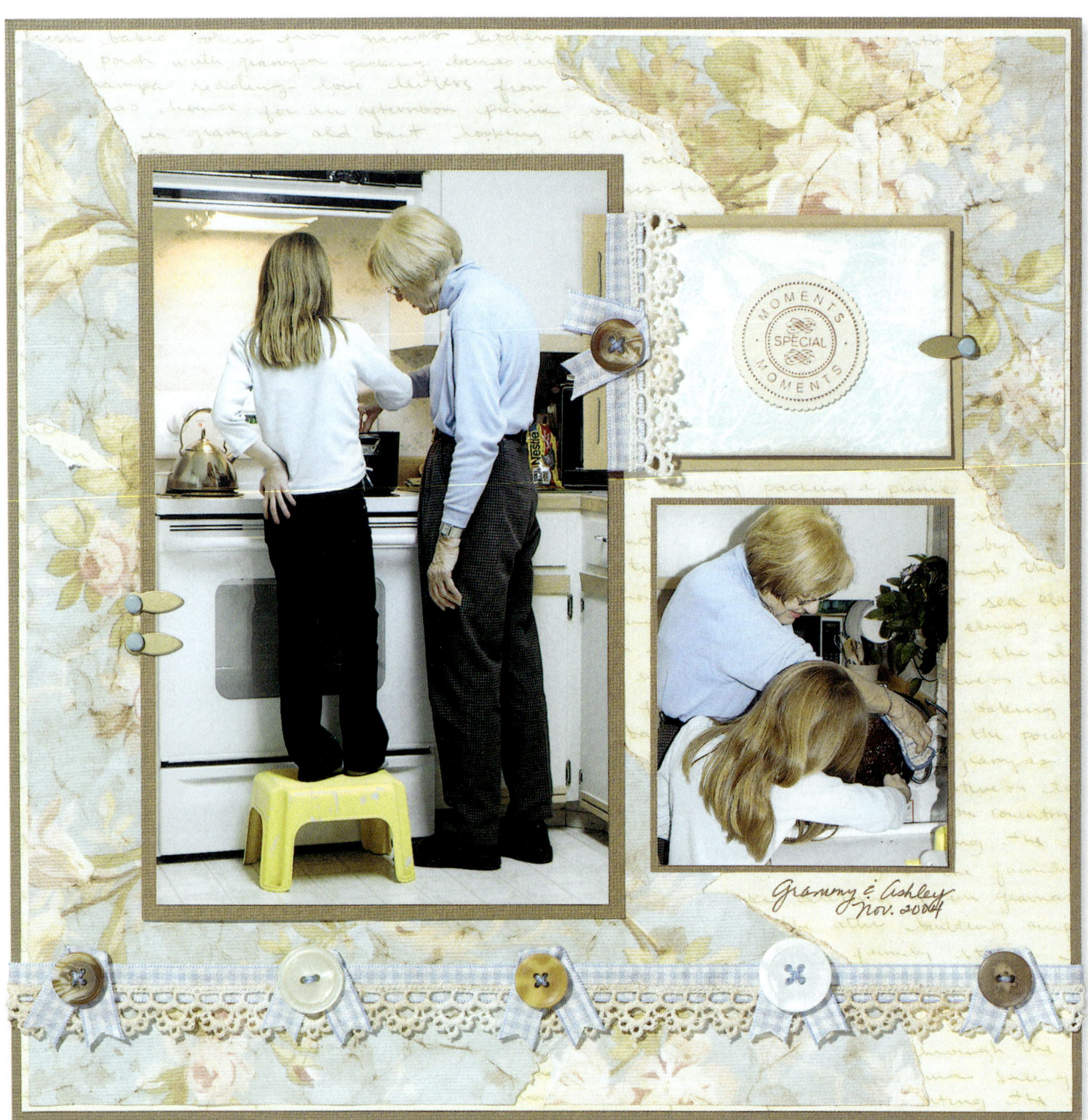

Making Fudge With Grammy

Supplies: Patterned paper, metal accent (K & Company); script patterned paper (EK Success); ribbon (Li'l Davis Designs); Fluid Chalk Ink (Clearsnap); stamp (Lazar Studiowerx); buttons (Jesse James); photo anchors (Making Memories); brads (Provo Craft); Fineliner pen (Staedtler); Fabro-Tac adhesive (Beacon Adhesives); Distress Ink (Ranger)

Have you ever tried to work with a certain paper and found it would not do because it was just a little too bright or lacked a certain character? Well, don't despair, as there is a very easy way to fix this problem! By dipping it into a bath of any brown-toned dye, you can give your paper a soft, muted look that will allow it to blend in nicely with most paper styles and colors. Throw in some quick crumpling and/or tearing before the dyeing process, and you can also give your paper additional "age" and dimensional interest.

You can use other types of dyes, but for this particular technique I like to use the Distress Ink refill bottles made to refresh stamp pads because it is so easy to create custom dye bath colors by adding a few drops of the concentrated liquid to a bowl of water. When you break the surface fibers of a piece of paper by crumpling or tearing it, the dye will concentrate in these areas and be darker than the rest of the surface. For a truly aged and distressed effect, take advantage of the altered texture of your paper after dyeing it and let the various tears and wrinkles that may result give your paper extra character.

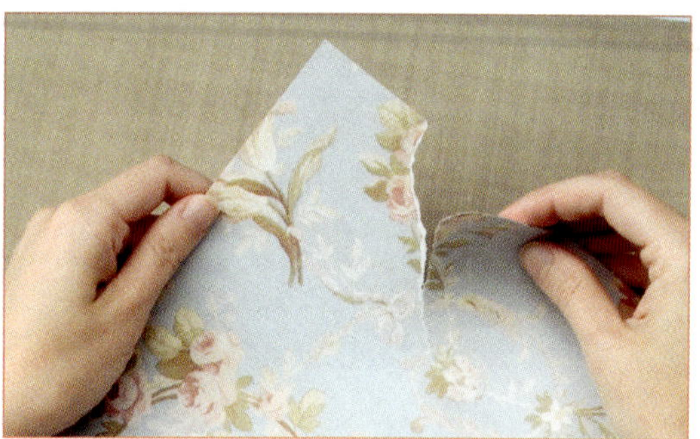

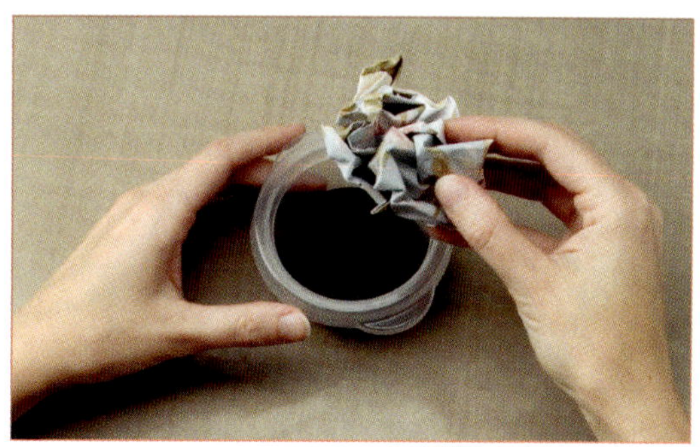

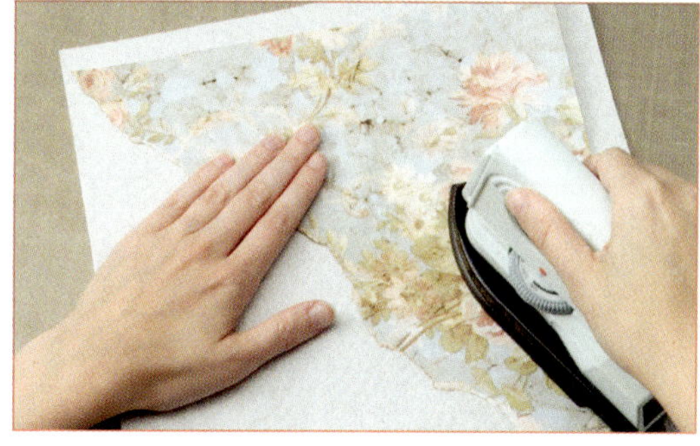

Tips & Tricks

- *Do not dip paper into hot water dye bath or your paper will quickly disintegrate into tattered shreds!*
- *Different types of papers and brands may accept the dye differently, so experiment with a test sample to see how long you need to saturate it to get the results you want.*
- *Other dye ink refill products may change color when water is added, so be sure to test first.*

1

Tear blue patterned paper into one large and one small triangle. Mist with water and crumple each piece into tight balls.

2

Dip each crumpled ball quickly into the dye bath, rotating and loosening the wrinkles if needed to make sure it is evenly covered with dye. Also dip portions of cream trim into dye and set aside to dry.

3

Gently spread out the wet paper onto paper towels and pat dry. Smooth flat with a craft iron or press under heavy books until completely dry.

Other Ideas to Try . . .

1. Experiment with different crumpling methods—crumple once for larger wrinkles, or smooth the paper out and re-crumple it several times for finer ones.

2. Drip or splatter a darker color of dye over paper to create "age spots" for a really old appearance.

3. Sand the raised edges of an embossed paper before putting it into the dye bath.

Dyed Embellishments

Hand-dyed paper flowers and a twill ribbon border were given a face-lift with dyes to create pretty embellishments for this simple but striking layout. The flowers were made even more interesting by crumpling the petals for dimension and adding word accents in the centers.

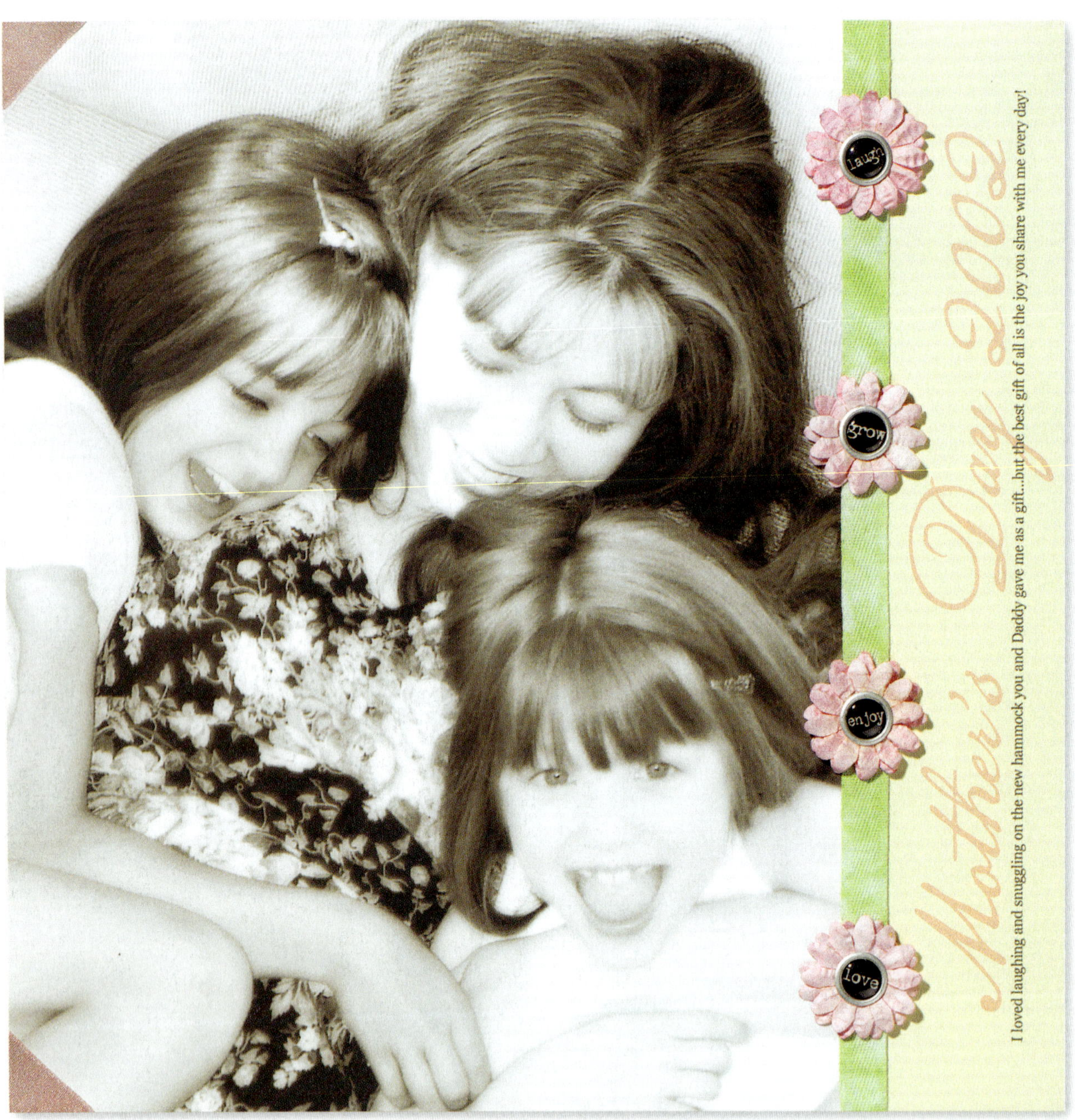

Mother's Day 2002

Supplies: Dyes (Making Memories); paper flowers (Prima); epoxy word stickers (K & Company); twill ribbon (Creek Bank Creations); photo corners (EK Success); glue dots (Glue Dots International); craft iron (Clover); Milwaukee heat tool (Wagner)

Another way dyes can be used for scrapbooking is to alter the color of premade embellishments such as ribbon and paper flowers. Natural materials such as cotton or twill fabrics used for tags and other accents are also good candidates for coloring with dyes.

Dyeing items a solid color in a dye bath is fine, but do not overlook the other ways you can create interesting effects with this medium! One variation is to control the way a portion of the object is exposed to the dye and the length of time you keep it in the color before removing it. For instance, you can give an embellishment a shaded look by quickly dipping it entirely into the dye, then re-dipping just the edges for several more seconds to create a darker tint. Or create a banded design by brushing on different colors in separate areas.

Another variation to try is the good old-fashioned tie-dyeing technique. Anything that can be wrapped with a rubber band or string is a great candidate to use. A monochromatic version of this method is one of my favorite ways to dress up plain ribbon, such as what I used on this layout.

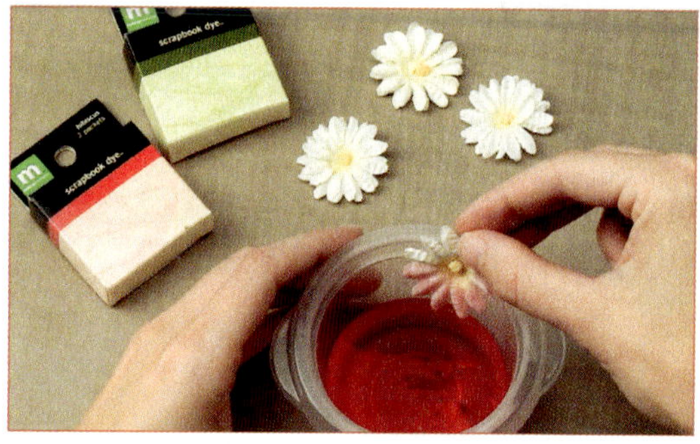

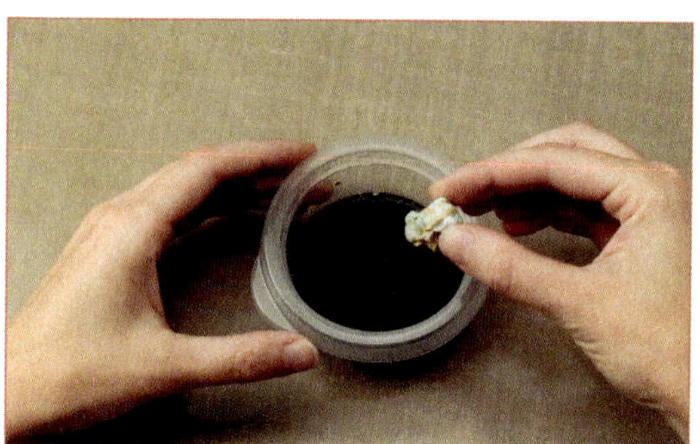

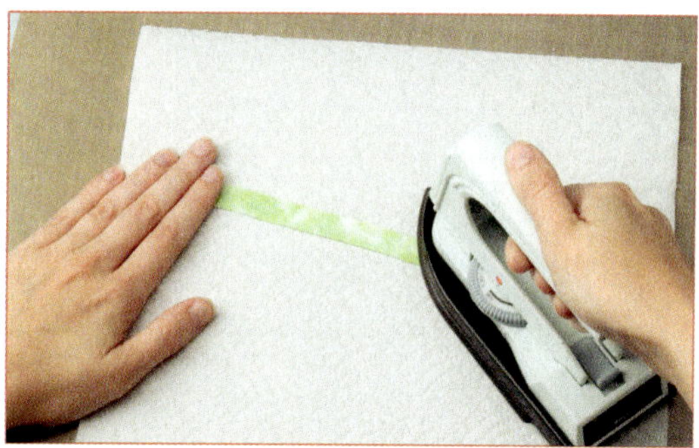

1

Dip white flowers into pink dye until completely colored. Manipulate with fingers to add dimension and dry with a heat tool to set the color.

2

Crunch white twill ribbon into a ball and secure tightly with a rubber band. Dip into green dye, remove rubber band and gently roll out.

3

Place damp ribbon onto a plain paper towel and iron until dry and straight to heat set the color permanently.

Tips & Tricks

- *Experiment with different ways of tying ribbon and flower petals with rubber bands, string, etc., to create various effects.*
- *Whenever possible, dry your items with a heat tool or iron to set the color and make it permanent.*
- *While flowers are still damp from the dye, crumple and fluff up the petals for added dimension and realism.*

Other Ideas to Try . . .

1. Double-dip flower petals so that just the tips are darkened for a pretty two-tone shading.
2. Use several colors and adjust the rubber band between dipping to create a more colorful, traditional-looking tie-dye design.
3. Dye wide strips or squares of fabric to use as photo mats.

Tinted Fabric & Chipboard

Who can resist these puppy dog eyes? Dyed and sewn fabric journal boxes are colorful ways to describe the happy nature of our beloved family pet. Chipboard discs were primed with gesso, then painted with the same dyes and sanded before the letters were stamped on with permanent ink.

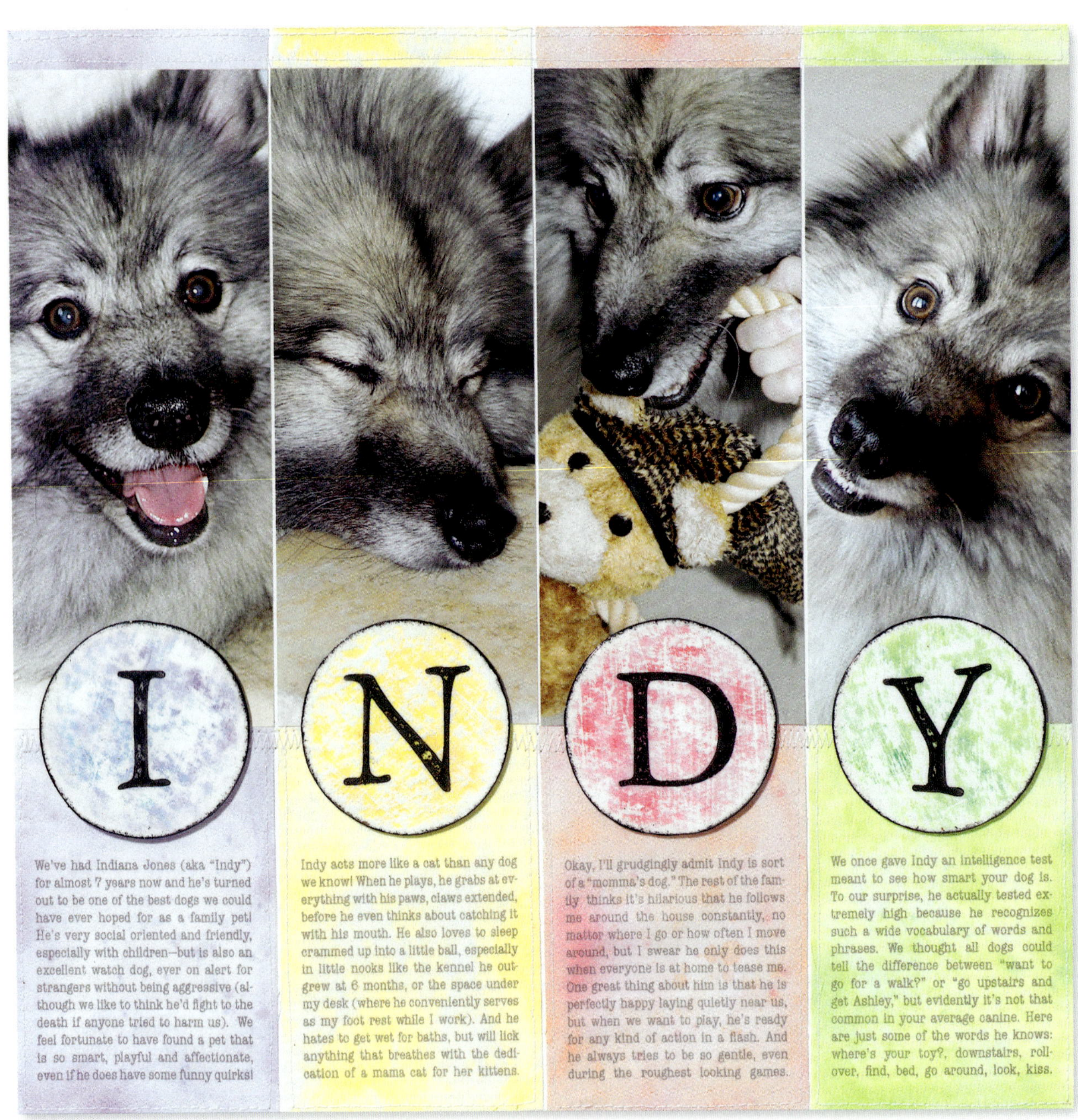

Indy *Supplies:* Dye-na-Flow paint and InkJet Printing Cotton fabric sheets (Jacquard Products); letter stamps (Purple Onion Designs); Staz-On solvent ink (Tsukineko); gesso (Delta); craft iron (Clover Needlecraft)

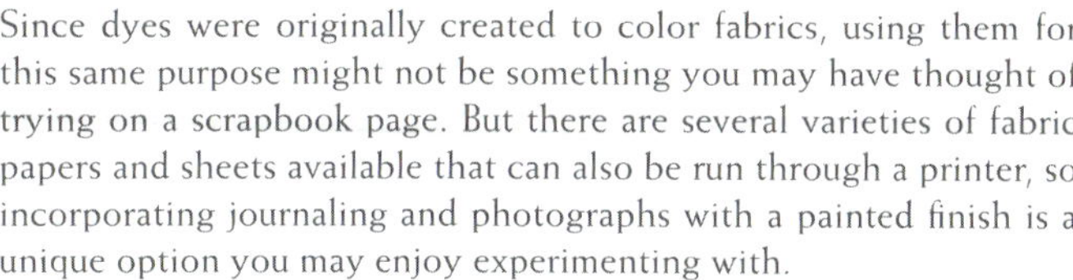

Since dyes were originally created to color fabrics, using them for this same purpose might not be something you may have thought of trying on a scrapbook page. But there are several varieties of fabric papers and sheets available that can also be run through a printer, so incorporating journaling and photographs with a painted finish is a unique option you may enjoy experimenting with.

It can be a fun and rewarding change of pace to include painted fabric in your designs, but do not limit yourself to using only dyes, as various other mediums, such as watercolors and acrylic paints, can also create wonderfully similar effects. For this particular technique, I chose to use an acid-free textile paint that acts more like a dye when applied to fabric or paper. Because it has dyelike properties, it can be thinned down to use like a watercolor and tends to bleed a lot, which is all part of its charm. As with regular dyes, this product is highly concentrated, so a little will go a long way.

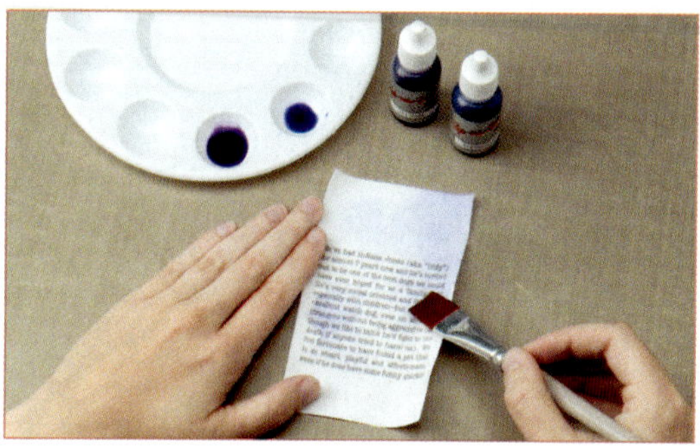

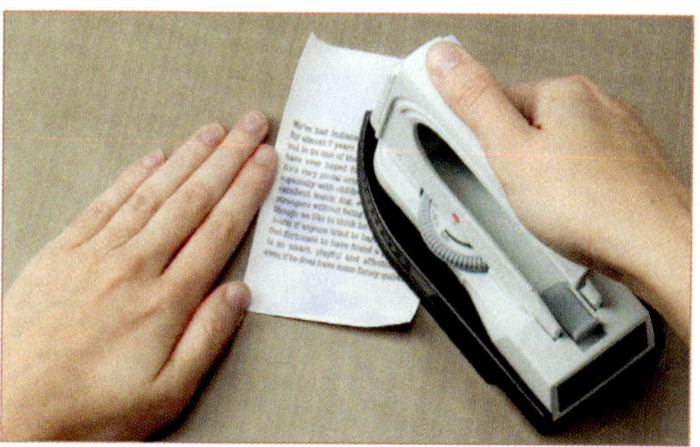

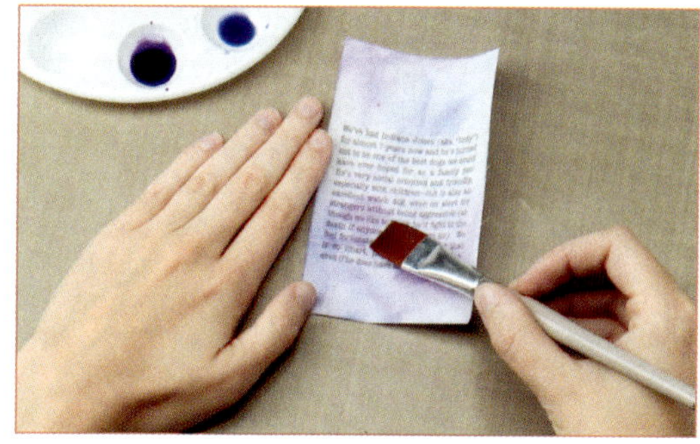

1

Print text onto fabric sheets made especially for inkjet printers (make sure your printer uses waterproof ink). Mist fabric with water. Dilute a few drops of textile paint with a little water and randomly brush onto damp fabric, concentrating around the outer edges. Also splatter on some color (see technique on page 39).

2

Iron both sides of fabric to flatten it back down, and heat set color.

3

Repeat painting process with second color. Remove paper backing if it becomes wrinkled, and finish ironing until fabric is completely dry.

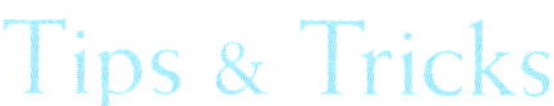

Tips & Tricks

- *You can also use dye inks that are normally used to refill stamp ink pads or watercolors with this technique. But test them first to make sure the colors will not change when water is added.*
- *Dyes will always appear much brighter when wet than when dry, so always do a test run to make sure you will get the color you want on your finished project.*
- *If the color is still too light, you can go back and add more color as often as needed to build up the color intensity.*

Other Ideas to Try . . .

1. Print a photograph onto fabric paper and tint around the edges or colorize special areas.

2. Color fabric or chipboard with just the splattering technique for a speckled background.

3. Hand-paint a design onto regular fabric to use as an accent piece or an entire layout background.

Etched Velvet Paper

Ashley's swimsuit fabric and the soft color shading in the water was the inspiration behind these velvety painted flower accents. Rickrack was machine-stitched on to create borders for this fun color-blocked design.

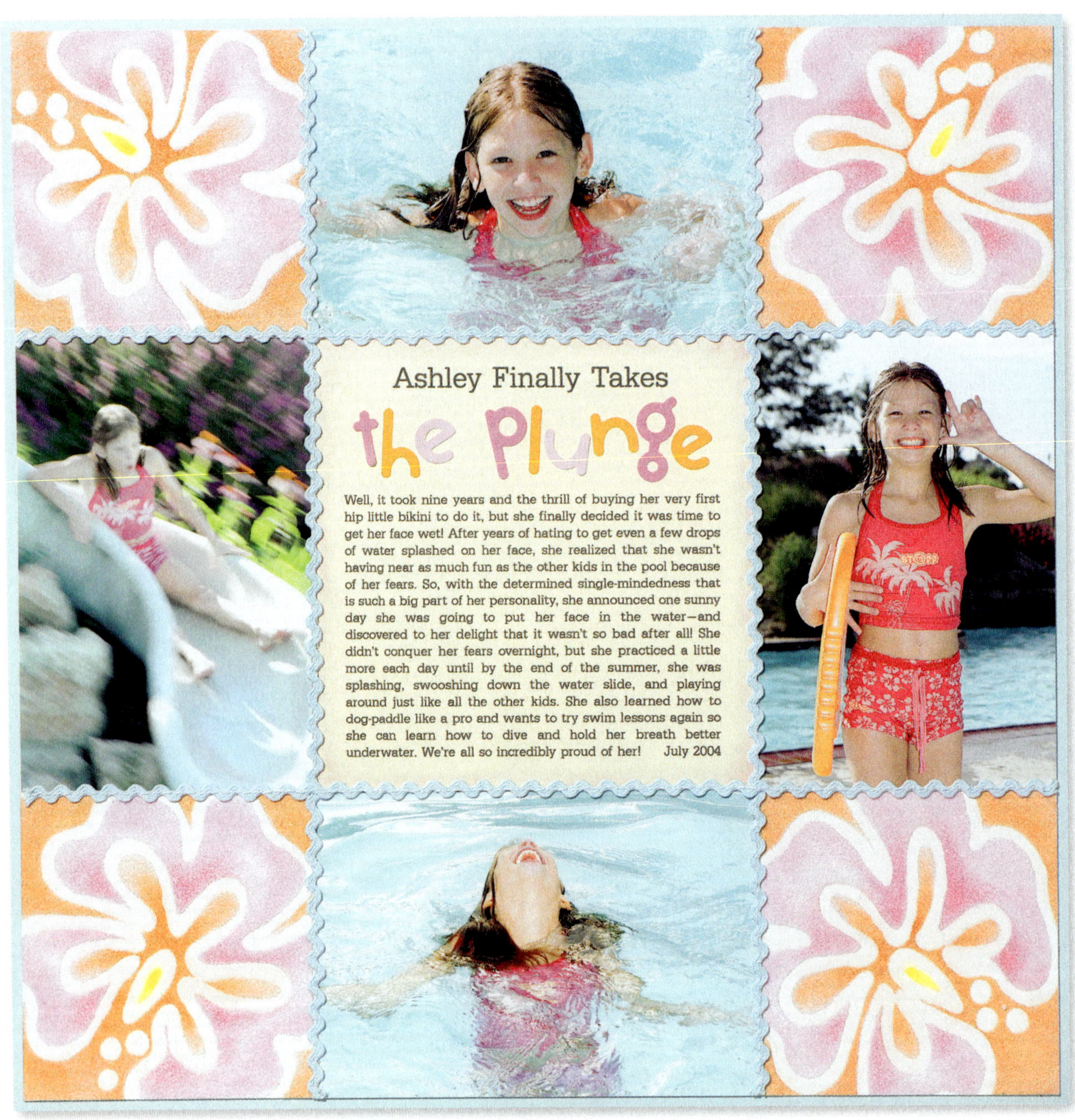

The Plunge *Supplies:* Rit Dyes (Phoenix Brands); AirPen Pro, Fiber Etch (Silk-paint Corp.); American Painter 1" Wash, #5 Round Golden Taklon brush (Loew-Cornell); craft iron (Clover); stamp (Rubber Stampede); suede paper (K & Company); rickrack (Wrights); letter stickers (KI Memories); shimmer chalks (Pebbles)

When I discovered a product called Fiber Etch, I was immediately intrigued by all of its possibilities. Originally used to remove fibers from cellulose fabrics like silk and cotton, it can now also be used on certain types of papers. Designs can be created freehand or with tools such as stamps and brushes without harming any non-cellulose surfaces such as plastic or metal.

After learning about the etching and dyeing techniques used on real velvet fabric, I couldn't wait to see if it also worked on faux velvet paper—and it did! After etching, I painted the designs with diluted liquid fabric dyes and the etched outlines worked like invisible "fences" that stopped color from migrating into other areas. Although you can apply Fiber Etch directly from the bottle, I used an AirPen Pro tool, which helps with large or intricate projects because it gives precise control and lessens hand fatigue. This versatile tool can be used to apply most other paints and mediums, too!

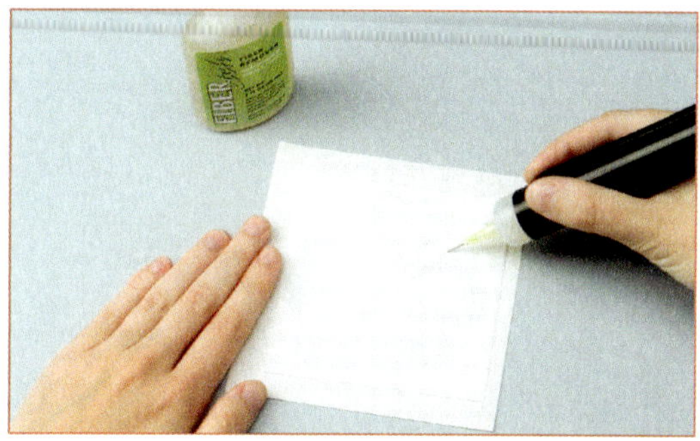

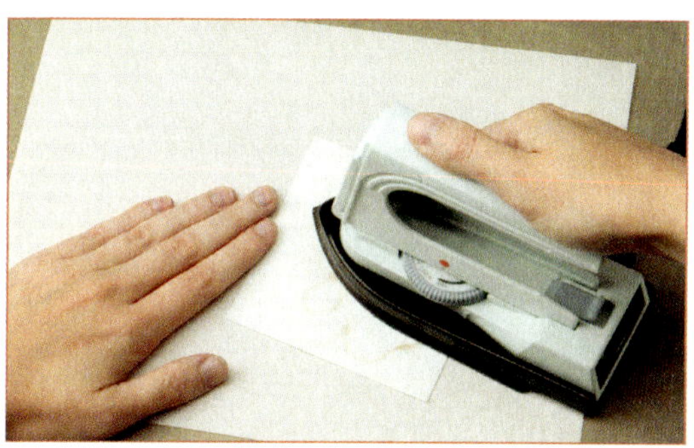

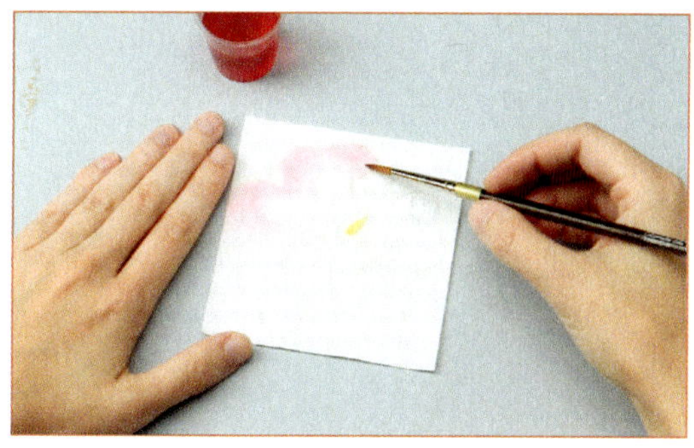

1

Stamp flower to use as a pattern and place under suede velvet paper. Apply Fiber Etch and allow to air dry or use a hair dryer on low until Fiber Etch no longer looks shiny or wet.

2

Lay suede paper facedown on plain newsprint and iron until Fiber Etch turns a light brown color. Or activate it in 210° oven for about 15 to 25 minutes. Rinse under running water and gently brush or rub off fibers under etched outlines.

3

Shake or pat off excess water and while paper is wet, dip brush into dye and touch tip to areas directly next to outlines and pull toward the center—the color will bleed down into a graded wash. Add more dye if a deeper or more uniform shade is desired in certain areas.

Tips & Tricks

- *Do not let the Fiber Etch get too brown or it may stain the paper.*
- *Like watercolors, dyes look darker when wet than they will when fully dry. Always test a sample before working on your actual project.*

Other Ideas to Try . . .

Bloom Book Cover

A stencil and special "carving paper" was used to create this floral design. It was soaked in a dye bath and embellished to decorate a small album cover.

Supplies: Rit Dyes (Phoenix Brands); Fiber Etch, carving paper (Silkpaint Corp.); daisy stencil (Delta); album, epoxy circle, metal disc (K & Company); sticker (Memories Complete); ribbon (Making Memories, Maya Road); stamp (Lazar Studiowerx); chalk fluid ink (Clearsnap); Milwaukee heat tool (Wagner); vellum

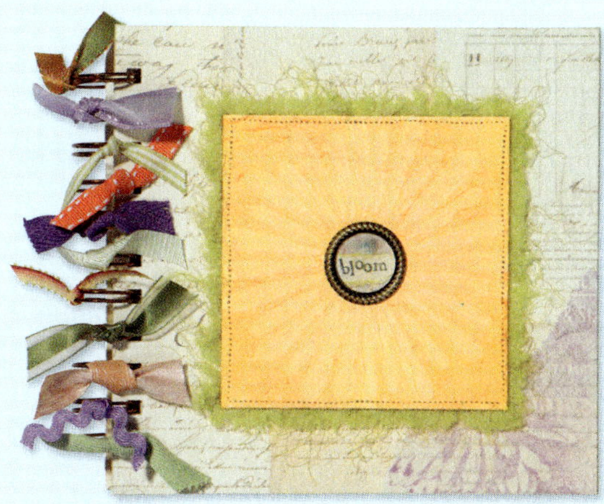

Wax Batik

This picture of my daughter Kaitlyn acting like she is going to kiss this frog always gives me the willies! But relax, she didn't really do it! The photo served as the inspiration for a batik background simulating the spotted look of the frog's body. The story about her little adventure is hidden behind the smaller photo.

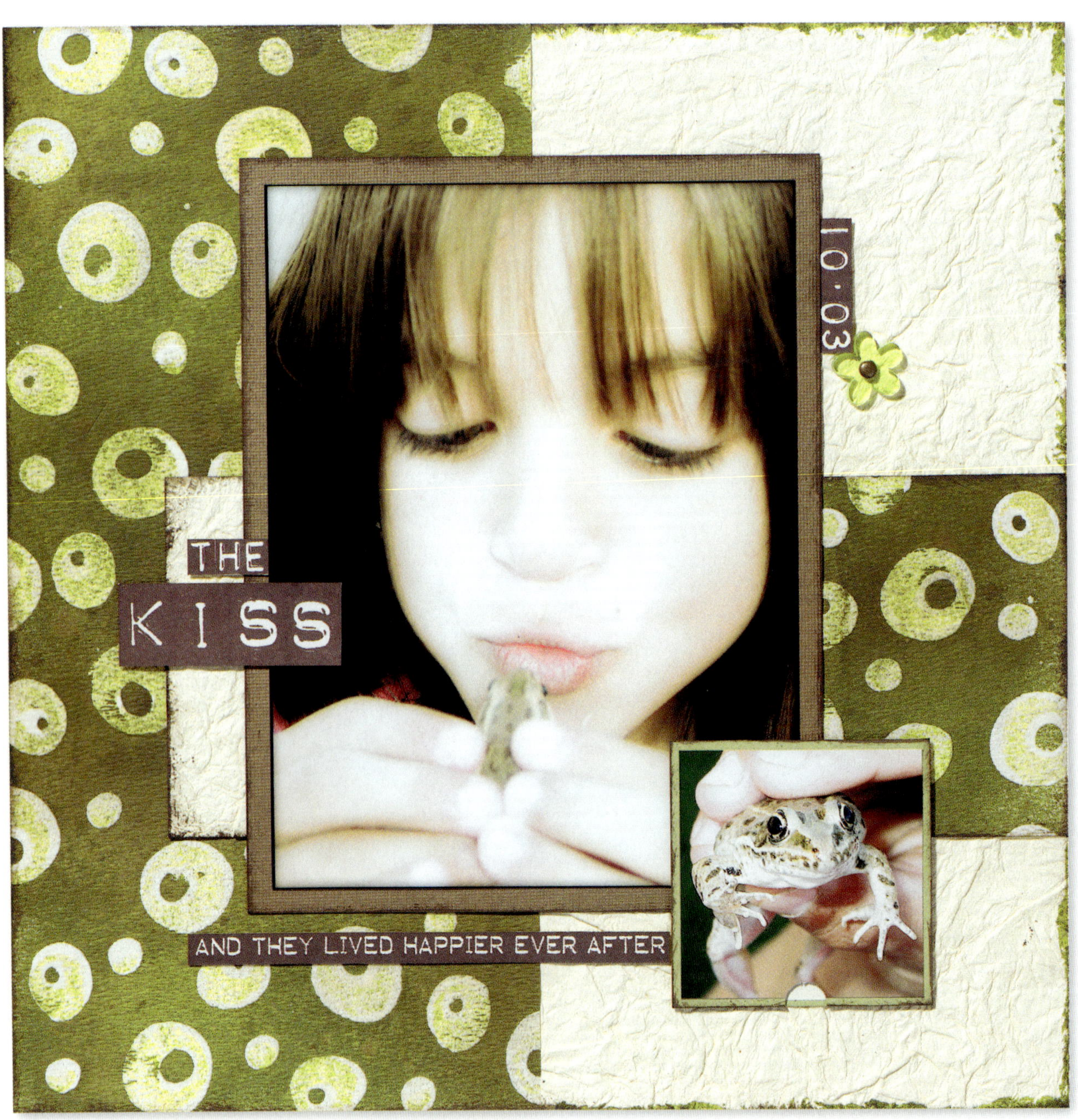

The Kiss *Supplies:* Adirondack Color Wash dyes, melting pot (Ranger); textured paper, brad (Provo Craft); 90 lb. watercolor paper (Strathmore); acrylic flower (KI Memories); quote stamp (Sunday International); letter stamps (Ma Vinci's Reliquary, Sunday International); Fluid Chalk Ink (Clearsnap); craft iron (Clover Needlecraft); wax block; newsprint

If you like the look of batik fabrics, then you will love this technique for creating your own batik papers! By using plain candle wax as a resist medium with simple, bold stamp designs and dyes, you can quickly create these beautiful backgrounds for your pages.

I used spray-on dyes with this technique, but you can also use dye baths or brush on the color. In addition to stamps, found objects like forks or leaves make great waxed impressions, or you can draw shapes freehand with a stick tool or an old brush. Use natural or white colored wax to avoid transferring any color to your paper.

Tips & Tricks

- *Rub stamp lightly on a section of the melting pot pan that does not have melted wax and it will help even out any excess wax for the best impression. You can also lightly blot waxed stamp on a paper towel before stamping if you want more dye to bleed through to the paper.*
- *Use a nonstick craft sheet underneath the newsprint to protect ironing surface from any dye or wax passing through to it.*
- *If you use a regular iron, move it around frequently to make sure you don't miss any waxy spots because of the vent holes on the plate of the iron.*

Other Ideas to Try . . .

Mini Album Cover

Borrow a child's crayons to draw on a more colorful resist effect! Crumple and smooth out the paper before adding dye so that the color will seep into the creases for a more traditional-looking batik design.

Supplies: Adirondack Color Wash dyes (Ranger); album, sticker, metal accent (K & Company); crayons (Crayola)

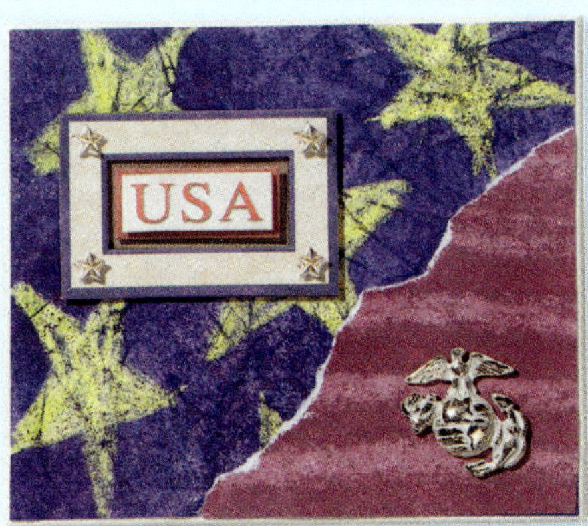

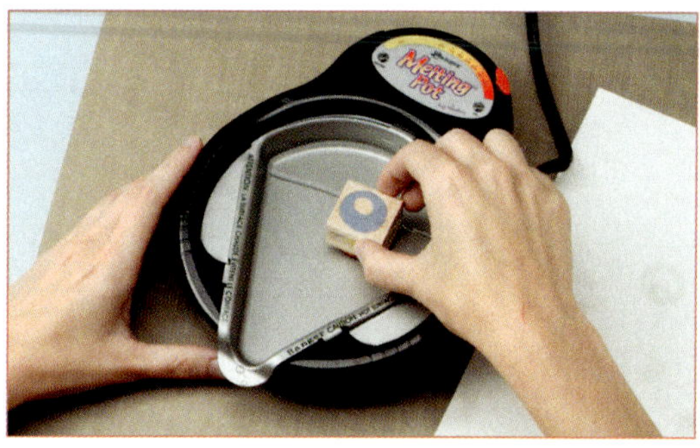

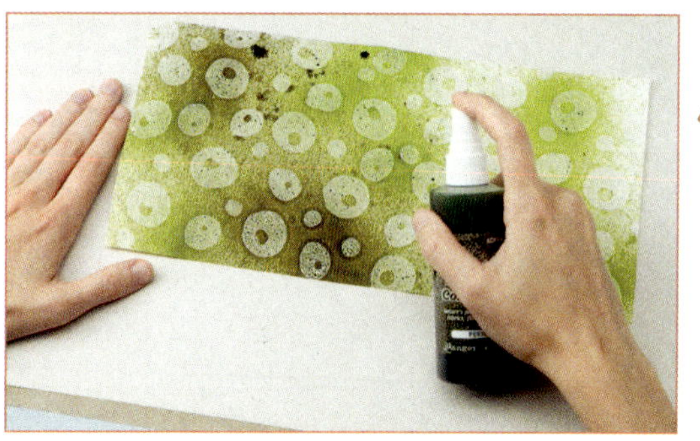

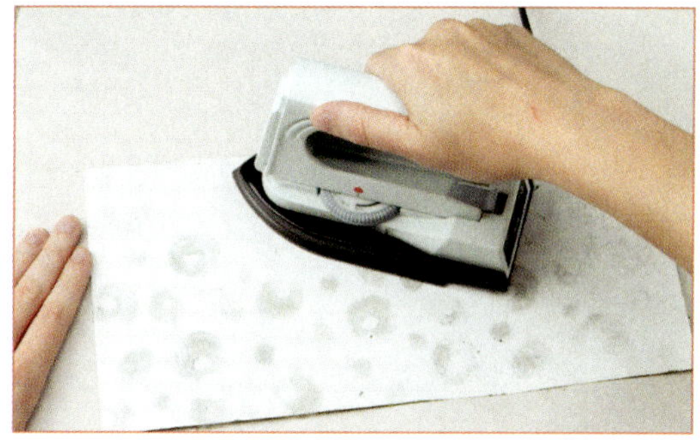

1

Lightly dip stamp into melted wax and press onto watercolor paper. Repeat this process in a random pattern with various sized stamps until background is completely covered.

2

Spray lighter green dye randomly over waxed designs. Apply a second layer of deeper green dye in just a few places for a mottled effect.

3

Wait a few seconds to allow the dye to saturate the paper, then lay damp paper facedown over plain newsprint and press evenly with a hot iron until all the wax has transferred to the newsprint.

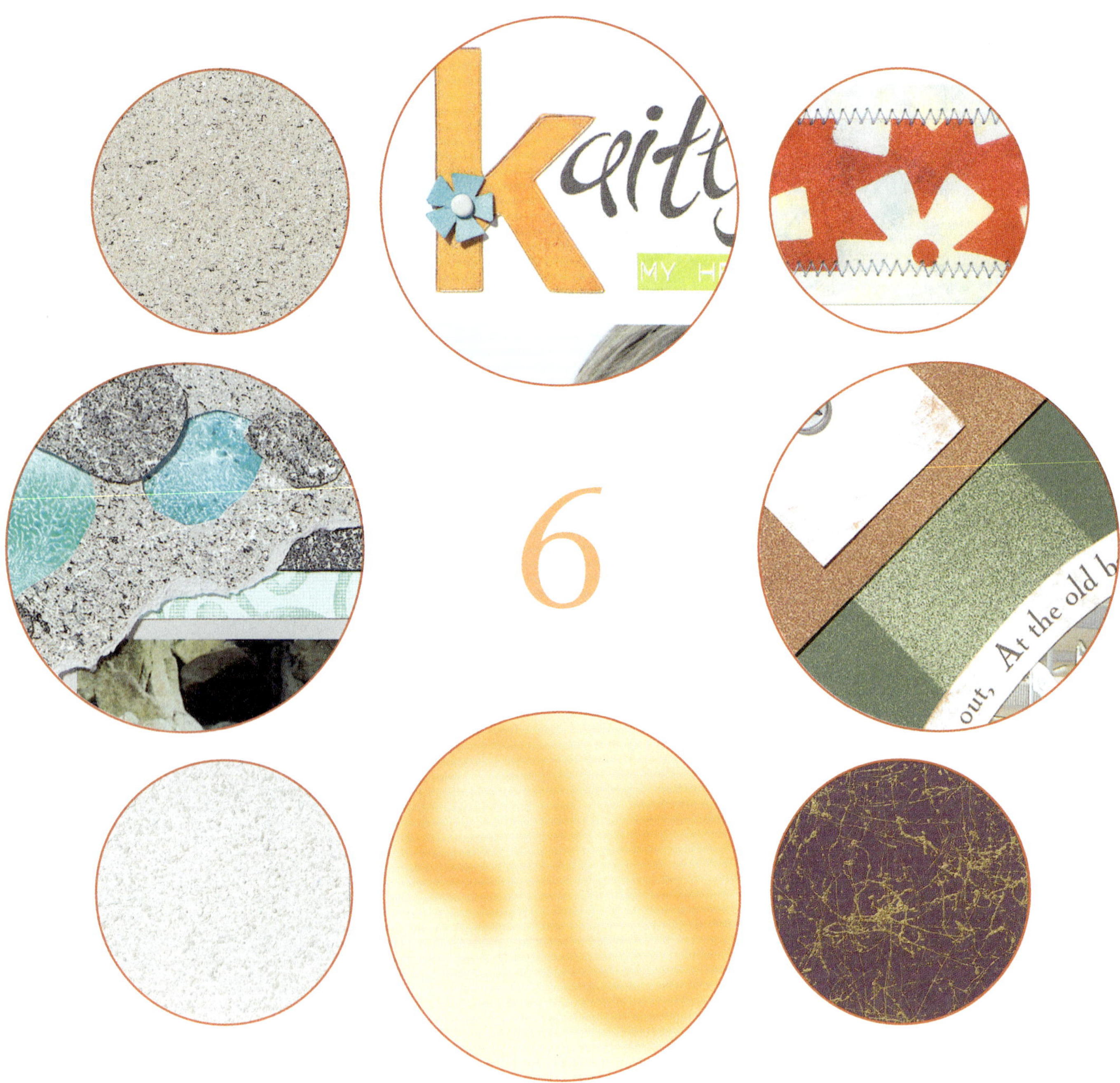

6

Spray Paints

When you think of spray painting, does the image of a gaudy muscle car or a graffiti-covered wall come to mind? Well, no need to panic, as this chapter is all about learning how to use these paints in much more refined and fun ways on our pages. While many brands contain materials that are considered unsafe for scrapbooking purposes, there are a few companies that offer paints that are not only acid-free, but have a variety of interesting textures and finishes that can easily be applied with the simple press of a button.

Although the directions on the label often recommend longer drying times, I've found that if I use light layers of paint on heavy cardstock, it is usually dry enough to handle in about 15 to 30 minutes. But I recommend spraying denser paints or multiple layers of color the night before and letting everything dry overnight for the best results. A spray booth is also very handy to keep out dust and prevent overspray from getting onto other surfaces.

Airbrushing is another great option for applying a sprayed-on finish because you can use several different types of artistic mediums with it. This tool uses thin paints to create seamless designs with soft edges, but you cannot apply any kind of thick or textured paints because it would clog up the spray nozzle. One key advantage is that you can mix up an infinite variety of custom colors and paint mixtures to use with it.

In addition to airbrushing, this chapter features spray paints with specialty finishes such as faux stone, suede, glass and webbing. There are also other paint types available that are not explored here, such as ones that contain glitter, pearlescent and antiquing finishes. After learning some of the techniques on the following projects, I am sure you will be searching your local craft store aisles for other spray painting products to experiment with and embellish your scrapbooks!

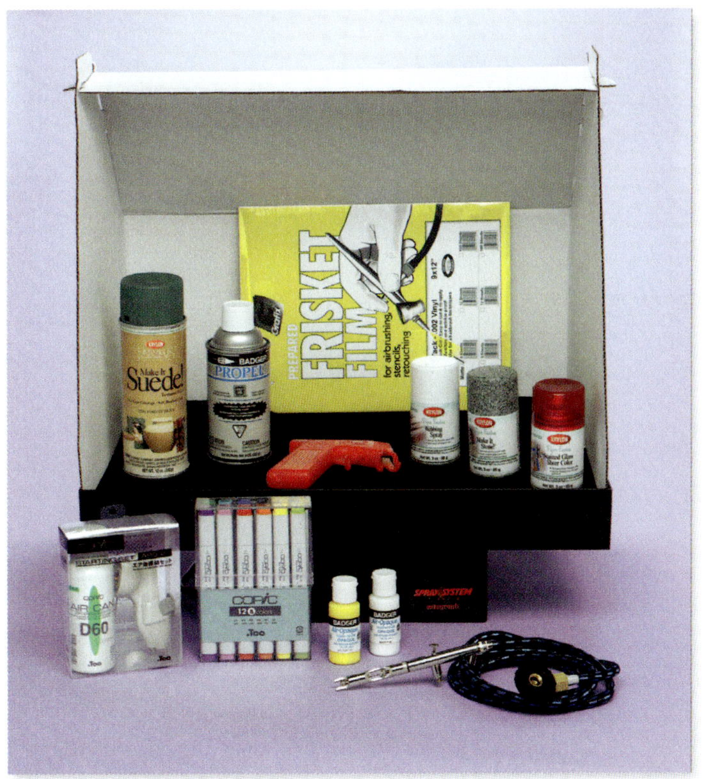

Featured Supplies

Textured Spray Paints

Stained Glass Spray Paints

Webbing Spray Paints

Traditional Airbrush Tools & Paints

Pen-Based Airbrush System

Low-Tack Frisket Film

Spray Booth

Spray Handle Attachment

Stained Glass & Masking

Bold, geometric borders tie together these two pages describing some of the unique characteristics of my daughter. The "K" is a clear acrylic accent that was also colored with spray paint and embellished with a flower accent.

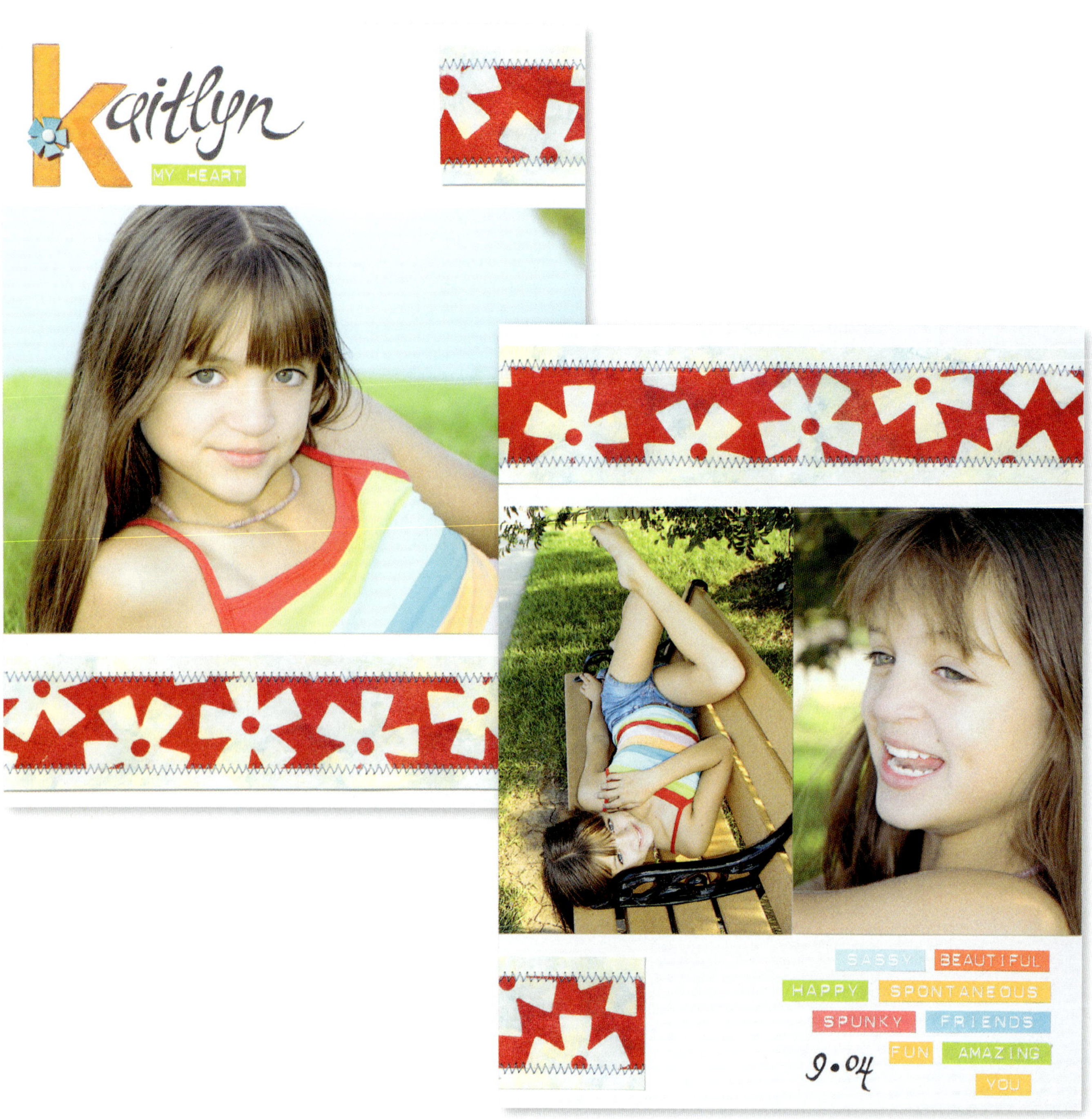

Kaitlyn *Supplies:* Stained Glass spray paint, all-purpose spray adhesive (Krylon); Low-Tack Frisket Film, Dura-Lar Wet Media Film (Grafix); Ceramcoat acrylic paint (Delta); Smooth Bristol paper (Strathmore); stickers (K & Company); flower die (Sizzix, Provo Craft); acrylic letter (Heidi Swapp); pen (EK Success); paper flower (Prima); brad (Limited Edition Rubber Stamps); sewing thread

Stained Glass is a translucent spray paint that gives any surface the look of real stained glass, and it is especially realistic when applied over clear transparencies or film. It comes in bright, primary colors that can also be combined with each other to create custom colors, either by applying them in coats over the same item or by layering two separately painted pieces.

Since real leading is not recommended for use on layouts, masking out shapes or borders with a product called "frisket" is a neat and safe alternative. This product is a self-adhesive, thin, clear film with a paper backing which makes it easy to cut, punch or die cut any shape to create a mask that will keep paint from adhering to the background. Low-tack frisket is the best kind to use over film because it won't leave any adhesive residue behind to mar the glossy finish and you can reuse it several times.

If you don't have access to frisket film, self-adhesive notes will work as long as you make sure to only use the part with the adhesive on it. There are also premade masks available featuring decorative designs that can be used with any type of spray paint.

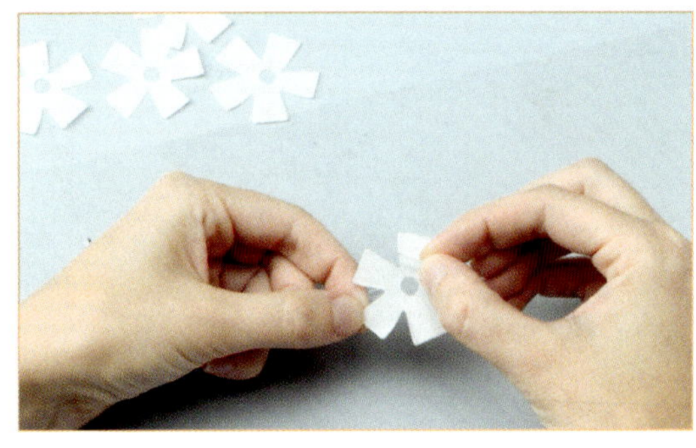

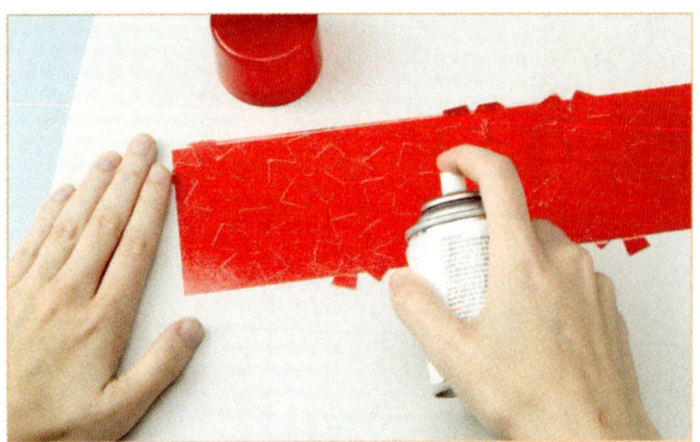

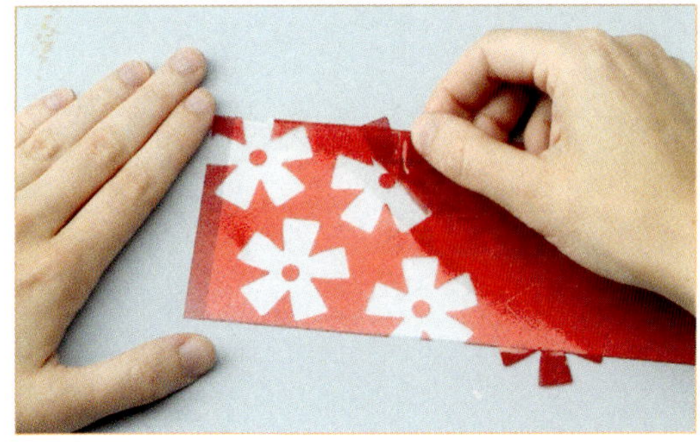

1

Die cut flower shapes from frisket film to create individual masks. Remove backing and attach to clear film. Make sure to remove any fingerprints before spraying with paint.

2

Spray a light coat of paint over film until evenly covered. Allow to dry 10 to 15 minutes and spray another coat if needed. Allow to dry completely according to label directions.

3

Remove frisket shapes and layer painted film over painted paper border (see directions for scumbling backgrounds on page 17).

Tips & Tricks

• Because the frisket film is so thin, it is helpful to back it with a plain sheet of paper while punching or die cutting shapes to get the crispest edges.

• The frisket film may be tricky to remove after painting. Try using the tip of a craft knife to help pry up an edge and then pull the rest of it off with your fingers or tweezers.

• I like to attach my film with the painted side facing down so that it will be protected from being damaged if I add other embellishments or photos over the top.

Other Ideas to Try . . .

1. Attach painted film with other accents such as brads, staples or eyelets.

2. Lay a sheet of film over a photograph and cut around a silhouetted shape to use as a colored background.

Stone & Webbing Textures

Realistic stone textured accents create a wonderfully interactive effect with photographs of a fun day exploring tide pools. Foam adhesive placed under smaller "rocks" and swirly stamped border strips also give a sense of playful motion.

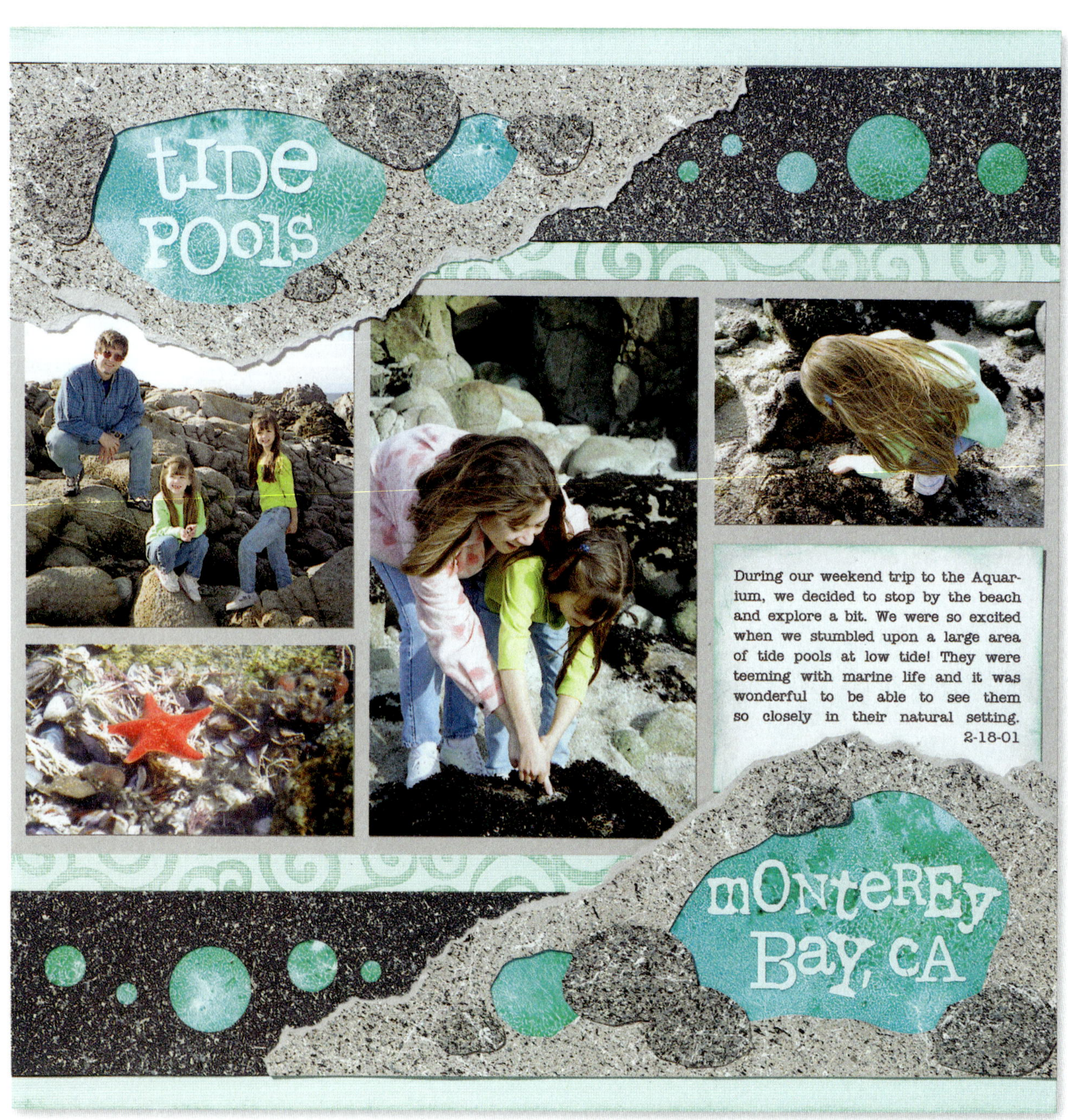

Tide Pools

Supplies: Make It Stone!, Stained Glass spray paints (Krylon); Dura-Lar Wet Media Film (Grafix); rub-on letters (Autumn Leaves); circle punches (EK Success, McGill); scroll stamp (Rubber Stampede); Fluid Chalk Ink (Clearsnap); glue dots (Glue Dots International)

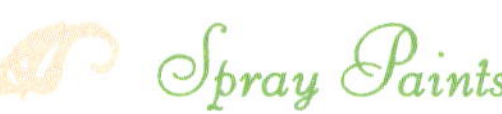

Even though visual texture can be painted on any surface with a variety of techniques and mediums, sometimes a design can benefit with the help of a little dimensional texture as well. Luckily, there are several types of unique spray paints that make it very easy to achieve this look on paper. One type of paint is called Make It Stone! and it creates a speckled quartzlike texture. The other is called Webbing Spray, and it can be used over Stone or other paints or on its own to create light, wispy strands of color. I love to mix and match these two paints to create a variety of realistic and abstract textural effects.

Tips & Tricks

- *Spray paint a few hours before you go to bed, then press between wax paper under heavy books overnight for completely flat and dry paper to work with the next day.*
- *The stone texture is rough and it can be tricky to get things to stick to its surface, so use extra strong gel or silicone type adhesives.*

Other Ideas to Try . . .

1. Layered earthy Stone colors create a sand or dirt texture.
2. Cut snowflakes or clouds from White Onyx stone paint.
3. Gold Metallic Webbing over dark cardstock.
4. Stone and Webbing paints look like natural quartz.

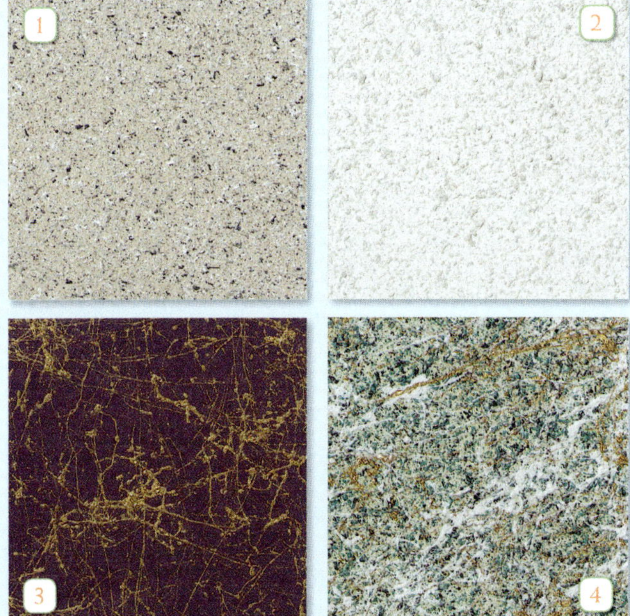

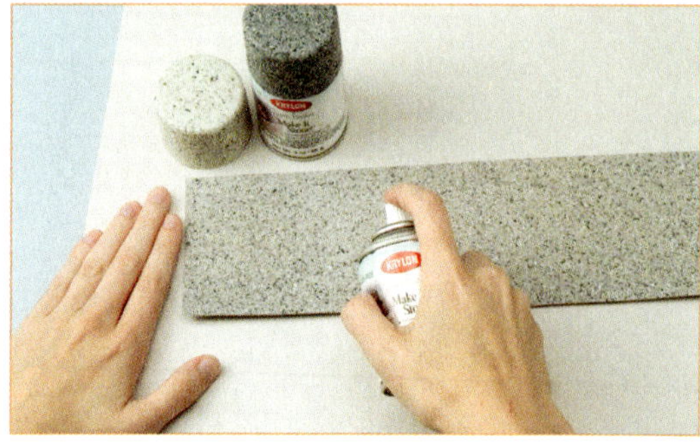

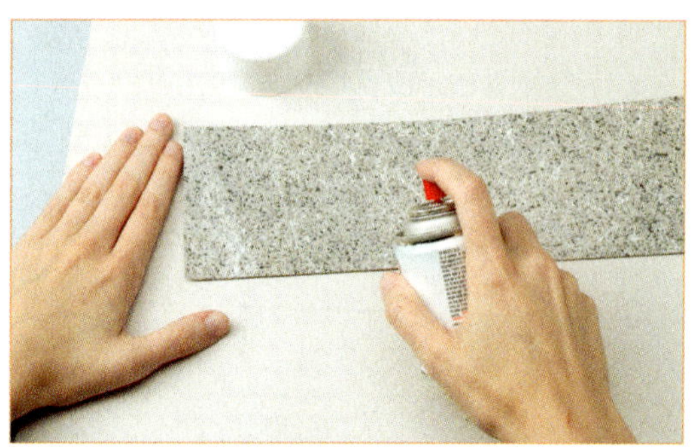

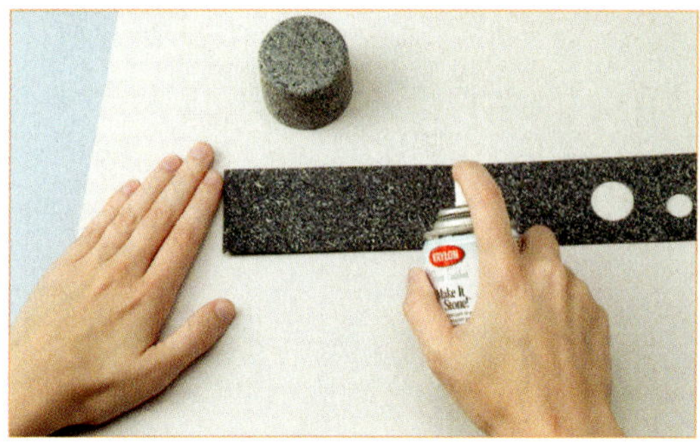

1

Spray gray cardstock with a light layer of Charcoal Sand Stone paint. Add a layer of Black Granite Stone paint in random areas for a mottled effect.

2

Add marbling "veins" by spraying white webbing paint so it gently floats down over the stone paint. Once dry, tear top edges and cut out "tide pool" openings with a craft knife.

3

Spray Black Granite Stone paint over black cardstock until completely covered; allow to dry. Punch circles and glue "water" texture film (spray blue and green Stained Glass paint over crackle medium and blot with a paper towel) to the back.

Suede Texture

Something about this classic song immediately brings to mind a great day spent at the ballpark, rooting for the home team! Journaling is hidden behind the hinged letter frame, which was also sprayed with green suede paint to coordinate with the striped background.

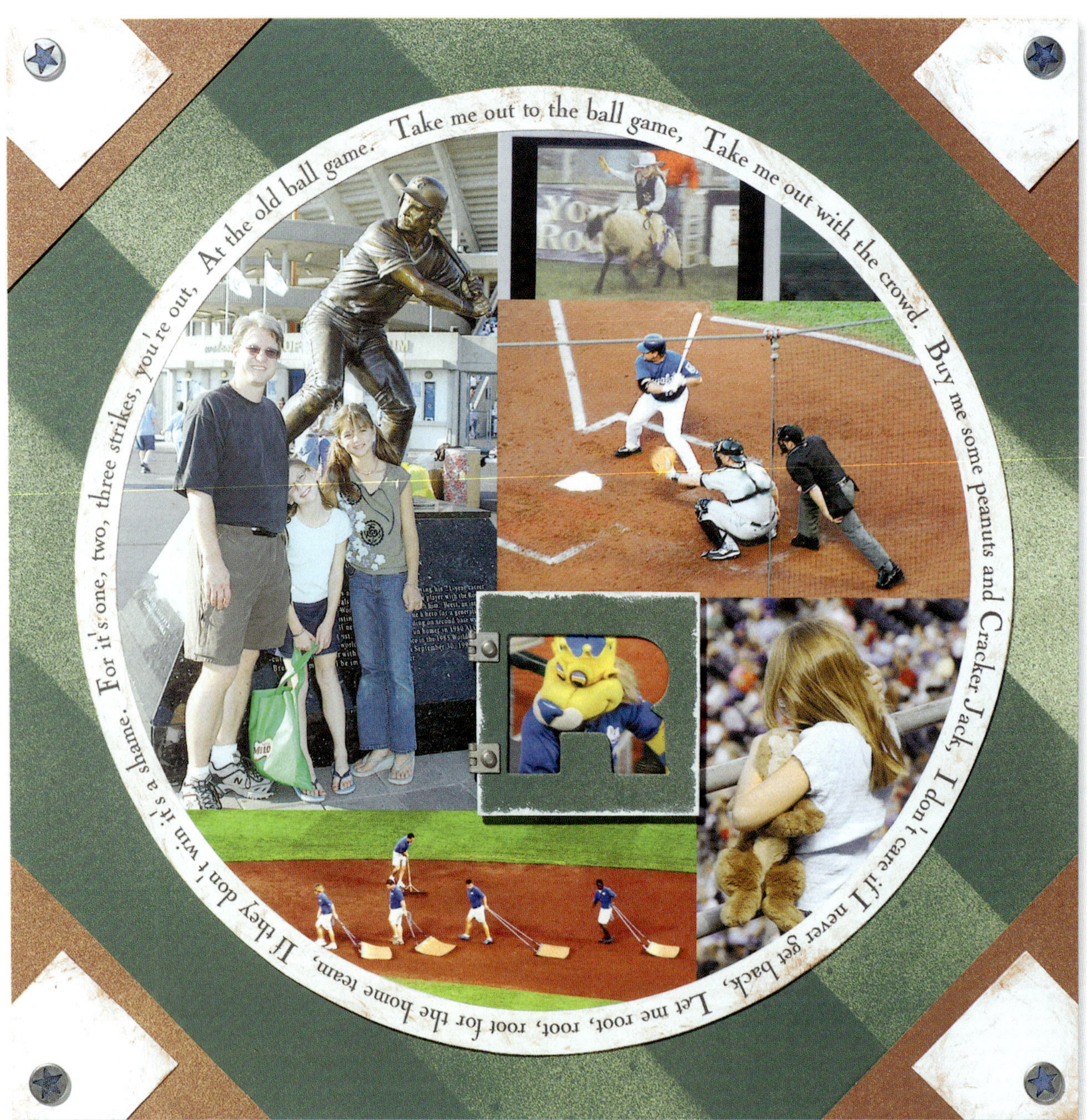

Take Me Out to the Ballgame . . .

Supplies: Make It Suede! spray paint (Krylon); Ceramcoat acrylic paint (Delta); tag die (Sizzix, Provo Craft); Spongit! tool (Loew-Cornell); chipboard letter, eyelets (Making Memories); painters tape (Henkel Consumer Adhesives)

I love the look of real leather, but unfortunately it is usually not safe to use with scrapbooking applications. However, there is a spray paint that creates the matte, brushed finish of suede and is perfectly safe to use on your pages.

But just because it is supposed to look like suede doesn't mean that you have to limit yourself to that specific texture on your designs. For instance, on this layout I was able to create the look of a freshly groomed baseball field with the help of a few strips of painters tape. I added a rubbed-on finish with a reddish-brown color to mimic the look of the dirt-covered areas.

Suede texture paints come in a variety of earthy colors and can also be layered under stone or webbing texture paints to create other interesting effects.

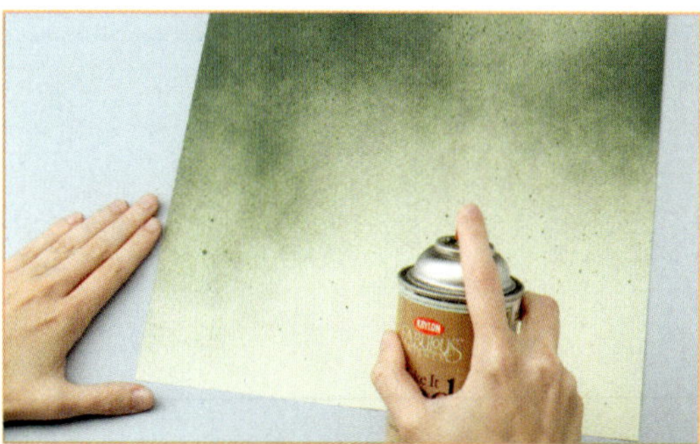

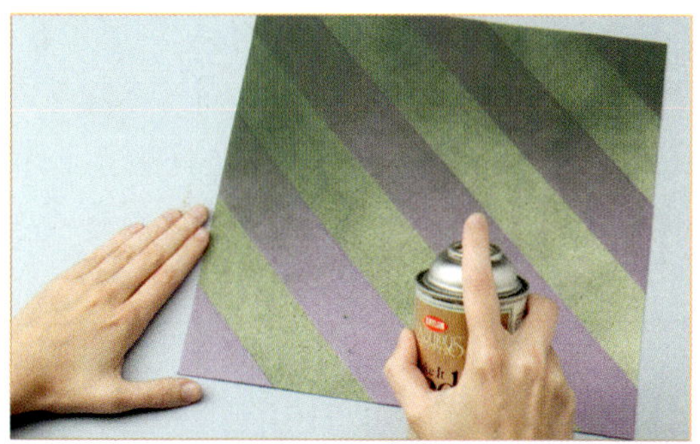

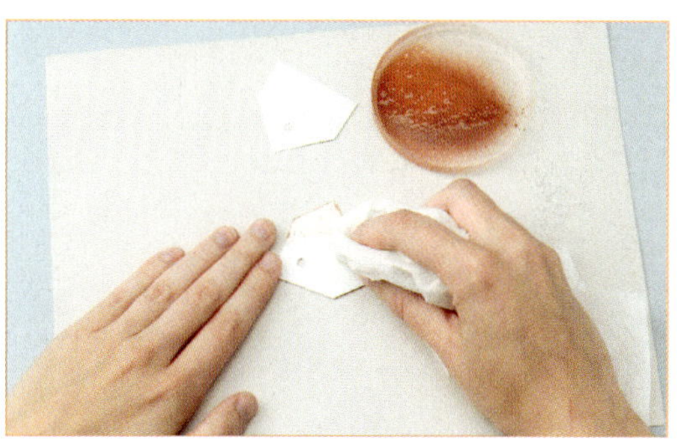

1

Spray a light coat of dark green suede spray paint over pale green cardstock; allow to dry.

2

Mask off diagonal stripes with painters tape and spray another coat of green suede paint; allow to dry and remove tape.

3

To paint "dirt" over text circle and corner base shapes (a modified tag die cut), spray sienna suede paint into a disposable plastic lid. Quickly dip a crumpled paper towel into the paint and rub over shapes to transfer color. Spray paint two 3" squares and cut into triangles for corner accents under the tags.

Tips & Tricks

- *This paint dries fairly quickly compared to other types of spray paints so you can apply several light coats within about 30 minutes.*
- *Use disposable palettes whenever possible, such as clean, used snack lids or fast food trays to reduce cleanup time.*
- *Use gloves or a trigger handle extension for spray cans when painting to avoid unsightly stains under your fingernails that may be hard to clean.*

Other Ideas to Try . . .

1. Instead of a paper towel, use crumpled plastic wrap for a more defined texture.
2. Stamp designs with a dark brown ink over tan suede paint to make faux "branded leather" backgrounds or accents.
3. Sponge on wet green paint to create a moss-covered or grassy look.
4. Mask out shapes and spray over cardstock that is the same color as the paint to simulate the look of embossed velvet.

Because airbrushing can apply such a soft, sheer layer of color, I was able to place a sheet of painted vellum over my journaling for a fun, peekaboo effect. Airbrushing also works great as a shading tool on the edges of this layout, and even mimics the look of freshly baked cookies.

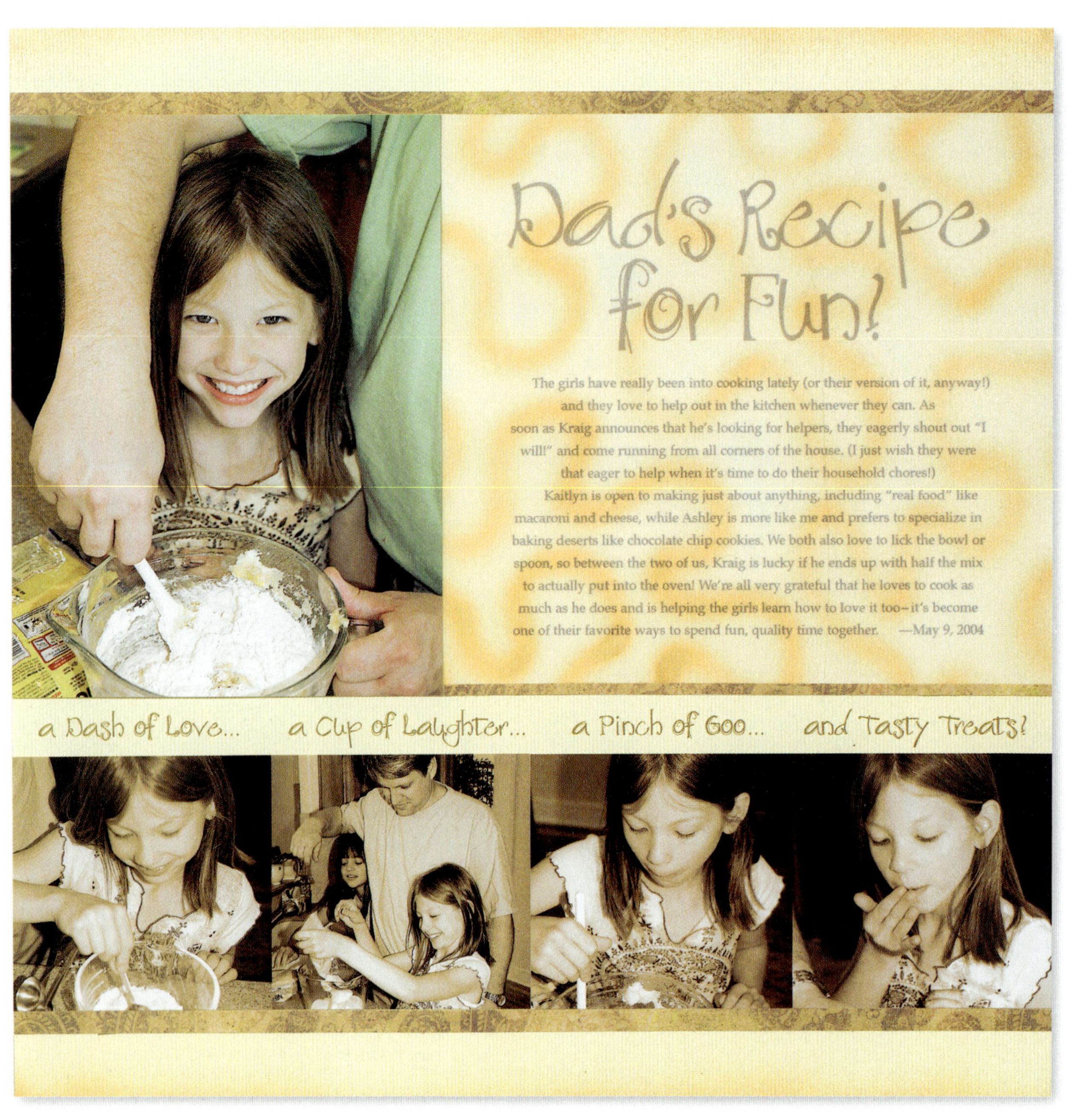

Dad's Recipe for Fun! *Supplies:* Airbrush tools, Air Opaque paint (Badger Air-Brush Co.); patterned paper (Creative Imaginations); vellum

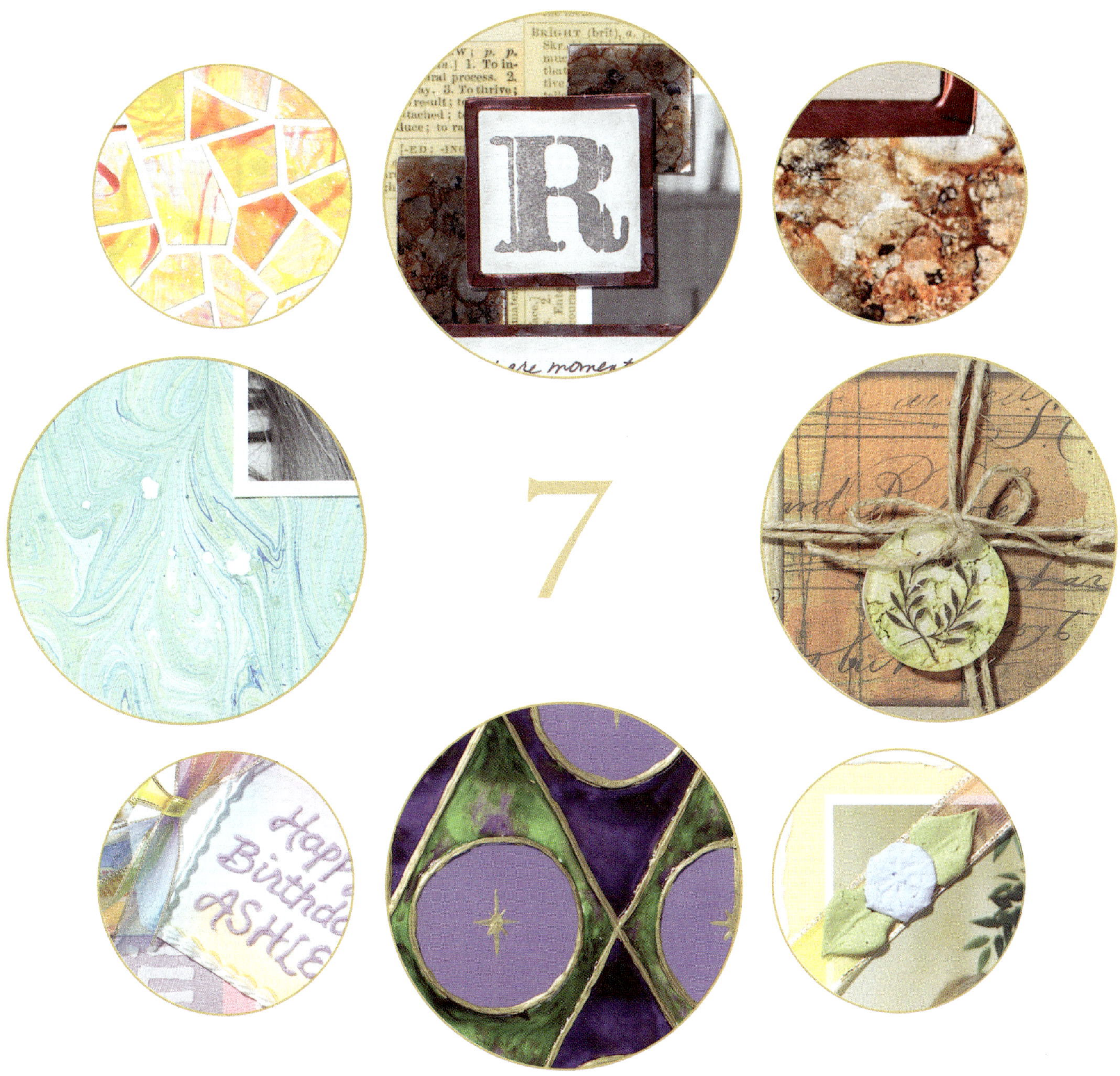

7

Airbrushing was one of those techniques that I'd always admired but was too intimidated to try because I thought it would be difficult to learn. But once I took the plunge and decided to play around with it, I was amazed at how easy it is to work with.

An airbrush tool applies paint basically in the same manner as regular spray cans, but the advantages are you can use a wider variety of mediums and there is more control over how hard or soft the paint is applied through the nozzle tip. You can use specific paints made for airbrushing or thin down paints you already have such as acrylics, watercolors or inks. The tool and a source of air power work together to apply a very fine mist of paint to create soft, dreamily shaded edges and blended color that would be very difficult to do with any other method.

The easiest way to get started is to purchase a basic kit that uses bottles of compressed air. If you find you enjoy using this medium, a dedicated air compressor might be something you could add to your toolbox.

Tips & Tricks

- *Multiple thin layers of paint will look nicer than one thick layer where the paint may drip or sag.*
- *A moderately priced airbrushing kit will probably have better components and achieve better results than the less expensive ones.*
- *Internet sites, such as www.howtoairbrush.com, can be great resources for information on learning airbrushing techniques.*

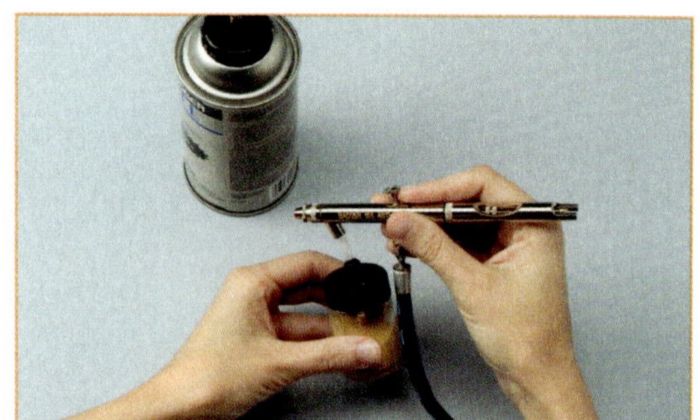

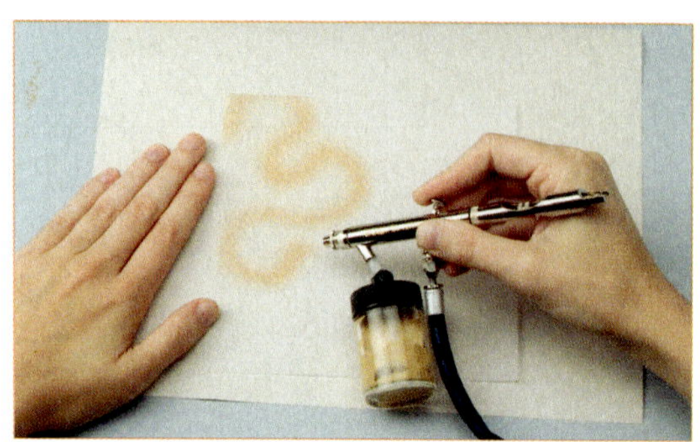

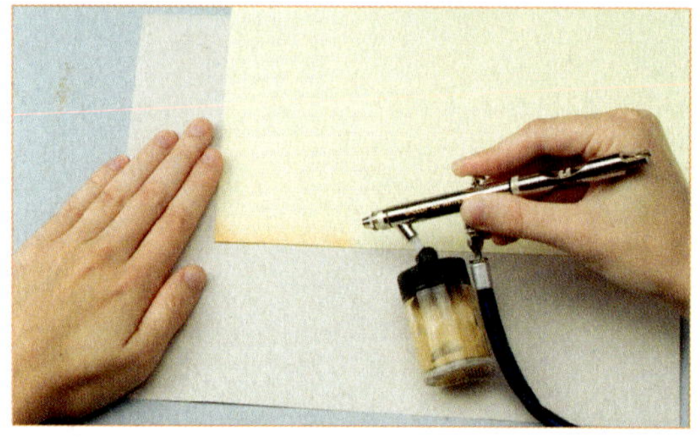

1

Fill jar with airbrush paint (or in this case, I mixed my own custom color) and attach it to the airbrush tool according to the manufacturer's directions.

2

Starting off the edge of the vellum, press trigger down to release paint; slowly and smoothly move your arm onto the paper. Use a continuous motion to create the random curvy lines until entire paper is covered; trim to size.

3

To shade the top and bottom edges of the background, start spraying before you hit the left side of the cardstock, then slowly paint along the edge and off the paper to the right side.

Other Ideas to Try . . .

Create Accent

Another way to create an airbrushed effect is with the Copic Air-Brushing System, which uses special pens instead of paint. They contain alcohol-based inks and work well on slick surfaces such as this metal accent.

Supplies: Copic Air-Brushing System (Imagination International); metal word (Making Memories)

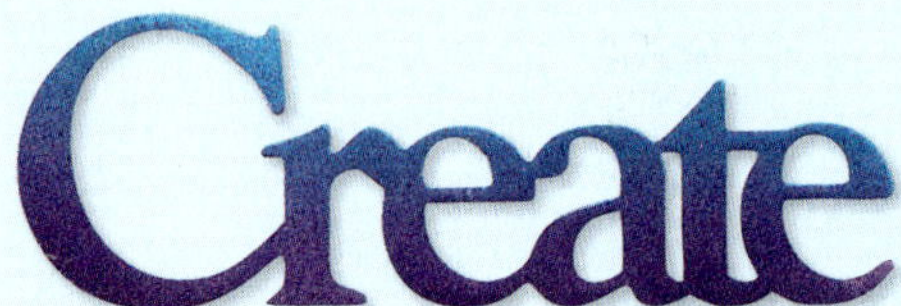

Specialty Paints

This chapter is devoted to a couple of products that did not seem to fit in any of the other previous categories but I thought deserved mentioning because they have unique characteristics that work with some wonderful painting techniques.

These products are marketed primarily as home décor, crafting or stamping mediums, but they have all been rated as acid-free and safe to use for scrapbooking applications. If you are skilled at cake decorating, Texture Magic will be right up your alley. If you can squeeze a tube and have a steady hand, Paint Jewels will make your heart flutter. If you can apply makeup or tap lightly on a table, you will love the magic of alcohol inks. And if you can wave a baton like a conductor or comb your hair, you can marbleize with enamels. It really doesn't sound that difficult or scary now, does it?

So if you are looking for some fun and unusual items to add to your painting toolbox, these may be the ones for you!

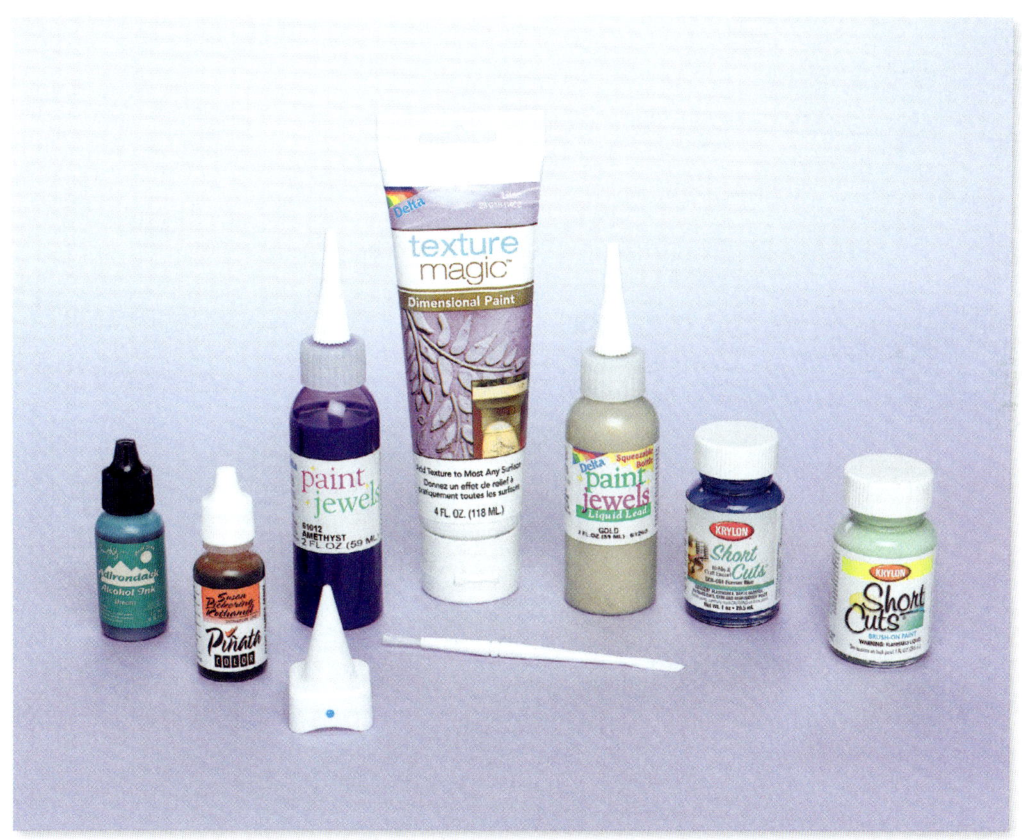

Featured Supplies

Alcohol Inks

Paint Jewels

Texture Magic Paint & Tools

Brush-On Enamel Paints

Alcohol Inks

My little brother, Robby—I never realized he was so cute when I was busy bossing him around and trying to keep him out of trouble! Geometric shapes create a simple "frame" around his photo, and a little chalk ink around the edges of the printed vellum background gives a soft, vintage feeling.

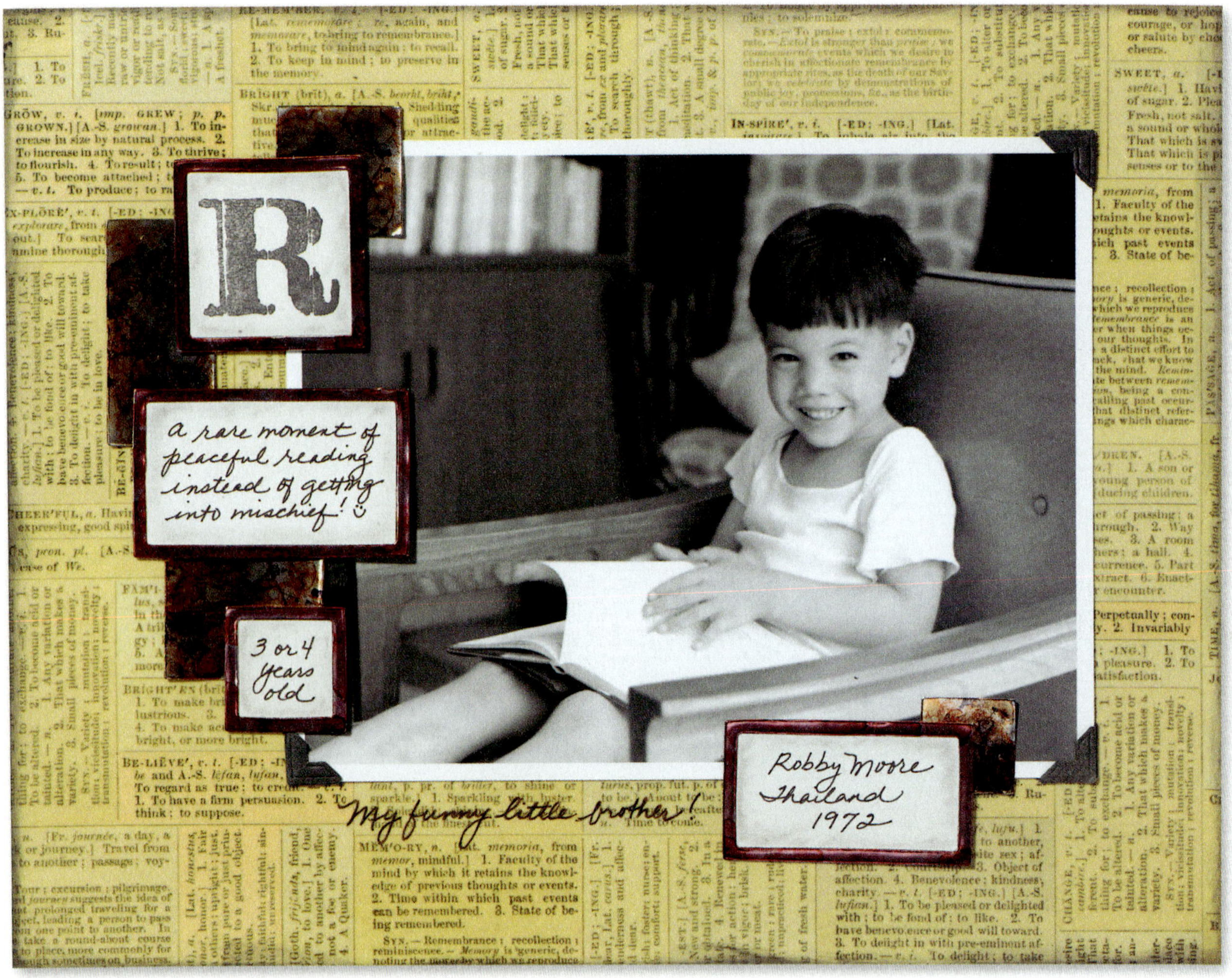

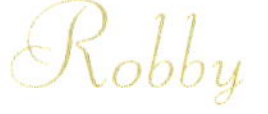

Supplies: Pinata alcohol inks (Jacquard Products); Art Emboss aluminum (AMACO); letter stamp (Technique Tuesday); Fluid Chalk Ink (Clearsnap); patterned vellum (K & Company); square and rectangle die (Sizzix, Provo Craft); Spongit tool (Loew-Cornell)

While alcohol inks may not technically be considered a type of paint, I included them in this category because they can create such gorgeous and translucent finishes on a variety of slick surfaces such as metal and acrylic. You can also use several painting techniques with these inks, such as sponging, splattering or brush painting, but one of the best ways to apply them is with a pouncing motion that allows them to naturally create the distinctive mottled patterning that is so typical of this medium.

Alcohol inks can be mixed together to create other colors, and their bold, concentrated hues can be thinned down with an extender or plain rubbing alcohol to create pastel tints or aid in blending colors over a surface. Because the alcohol in these inks evaporates very quickly, timing can be critical when working with them. But they are forgiving of mistakes and you can often go back several times to add or remove color until you achieve the desired effect.

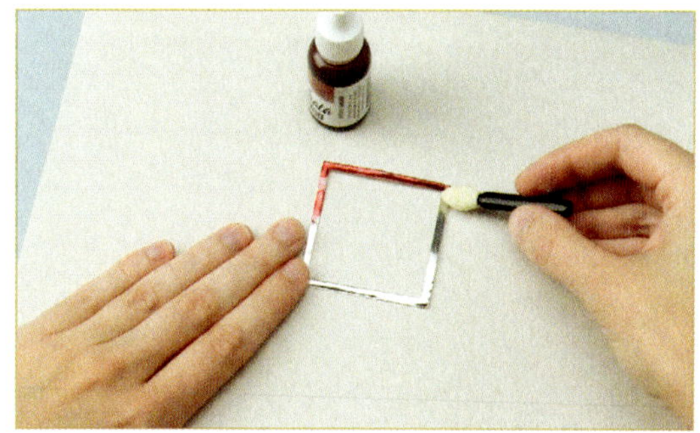

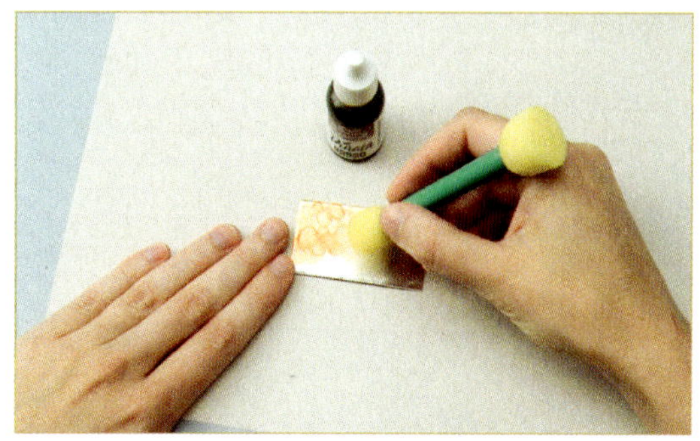

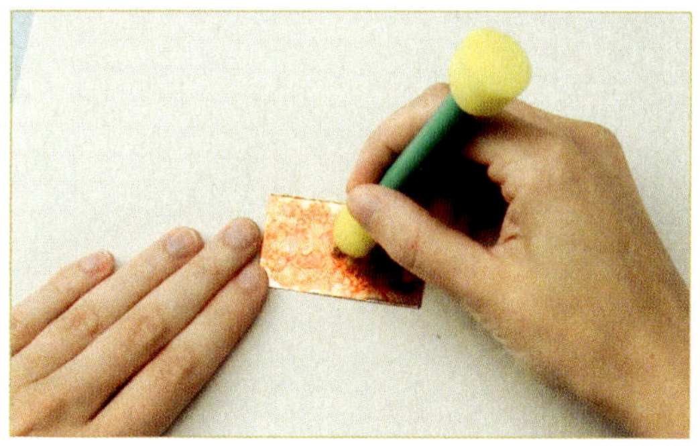

1

Add a drop of Sangria alcohol ink to a Spongit applicator and apply color to the metal frames with a light rubbing motion.

2

Pounce Havana Brown ink over the solid metal shapes; repeat process with a second layer of Burro Brown ink, but with less coverage so that some of the first color still shows through.

3

Add a very tiny drop of black ink and 1 to 2 drops of Claro Extender to the applicator and randomly pounce color over metal shapes, then set aside to let the colors blend and dry.

Tips & Tricks

- *Alcohol inks can be combined with metallic pens to create elegant and dramatic effects.*
- *These inks can stain fingers and clothing, so use with caution if you want to preserve that manicure!*

Other Ideas to Try . . .

Everlasting Love Album Cover

Glass paints also work best on slick surfaces and have a sheer color. The back of this clear acrylic tag was stippled with two colors of glass paint, then the entire back was sealed with acrylic paint so that the colors pop and almost appear to be floating inside. A rub-on was added on the front for the finishing touch.

Supplies: Vitrea 160 glass paint (Pebeo); Ceramcoat acyric paint (Delta); acrylic circle tag (Creek Bank Creations); rub-on letters (K & Company); Versamagic stamping ink (Tsukineko); album (7 Gypsies)

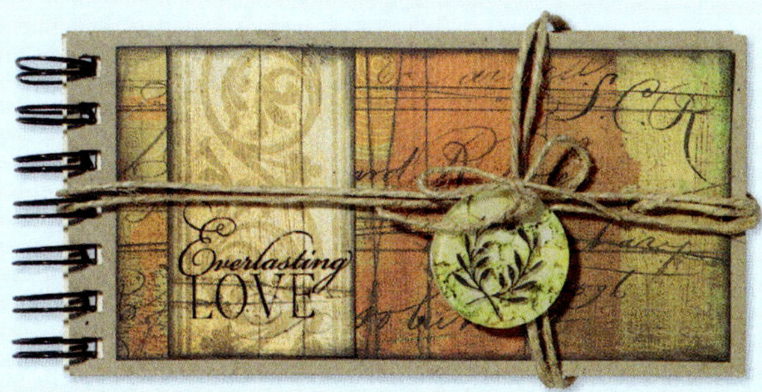

Texture Magic Paint

I can't believe my "baby girl" is another year older! The dimensional tag is decorated with "frosting," and airbrushing just like the cake from her party and a sweet little "icing" flower over sheer ribbon make a unique photo corner accent.

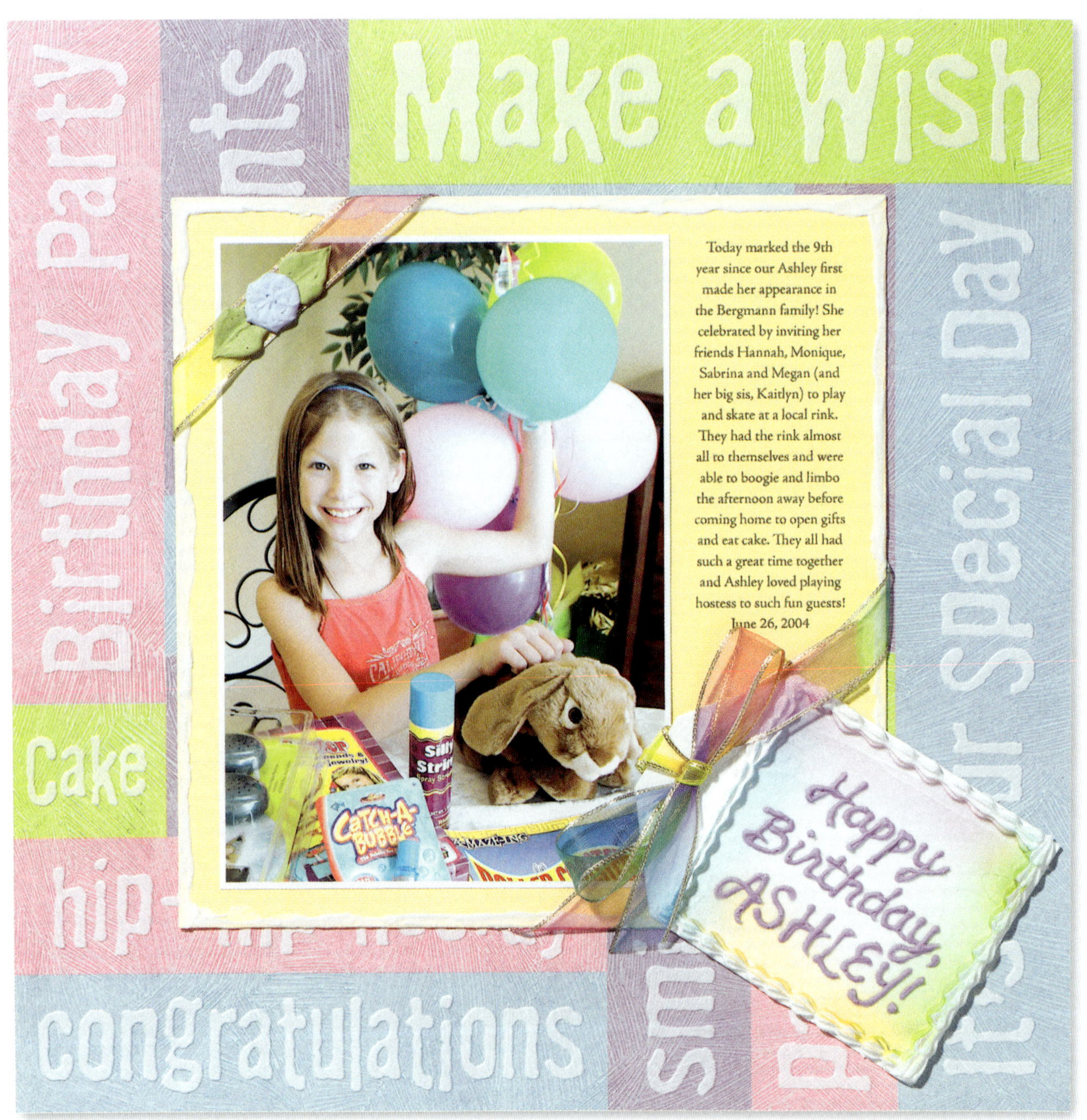

Happy Birthday, Ashley!

Supplies: Texture Magic paint, decorative tips (Delta); 140 lb. watercolor paper (Strathmore); Copic Airbrush System, markers (Imagination International); embossed paper (K & Company); die-cut tag (Provo Craft), ribbon (Offray); glue dots (Glue Dots International); nonstick craft sheet (Ranger)

If you like decorating cakes, then you will love working with this paint! This product is very similar to Light Modeling Paste, but comes already pre-tinted in tubes that you can use with special tip attachments to create patterns and designs. You can also mix it with other paints to make custom colors or apply it to backgrounds with tools like a palette knife or faux finishing comb on a variety of surfaces.

Another way you can use this product is to create individual embellishments. Since the special decorator tips look and work just like regular cake decorating tools, you can even use their patterns and techniques to create traditional icing accents such as roses, leaves and stars. The best part is they will remain soft and flexible and will never grow stale! So you can make an entire batch and save them for later use on other projects.

Tips & Tricks

- *I like to make free-standing accent designs on a nonstick craft sheet so they can be easily removed and applied anywhere I want on my layout.*
- *Use Texture Magic in place of glue to hold embellishments such as beads and buttons.*
- *This product dries fairly quickly, so be sure to wash off your tools as soon as possible to avoid paint hardening on them.*

Other Ideas to Try . . .

1. Apply Texture Magic with a palette knife over a stencil to create an all-over background design, photo corners or borders.
2. Use found objects such as wooden spools or pencil erasers to stamp texture over a smooth layer of paint.
3. Press dried botanicals into wet paint for a natural, organic design.
4. Blend and scrape several colors together with a palette knife to create a marbled effect.

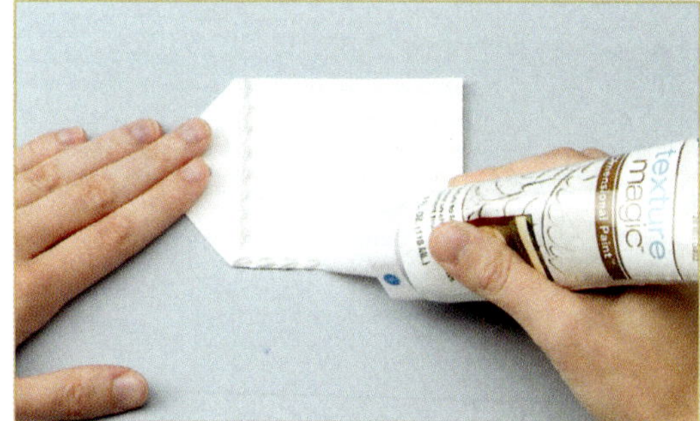

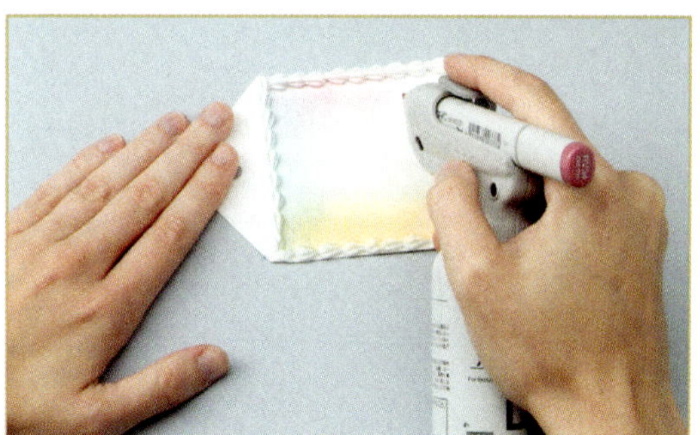

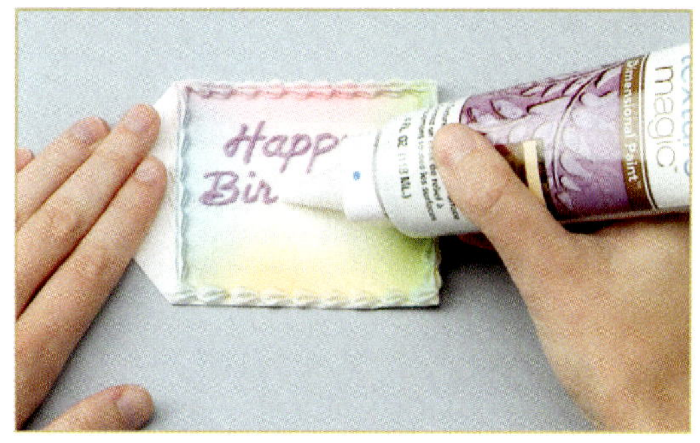

1

Die cut tag shape from watercolor paper. Use a palette knife to spread white paint over the tag so it looks like cake frosting. Also spread a little paint around the edges of the yellow cardstock journal box and allow both pieces to dry. Replace regular paint tube cap with the star decorator tip and create a ruffled border around the edge of the tag.

2

Airbrush the inner edges of the "cake" tag with four coordinating colors.

3

Attach the small dot decorator tip to the Lilac tube and write a message in the center of the tag.

Paint Jewels

Designer Nicole Gartland wanted to create a page showing how precious her beautiful baby, Naomi, is to her. The jewel tones she used to create an elegant background really make this neutral-colored photograph pop.

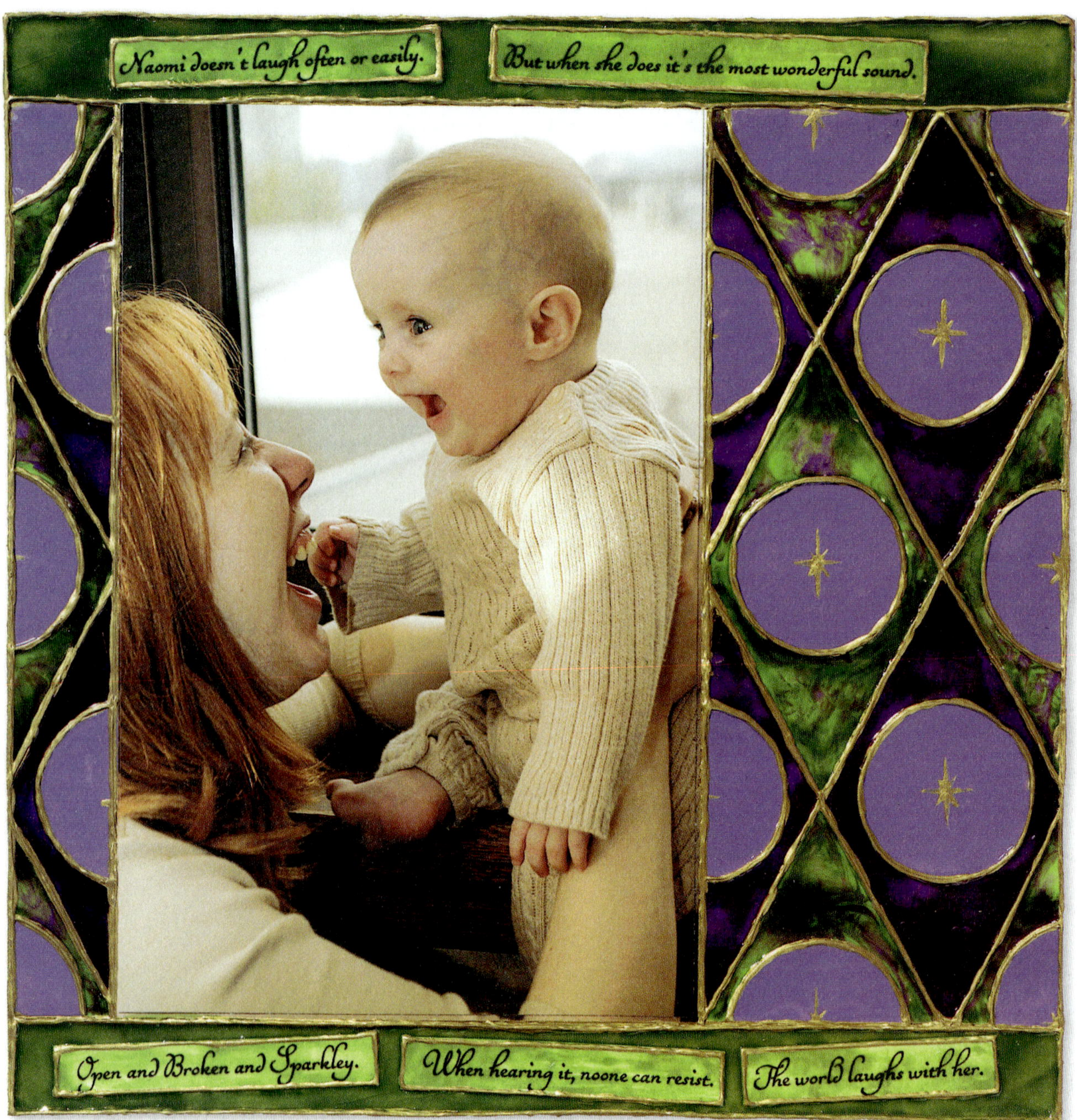

Naomi's Laugh

Supplies: Amethyst, Lilac Quartz and Jade Green Paint Jewel paints, Gold Liquid Lead (Delta); star stencil (Club Scrap)

Nicole Gartland, Portland, Oregon

I adore the jewel-like glow of a beautiful stained-glass window and was thrilled to discover a line of dimensional paints that can re-create this look on paper. They come in squeezable bottles, are available in a wide range of colors that even offer several types of faux leading and dry to a high gloss, transparent finish.

To achieve the most realistic stained-glass look, use designs that have strongly defined shapes, such as quilting or coloring books or real stained-glass patterns. You can fill in each shape in a variety of ways, ranging from simple, solid colors to intricate-looking marbleized swirls. Either way, it is a deceptively easy process, and you will be amazed at the stunning results!

Tips & Tricks

- *When applying the "leading" paint, try to stop and start at places where it will look like a traditional solder joint.*
- *Practice applying and blending these paints. You may be surprised at the way they change after they have dried.*
- *Heavy, glossy papers are my favorite surfaces to use with these paints.*

Other Ideas to Try . . .

Mosaic Monogram

Squeeze out several colors over a sheet of glossy cardstock and roughly blend them together with an old or disposable brush. Drizzle on an accent color and allow to dry, then cut into small pieces that resemble broken tiles. Arrange over a painted monogram square and leave narrow spaces between each piece to create "grout" lines.

Supplies: Paint Jewel paints, gesso, Ceramcoat acrylic paint (Delta); chipboard letter (Heidi Swapp); white glossy paper (Ranger); textured cardstock (DieCuts with a View)

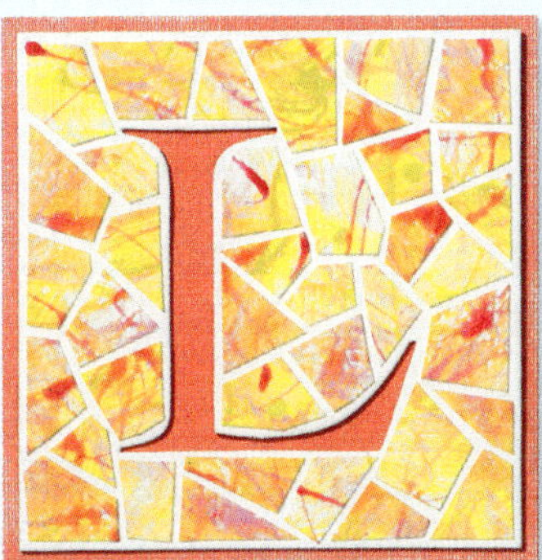

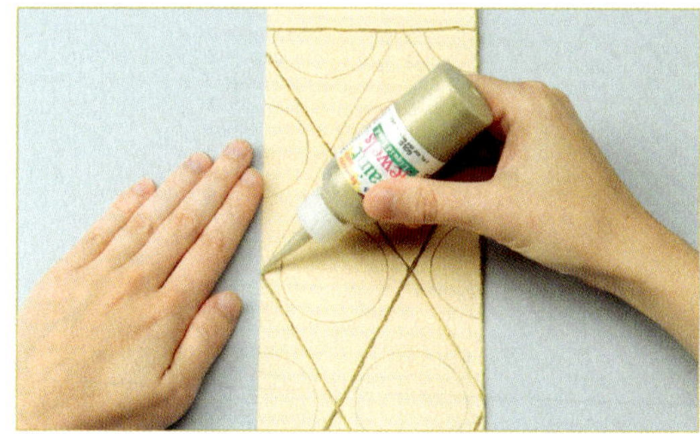

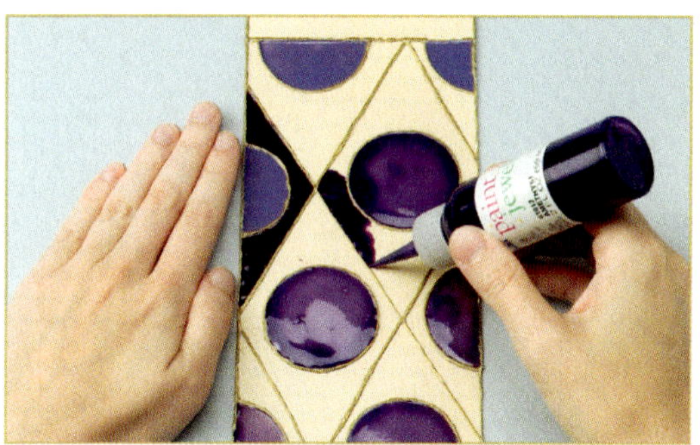

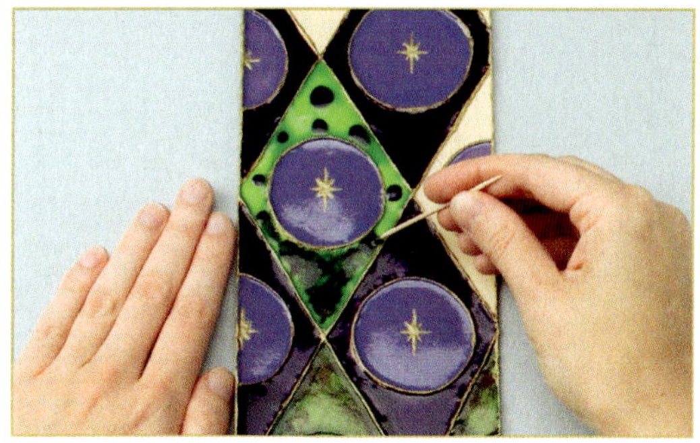

1

Draw design lightly in pencil. Hold Gold Leading nozzle about ¼" away from the paper and trace over lines; allow to dry.

2

Fill circles with Lilac Quartz and alternating rows of diamonds with Amethyst paint; allow to dry. Stencil gold stars in center of circles with Gold Leading.

3

Create swirl painted diamonds by laying down a thick coat of the primary color (in this case, Jade Green), then add large drops of the secondary color (Amethyst) and quickly swirl them together with a toothpick.

Marbleizing

I love how the delicate patterns of the marbleized papers work so well with the textured cardstock. The simplicity of this stitched and color-blocked background creates such a pretty frame around the joyful faces of my two daughters—no other embellishments are needed except a few tiny flowers.

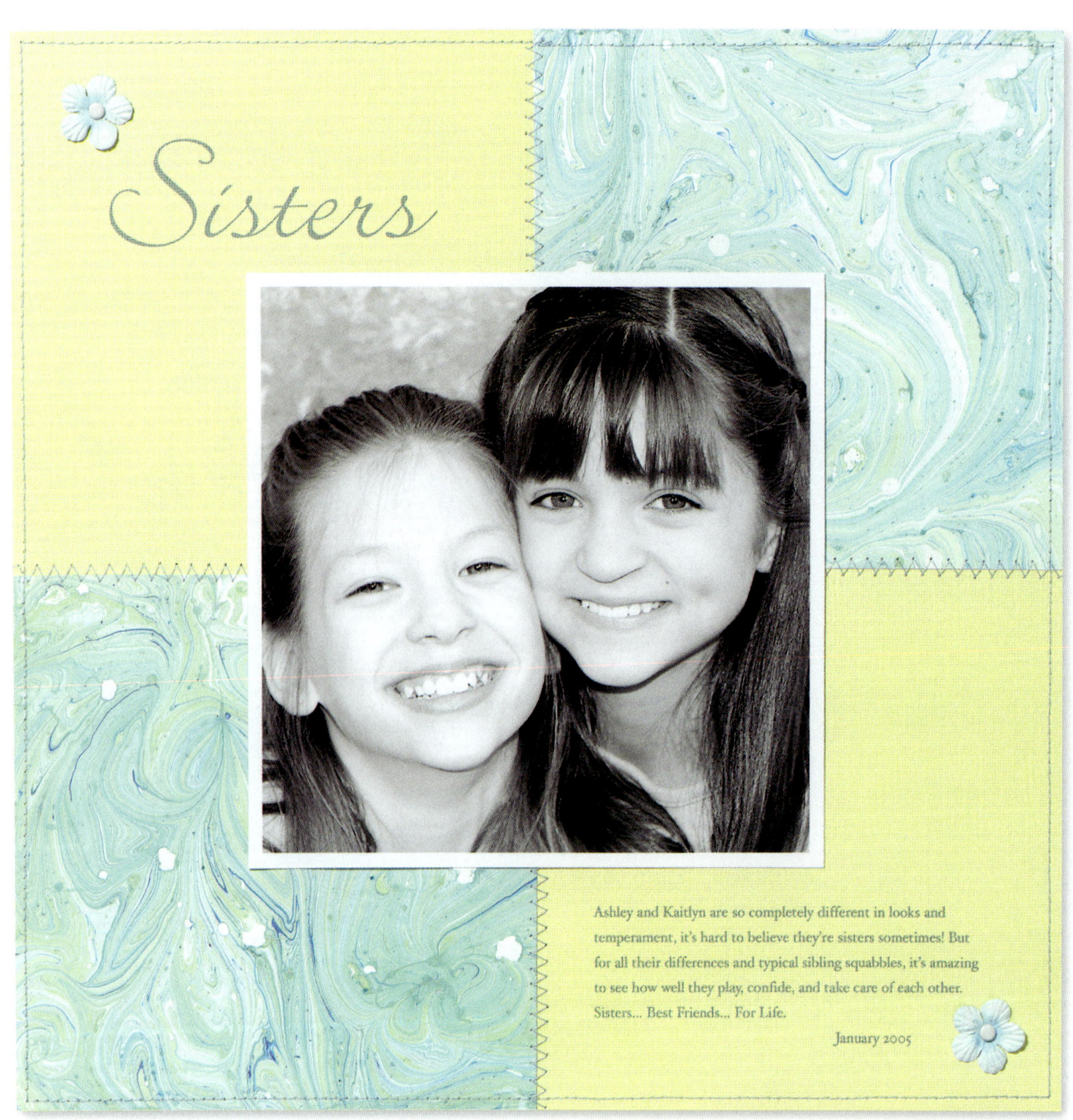

Sisters *Supplies:* Short Cuts enamel paint (Krylon); textured cardstock (DieCuts with A View); paper flowers (Prima); brads (Limited Edition Rubberstamps); 20 Mule Team Borax (Dial Corp.)

Enamel paints are not something I normally think to use for scrapbooking techniques, but when I heard that there was a line that is acid-free and archival, I thought it would be a great product to use on items such as metal and acrylic embellishments. Although the glossy, enameled finish they create is well worth the extra effort, these paints are not your typical soap-and-water cleanup jobs. So I always make sure to have special paint remover wipes or mineral spirits on hand in case I get a little messy while I'm working with them. Also keep strips of newspaper on hand to clean out the pan in between applications.

One of the special properties of enamel paints is that they can be used as a marbleizing medium when applied over a simple mixture of water and a natural product called borax. Borax acts as a suspension agent that allows the paint to float and disperse over the water, and it can usually be found in the water softener or laundry detergent aisle of your local grocery store. Marbleizing patterns are created by stirring or pulling a tool such as an old plastic comb, thin sticks or even feathers through the paint. The way a tool is applied can create specific designs ranging from traditional bookplate patterns to abstract free-form shapes.

Tips & Tricks

• Work very quickly, as these paints tend to skim up and separate in about 15 to 30 seconds. If this happens, remove paint and start over.

• Have several new stir sticks on hand and use a different one in each paint color to keep them from contaminating each other.

• Test the water to make sure you have enough borax mixed in by adding a few drops of paint. If the drops sink to the bottom, add a little more borax until the paint floats on the top.

Other Ideas to Try . . .

1. Mix in a few drops of metallic paint for an elegant touch.

2. Marbleize coordinating embellishments such as slide holders, metal border strips and tags.

3. You can also use Stained Glass spray paints for marbleizing by spraying over plain water (no borax needed), but your color options are more limited.

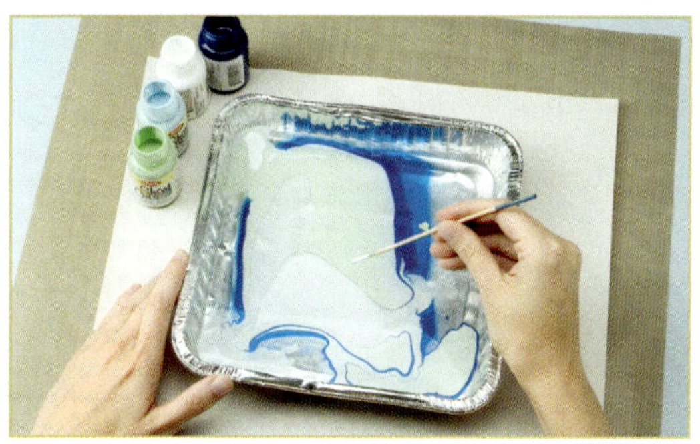

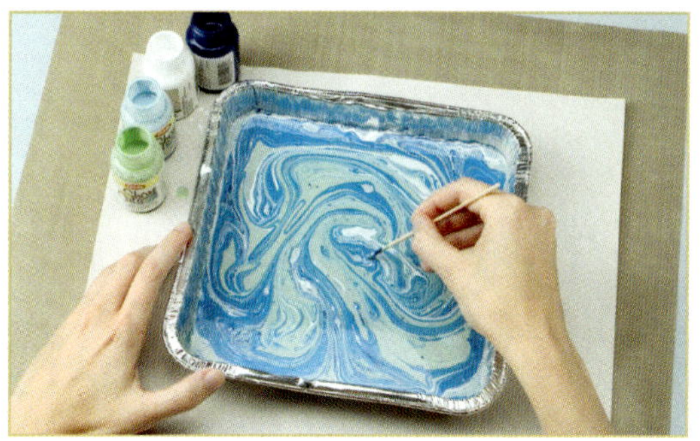

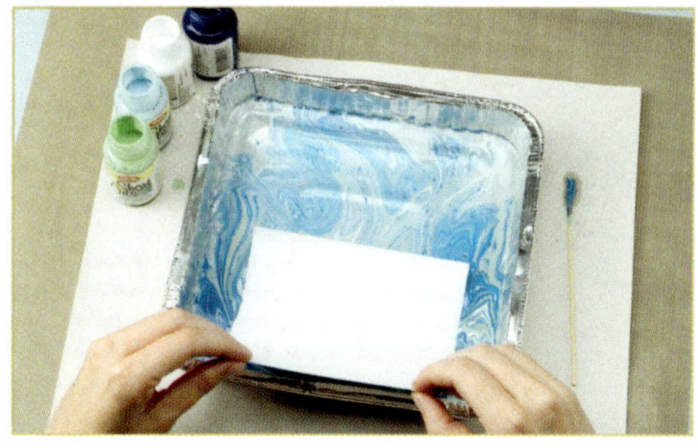

1

Dissolve about 1 ounce of borax into 1 gallon of warm water and pour into a disposable pan. Add a few drops of each paint color randomly over water.

2

When all the paint colors have been added, quickly swirl them together, using a random serpentine or back-and-forth motion, depending on the pattern you want to create.

3

When you reach the desired look, stop stirring and drop in the paper, starting slowly at one end until entire sheet is in contact with the water. Tap a few times to remove any air bubbles and slowly pull across and out of the pan.

Additional Credits & Supplies

Cover

Natural Beauty

Stained Glass spray paint, Short-Cuts enamel paints, All Purpose Spray Adhesive (Krylon); Low-Tack Frisket Film, Dura-Lar Wet Media Film (Grafix); metal letter, molding strip (Making Memories); die-cut charm (Sizzix); Light Molding Paste (Golden); Ceramcoat acrylic paints, Sheer Gold Glaze, scroll stencil (Delta); Smooth Bristol and 140 lb. watercolor papers (Strathmore); watercolors (Daler-Rowney); letter stamps (River City Rubber Works); black Fineliner pen (Staedtler)

Painted Swatches

Page 19
Ceramcoat acrylic paint (Delta); Acrylic Glazing Liquid (Golden); Dura-Lar Wet-Media Film (Grafix); stamp (Rubber Stampede); wood-grain tool (Plaid)

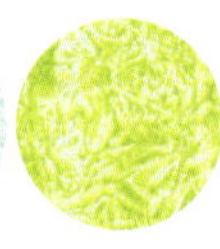

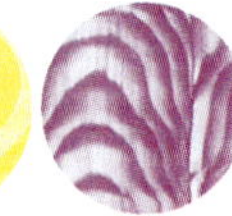

Page 29
Blended fibers, glass beads, resin sand texture gels (Liquitex); fine garnet gel (Golden)

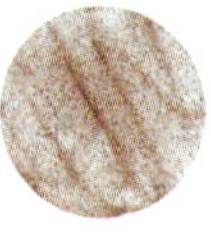

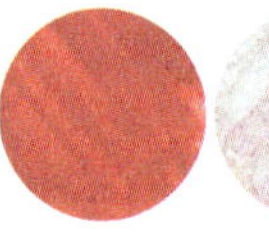

Page 77
Make It Stone!, webbing spray paints (Krylon)

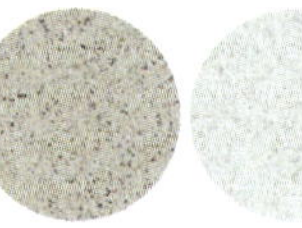

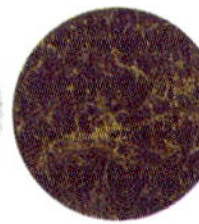
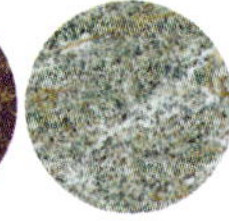

Page 27
Matte Soft Gel, Gloss Soft Gel, Semi-Gloss Gel (Golden)

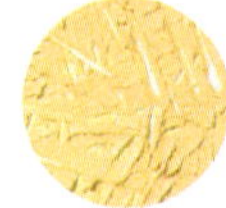
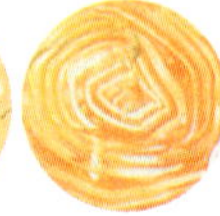

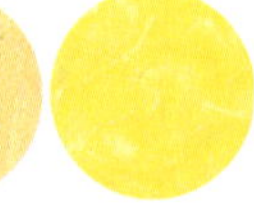

Page 47
Granulation and Texture Mediums for Water Colour (Winsor & Newton)

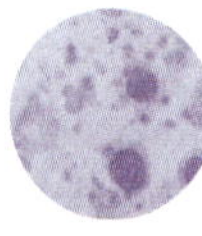
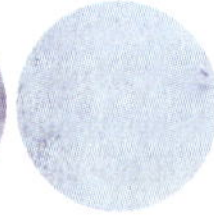
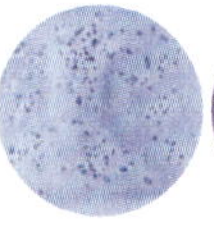

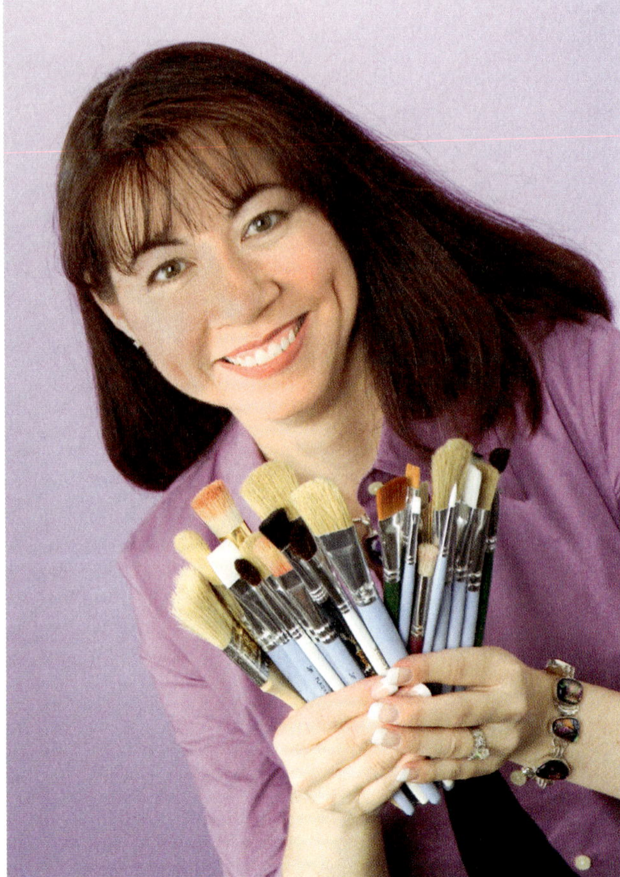

About the Author

As a child, Lori Bergmann could always be found drawing, painting, crafting, reading or singing—sometimes even attempting all of them at once! As she grew up, she continued her love of anything involving the creative arts and still has a collection of many of her original creations she made "just for fun!" She earned a degree in Visual Art and worked as a professional graphic designer before becoming "obsessed" with scrapbooking in 1998, which she now does full-time from her home studio.

With over seven years of dedicated involvement and recognition in the scrapbooking and paper crafting industries, Lori is known for her innovative use of a wide variety of artistic techniques. She has published over 350 projects and has written feature articles for magazines such as *Creating Keepsakes*, *Scrapbooks Etc.* and *Paper Crafts*, was an original "Hall of Fame" contest winner, and has made several guest appearances on the "DIY Scrapbooking" television show. Lori also enjoys working as a freelance designer and consultant, creates licensed product designs, and teaches and demonstrates at local stores and national events around the country.

Lori currently lives in Kansas with her college sweetheart and husband, Kraig, their two beautiful daughters, Kaitlyn and Ashley, and a lovable fur ball named Indiana Jones. When she's not scrapbooking or painting, she can usually be found curled up on the sofa reading a good book, searching antique stores or craft shops for that "perfect find," redecorating her home, or dreaming of traveling to Europe for another wonderful adventure.

Source Guide

The following companies manufacture products featured in this book. Please check your local retailers to find these materials, or go to a company's Web site for the latest product. In addition, we have made every attempt to properly credit the items mentioned in this book. We apologize to any company that we have listed incorrectly, and we would appreciate hearing from you.

7 Gypsies
(800) 588-6707
www.7gypsies.com

American Art Clay Co. (AMACO)
(800) 374-1600
www.amaco.com

Artograph, Inc.
(888) 975-9555
www.artograph.com

Autumn Leaves
(800) 588-6707
www.autumnleaves.com

Avery Dennison Corporation
(800) GO-AVERY
www.avery.com

Badger Air-Brush Company
(847) 678-3104
www.badgerairbrush.com

Bazzill Basics Paper
(480) 558-8557
www.bazzillbasics.com

Beacon Adhesives
(800) 865-7238
www.beaconcreates.com

Berwick Offray, LLC
(800) 344-5533
www.offray.com

Canson®, Inc.
(800) 628-9283
www.canson-us.com

Carma
www.carma.biz

Carolee's Creations®
(435) 563-1100
www.ccpaper.com

Clearsnap, Inc.
(360) 293-6634
www.clearsnap.com

Clover Needlecraft, Inc.
www.clover-usa.com

Club Scrap™, Inc.
(888) 634-9100
www.clubscrap.com

Coats & Clark
(800) 648-1479
www.coatsandclark.com

Crayola®
www.crayola.com

Creative Imaginations
(800) 942-6487
www.cigift.com

Creative Memories®
(800) 468-9335
www.creativememories.com

Creek Bank Creations, Inc.
(217) 427-5980
www.creekbankcreations.com

Cruddas Innovations
www.cruddas4innovation.co.uk

C-Thru® Ruler Company, The
(800) 243-8419
www.cthruruler.com

Daisy D's Paper Company
(888) 601-8955
www.daisydspaper.com

Daler-Rowney USA
(609) 655-5252
www.daler-rowney.com

DecoArt™ Inc.
(800) 367-3047
www.decoart.com

Delta Technical Coatings, Inc.
(800) 423-4135
www.deltacrafts.com

Deluxe Designs
(480) 497-9005
www.deluxedesigns.com

Dial Corporation, The
(800) 258-3425
www.dialcorp.com

DieCuts with a View™
(877) 221-6107
www.dcwv.com

DMC Corp.
(973) 589-0606
www.dmc.com

Dr. Ph. Martin's
(800) 843-8293
www.docmartins.com

Dymo
(800) 426-7827
www.dymo.com

EK Success™, Ltd.
(800) 524-1349
www.eksuccess.com

Faber-Castell
(800) 642-2288
www.faber-castellusa.com

Fiskars®, Inc.
(800) 950-0203
www.fiskars.com

Glue Dots® International
(888) 688-7131
www.gluedots.com

Golden Artist Colors, Inc.
(800) 959-6543
www.goldenpaints.com

Grafix®
(800) 447-2349
www.grafix.com

Hampton Art Stamps, Inc.
(800) 229-1019
www.hamptonart.com

Heidi Swapp/Advantus Corporation
(904) 482-0092
www.heidiswapp.com

Henkel Consumer Adhesives, Inc.
(800) 321-0253
www.ducktapeproducts.com

Heritage Handcrafts
(303) 683-0963
www.heritagehandcrafts.com

Hero Arts® Rubber Stamps, Inc.
(800) 822-4376
www.heroarts.com

Imagination International, Inc.
(866) 662-6742
www.copic.com

Jaquard Products/Rupert, Gibbon & Spider, Inc.
(800) 442-0455
www.jacquardproducts.com

Jesse James & Co., Inc.
(610) 435-0201
www.jessejamesbutton.com

JewelCraft, LLC
(201) 223-0804
www.jewelcraft.biz

K & Company
(888) 244-2083
www.kandcompany.com

Karen Foster Design
(801) 451-9779
www.karenfosterdesign.com

KI Memories
(972) 243-5595
www.kimemories.com

Krylon®
(216) 566-200
www.krylon.com

Lazar Studiowerx, Inc.
(866) 478-9379
www.lazarstudiowerx.com

Li'l Davis Designs
(949) 838-0344
www.lildavisdesigns.com

Limited Edition Rubberstamps
(650) 594-4242
www.limitededitionrs.com

Lindy's Stamp Gang
(360) 785-4588
www.lindystampgang.com

Liquitex® Artist Materials
(888) 4-ACRYLIC
www.liquitex.com

Loew-Cornell, Inc.
(201) 836-7070
www.loew-cornell.com

Lyra USA, LLC
(888) 736-5972
www.lyra.de

Magic Scraps™
(972) 238-1838
www.magicscraps.com

Making Memories
(800) 286-5263
www.makingmemories.com

Marvy® Uchida/ Uchida of America, Corp.
(800) 541-5877
www.uchida.com

Masquepen
(415) 453-1389
www.masquepen.com

Ma Vinci's Reliquary
http://crafts.dm.net/mall/reliquary/

Maya Road, LLC
(214) 488-3279
www.mayaroad.com

McGill, Inc.
(800) 982-9884
www.mcgillinc.com

Memories Complete™, LLC
(866) 966-6365
www.memoriescomplete.com

Mohawk Paper Mills, Inc.
(800) THE-MILL
www.strathmore.com

Morex Corporation
(717) 852-7771
www.morexcorp.com

Mustard Moon™
(408) 299-8542
www.mustardmoon.com

Offray - see Berwick Offray, LLC

One Heart...One Mind®, LLC
(888) 414-3690

Paper Loft
(866) 254-1961
www.paperloft.com

pcCrafter
(801) 221-8875
www.pccrafter.com

Pebbles Inc.
(801) 224-1857
www.pebblesinc.com

Pebéo of America
(801) 235-1520
www.pebeo.com

Phoenix Brands, LLC
(866) 794-0800
www.ritdye.com

Plaid Enterprises, Inc.
(800) 842-4197
www.plaidonline.com

Prima Marketing, Inc.
(909) 627-5532
www.mulberrypaperflowers.com

Provo Craft®
(888) 577-3545
www.provocraft.com

Prym-Dritz Corporation
www.dritz.com

Purple Onion Designs
www.purpleoniondesigns.com

Ranger Industries, Inc.
(800) 244-2211
www.rangerink.com

Rit® Dyes - see Phoenix Brands, LLC

River City Rubber Works
(877) 735-2276
www.rivercityrubberworks.com

Rubber Stampede
(800) 423-4135
www.deltacrafts.com

Salis International, Inc. - see Dr. Ph. Martin's

Sanford® Corporation
(800) 323-0749
www.sanfordcorp.com

Silkpaint Corporation®
(800) 563-0074
www.silkpaint.com

Sizzix®
(866) 742-4447
www.sizzix.com

Speedball® Art Products Company
(800) 898-7224
www.speedballart.com

Staedtler®, Inc.
(800) 927-7723
www.staedtler.us

Stamp Doctor, The
(866) 782-6737
www.stampdoctor.com

Stampendous!®
(800) 869-0474
www.stampendous.com

Stewart Gill Ltd.
www.stewartgill.com

Strathmore Papers
(also see Mohawk Paper Mills)
(800) 628-8816
www.strathmore.com

Sunday International
(800) 401-8644
www.sundayint.com

Tandy Leather Company
(800) 433-3201
www.tandyleather.com

Technique Tuesday, LLC
(503) 644-4073
www.techniquetuesday.com

Therm O Web, Inc.
(800) 323-0799
www.thermoweb.com

Tombow®
(800) 835-3232
www.tombowusa.com

Tsukineko®, Inc.
(800) 769-6633
www.tsukineko.com

USArtQuest, Inc.
(517) 522-6225
www.usartquest.com

Wagner
(800) 328-8251
www.wagnerspraytech.com

Winsor & Newton™
www.winsornewton.com

Wrights® Ribbon Accents
(877) 597-4448
www.wrights.com

Xyron
(800) 793-3523
www.xyron.com

Index

Learn more with the authors of these fine titles from Memory Makers Books!

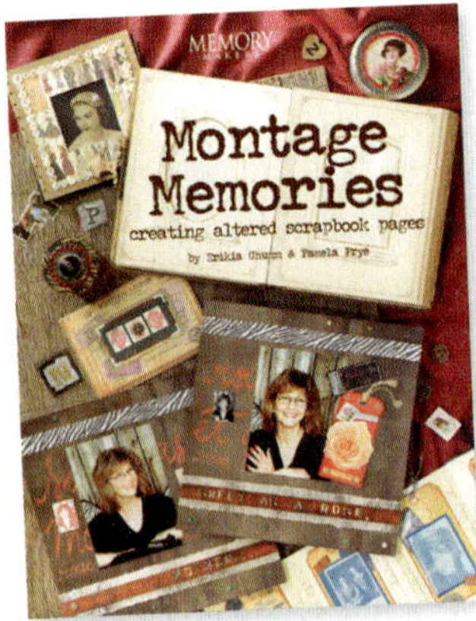

Montage Memories
ISBN-13: 978-1-89212-732-7,
ISBN-10: 1-89212-732-6,
paperback, 112 pgs., #32895

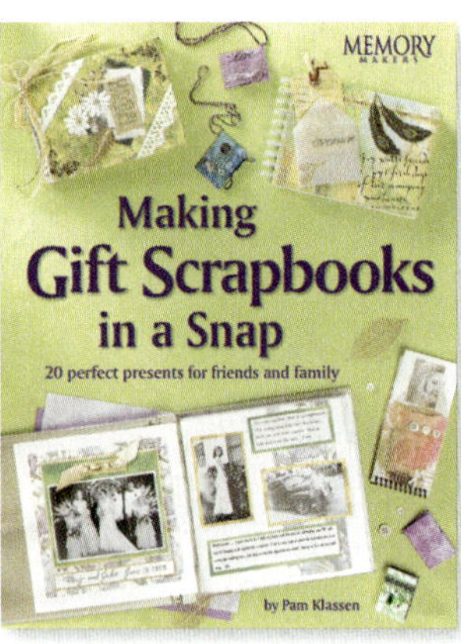

Making Gift Scrapbooks in a Snap
ISBN-13: 978-189212-736-5,
ISBN-10: 1-89212-736-9,
paperback, 96 pgs., #32994

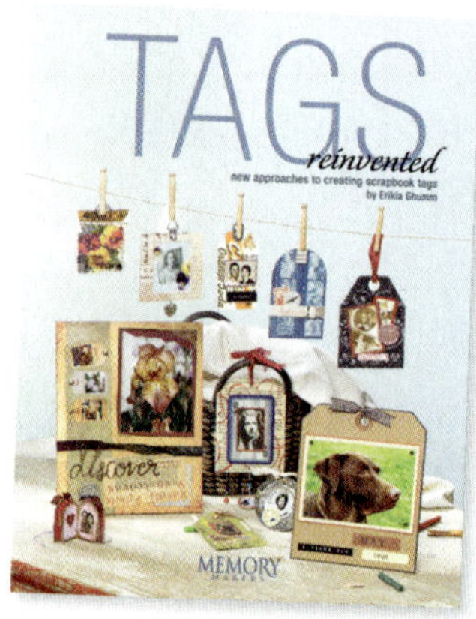

Tags Reinvented
ISBN-13: 978-1-89212-747-1,
ISBN-10: 1-89212-747-4,
paperback, 96 pgs., #33212

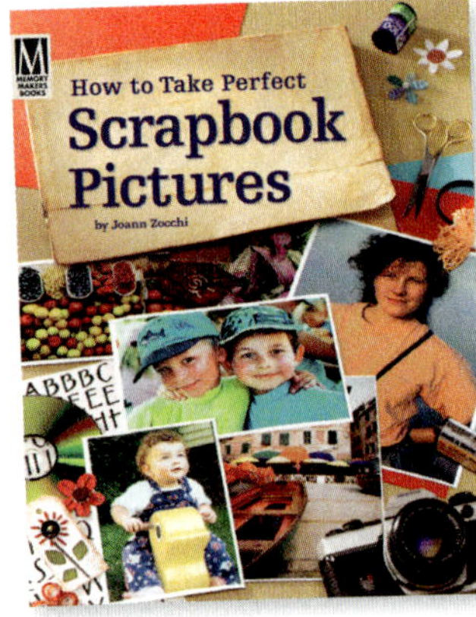

How to Take Perfect Scrapbook Pictures
ISBN-13: 978-1-89212-740-2,
ISBN-10: 1-89212-740-7,
paperback, 112 pgs., #33159

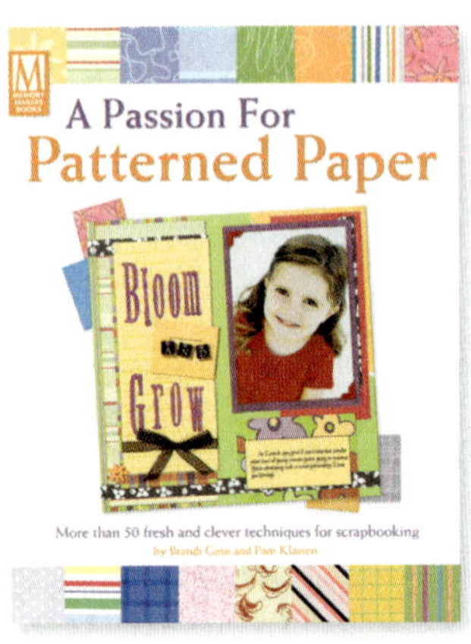

A Passion for Patterned Paper
ISBN-13: 978-1-89212-751-8,
ISBN-10: 1-89212-751-2,
paperback, 96 pgs., #33265

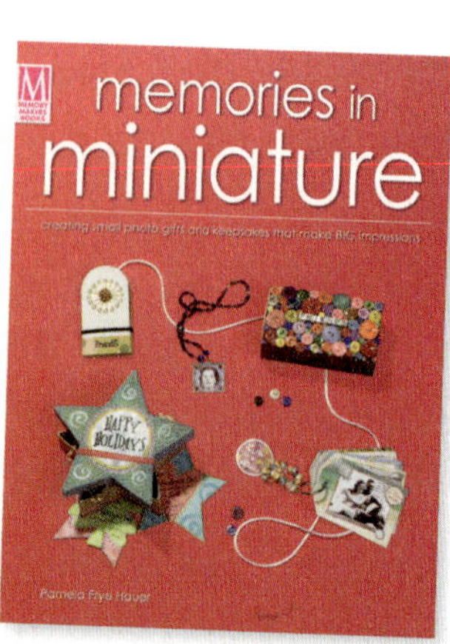

Memories in Miniature
ISBN-13: 978-1-89212-750-1,
ISBN-10: 1-89212-750-4,
paperback, 96 pgs., #33266

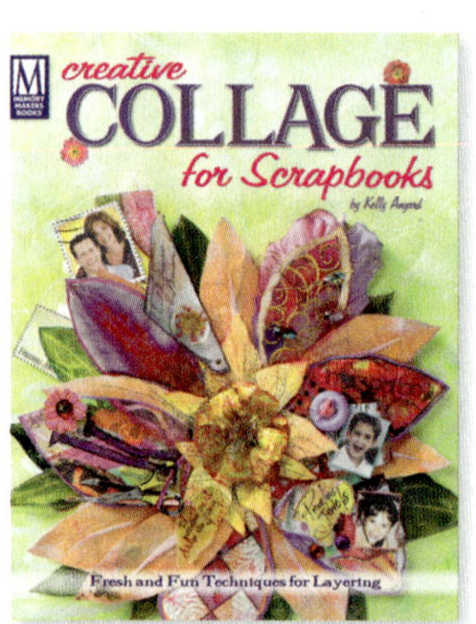

Creative Collage for Scrapbooks
ISBN-13: 978-1-89212-7-58-X,
ISBN-10: 1-892127-58-X,
paperback, 128 pgs., #33419

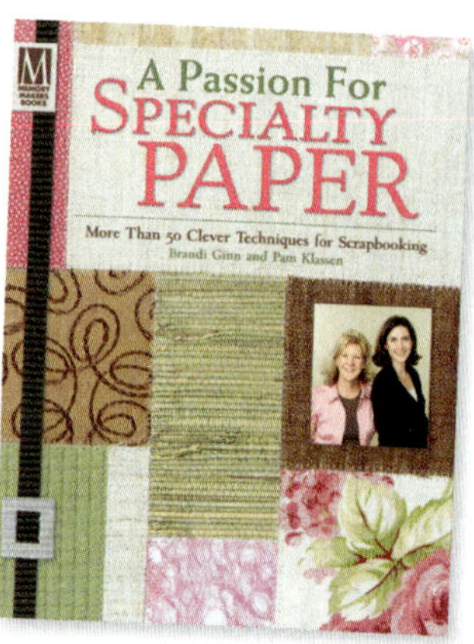

A Passion for Speciality Paper
ISBN-13: 978-1-892127-61-X,
ISBN-10: 1-892127-61-X,
paperback, 96 pgs., #33460

These books and other fine Memory Makers Books titles are available from your local art or craft retailer, bookstore or online supplier. Please see page 2 of this book for contact information for Canada, Australia, the U.K. and Europe.